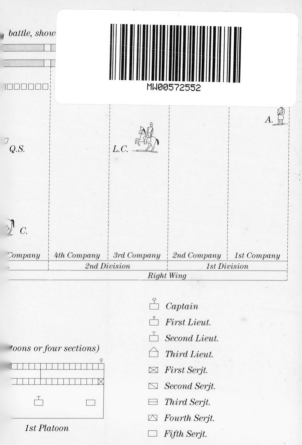

battle, show

A.

Q.S.

L.C.

C.

5th Company	4th Company	3rd Company	2nd Company	1st Company
	2nd Division		1st Division	
		Right Wing		

(platoons or four sections)

1st Platoon

Captain

First Lieut.

Second Lieut.

Third Lieut.

First Serjt.

Second Serjt.

Third Serjt.

Fourth Serjt.

Fifth Serjt.

The

1863

U.S. INFANTRY TACTICS

INFANTRY OF THE LINE,
LIGHT INFANTRY, AND RIFLEMEN

BY

U.S. War Department

STACKPOLE
BOOKS

Published by
STACKPOLE BOOKS
5067 Ritter Road
Mechanicsburg, PA 17055-6921
www.stackpolebooks.com

Printed in China

Cover design by Wendy Reynolds

10 9 8 7 6 5 4 3 2

Library of Congress Cataloging-in-Publication Data

United States. War Dept.
 [U.S. infantry tactics]
 The 1863 U.S. infantry tactics : infantry of the line, light infantry,
and rifleman / by U.S. War Department.
 p. cm.
 Originally published: U.S. infantry tactics / prepared under the
direction of the War Department. Philadelphia : J.B. Lippincott,
1863.
 Includes index.
 ISBN 0-8117-0021-6 (alk. paper)
 1. United States. Army. Infantry–Drill and tactics. I. Title.

UD160 .U55 2002
356'.1154-dc21   2002020607
ISBN 9780-8117-0021-4

[BY AUTHORITY.]

U. S. INFANTRY TACTICS,

FOR THE

INSTRUCTION, EXERCISE, AND MANŒUVRES

OF THE

UNITED STATES INFANTRY,

INCLUDING

𝕴nfantry of the 𝕷ine, 𝕷ight 𝕴nfantry,
and 𝕽iflemen.

PREPARED UNDER THE DIRECTION OF THE
WAR DEPARTMENT,

AND AUTHORIZED AND ADOPTED BY

THE SECRETARY OF WAR,

MAY 1, 1861.

CONTAINING

THE SCHOOL OF THE SOLDIER; THE SCHOOL OF THE
COMPANY; INSTRUCTION FOR SKIRMISHES; THE
GENERAL CALLS, THE CALLS FOR SKIRMISHES,
AND THE SCHOOL OF THE BATTALION;
INCLUDING THE ARTICLES OF WAR AND A DICTIONARY
OF MILITARY TERMS.

PHILADELPHIA:

J. B. LIPPINCOTT & CO.

1863.

☞ *The numbers under the illustrations in the School
of the Soldier refer to the paragraphs.*

War Department,
Washington, May 1, 1861.

This system of United States Infantry Tactics, prepared under the direction of the War Department, having been approved by the President, is adopted for the instruction of the troops and for the observance of the militia when so employed.

SIMON CAMERON,
Secretary of War.

PREFACE.

THE following system of Infantry Tactics, based upon the latest improvements in French military experience, and adapted to the peculiar wants of our service, has been prepared by order of the United States Government, and is now, after the most satisfactory evidence of its efficiency, authorized and adopted by the Secretary of War for the instruction of the troops.

Infantry is divided into Heavy Infantry—also called Infantry of the Line—and Light Infantry. The difference between Heavy and Light Infantry is twofold: 1st. In their weapons and equipment, the former being armed with the musket, and the latter with the rifle, when it may be had. 2d. In the order of battle, Heavy Infantry being in compact order, while Light Infantry is dispersed or deployed as skirmishers, the men being separated and more independent in delivering their fire as sharpshooters.

In the school of the company and of the battalion, *the instruction for Heavy and Light Infantry is the same,* every regiment of Infantry having one company of Light Infantry as a part of its organization, and all these companies being drilled as Infantry of the Line.

The system now presented gives a complete course of instruction for both kinds of Infantry, in the schools of the company and battalion, and has besides a special drill for Light Infantry when employed as skirmishers.

The advantages claimed by this system of tactics over former ones are numerous and decided: greater celerity in movements, forming in line from column without halting, changing direction from front to rear while marching, doubling the files when marching by a flank, the omission of unnecessary commands, or parts of commands, more varied formation of squares against cavalry, and many others.

A complete manual of arms for the *musket* will be found at the end of the school of the soldier, p. 74.

It is believed that, with the same *matériel*, this system will render a company or regiment much more effective than any other.

With a view to insure uniformity in a system of instruction the merits of which are acknowledged by the highest authority, it is now presented to the volunteers and militia called into service, as the authorized drill for the United States Infantry, and that by which they will be instructed and disciplined.

WASHINGTON, D.C., May 1, 1861.

United States Infantry Tactics.

TITLE FIRST.

ARTICLE FIRST.

Formation of a Regiment in order of battle, or in line.

1. A REGIMENT is composed of ten companies, which will habitually be posted from right to left, in the following order: first, sixth, fourth, ninth, third, eighth, fifth, tenth, seventh, second, according to the rank of captains.

2. With a less number of companies the same principle will be observed, viz.: the first captain will command the right company, the second captain the left company, the third captain the right centre company, and so on.

3. The companies thus posted will be designated from right to left, *first* company, *second* company, &c. This designation will be observed in the manœuvres.

4. The first two companies on the right, whatever their denomination, will form the *first division*; the next two companies the *second division*; and so on, to the left.

5. Each company will be divided into two equal parts, which will be designated as the first and second platoon, counting from the right; and each platoon, in like manner, will be subdivided into two sections.

6. In all exercises and manœuvres, every regiment,

or part of a regiment, composed of two or more companies, will be designated as a battalion.

7. The color, with a guard to be hereinafter designated, will be posted on the left of the right centre battalion company. That company, and all on its right, will be
denominated the *right wing* of the battalion; the remaining companies the *left wing*.

8. The formation of a regiment is in two ranks; and
each company will be formed into two ranks, in the following manner: the corporals will be posted in the front
rank, and on the right and left of platoons, according to
height; the tallest corporal and the tallest man will form
the first file, the next two tallest men will form the second
file, and so on to the last file, which will be composed of
the shortest corporal and the shortest man.

9. The odd and even files, numbered as one, two, in
the company, from right to left, will form groups of four
men, which will be designated *comrades in battle*.

10. The distance from one rank to another will be
thirteen inches, measured from the breasts of the rear
rank men to the backs or knapsacks of the front rank
men.

11. For manœuvring, the companies of a battalion
will always be equalized, by transferring men from the
strongest to the weakest companies.

Posts of Company Officers, Sergeants and Corporals.

12. The company officers and sergeants are nine in
number, and will be posted in the following manner:

13. The *captain* on the right of the company, touching with the left elbow.

14. The *first sergeant* in the rear rank, touching with
the left elbow, and covering the captain. In the manœuvres he will be denominated *covering sergeant*, or *right
guide* of the company.

15. The remaining officers and sergeants will be

posted as file closers, and two paces behind the rear rank.

16. The *first lieutenant*, opposite the centre of the fourth section.

17. The *second lieutenant*, opposite the centre of the first platoon.

18. The *third lieutenant*, opposite the centre of the second platoon.

19. The *second sergeant*, opposite the second file from the left of the company. In the manœuvres he will be designated *left guide* of the company.

20. The *third sergeant*, opposite the second file from the right of the second platoon.

21. The *fourth sergeant*, opposite the second file from the left of the first platoon.

22. The *fifth sergeant*, opposite the second file from the right of the first platoon.

23. In the left or tenth company of the battalion, the second sergeant will be posted in the front rank, and on the left of the battalion.

24. The corporals will be posted in the front rank, as prescribed No. 8.

25. Absent officers and sergeants will be replaced, officers by sergeants, and sergeants by corporals. The colonel may detach a first lieutenant from one company to command another, of which both the captain and first lieutenant are absent; but this authority will give no right to a lieutenant to demand to be so detached.

Posts of Field Officers and Regimental Staff.

26. The field officers, colonel, lieutenant colonel and major, are supposed to be mounted, and on active service shall be on horseback. The adjutant, when the battalion is manœuvring, will be on foot.

27. The colonel will take post thirty paces in rear of the file closers, and opposite the centre of the battalion.

This distance will be reduced whenever there is a reduction in the front of the battalion.

28. The lieutenant colonel and the major will be opposite the centres of the right and left wings respectively, and twelve paces in rear of the file closers.

29. The adjutant and sergeant major will be opposite the right and left of the battalion, respectively, and eight paces in rear of the file closers.

30. The adjutant and sergeant major will aid the lieutenant colonel and major, respectively, in the manœuvres.

31. The colonel, if absent, will be replaced by the lieutenant colonel, and the latter by the major. If all the field officers be absent, the senior captain will command the battalion; but if either be present, he will not call the senior captain to act as field officer, except in case of evident necessity.

32. The quarter-master, surgeon, and other staff officers, in one rank, on the left of the colonel, and three paces in his rear.

33. The quarter-master sergeant, on a line with the front rank of the field music, and two paces on the right.

Posts of Field Music and Band.

34. The buglers will be drawn up in four ranks, and posted twelve paces in rear of the file closers, the left opposite the centre of the left centre company. The senior principal musician will be two paces in front of the field music, and the other two paces in the rear.

35. The regimental band, if there be one, will be drawn up in two or four ranks, according to its numbers, and posted five paces in rear of the field music, having one of the principal musicians at its head.

Color-guard.

36. In each battalion the color-guard will be com-

posed of eight corporals, and posted on the left of the right centre company, of which company, for the time being, the guard will make a part.

37. The front rank will be composed of a sergeant, to be selected by the colonel, who will be called, for the time, *color-bearer*, with the two ranking corporals, respectively, on his right and left; the rear rank will be composed of the three corporals next in rank; and the three remaining corporals will be posted in their rear, and on the line of file closers. The left guide of the color-company, when these three last named corporals are in the rank of file closers, will be immediately on their left.

38. In battalions with less than five companies present, there will be no color-guard, and no display of colors, except it may be at reviews.

39. The corporals for the color-guard will be selected from those most distinguished for regularity and precision, as well in their positions under arms as in their marching. The latter advantage, and a just carriage of the person, are to be more particularly sought for in the selection of the color-bearer.

General Guides.

40. There will be two *general* guides in each battalion, selected, for the time, by the colonel, from among the sergeants (other than first sergeants) the most distinguished for carriage under arms, and accuracy in marching.

41. These sergeants will be respectively denominated, in the manœuvres, *right general guide*, and *left general guide*, and be posted in the line of file closers; the first in rear of the right, and the second in rear of the left flank of the battalion.

ARTICLE SECOND.

Instruction of the Battalion.

42. Every commanding officer is responsible for the instruction of his command. He will assemble the officers together for theoretical and practical instruction as often as he may judge necessary, and when unable to attend to this duty in person, it will be discharged by the officer next in rank.

43. Captains will be held responsible for the theoretical and practical instruction of their non-commissioned officers, and the adjutant for the instruction of the non-commissioned staff. To this end, they will require these tactics to be studied and recited lesson by lesson; and when instruction is given on the ground, each non-commissioned officer, as he explains a movement, should be required to put it into practical operation.

44. The non-commissioned officers should also be practised in giving commands. Each command, in a lesson, at the theoretical instruction, should first be given by the instructor, and then repeated, in succession, by the non-commissioned officers, so that while they become habituated to the commands, uniformity may be established in the manner of giving them.

45. In the school of the soldier, the company officers will be the instructors of the squads; but if there is not a sufficient number of company officers present, intelligent sergeants may be substituted; and two or three squads, under sergeant instructors, be superintended, at the same time, by an officer.

46. In the school of the company, the lieutenant colonel and the major, under the colonel, will be the principal instructors, substituting frequently the captain of the company, and sometimes one of the lieutenants; the substitute, as far as practicable, being superintended by one of the principals.

47. In the school of the battalion, the brigadier general may constitute himself the principal instructor, frequently substituting the colonel of the battalion, sometimes the lieutenant colonel or major, and twice or thrice, in the same course of instruction, each of the three senior captains. In this school, also, the substitute will always, if practicable, be superintended by the brigadier general or the colonel, or (in case of a captain being the instructor) by the lieutenant colonel or major.

48. Individual instruction being the basis of the instruction of companies, on which that of the regiment depends, and the first principles having the greatest influence upon this individual instruction, classes of recruits should be watched with the greatest care.

49. Instructors will explain, in a few clear and precise words, the movement to be executed; and not to overburden the memory of the men, they will always use the same terms to explain the same principles.

50. They should often join example to precept, should keep up the attention of the men by an animated tone, and pass rapidly from one movement to another, as soon as that which they command has been executed in a satisfactory manner.

51. The sabre bayonet should only be fixed when required to be used, either for attack or defence; the exercises and manœuvres will be executed without the bayonet.

52. In the movements which require the bayonet to be fixed, the chief of the battalion will cause the signal *to fix bayonet*, to be sounded; at this signal the men will fix bayonets without command, and immediately replace their pieces in the position they were before the signal.

Instruction of Officers.

53. The instruction of officers can be perfected only by joining theory to practice. The colonel will often practise them in marching and in estimating distances, and he will carefully endeavor to cause them to take steps equal in length and swiftness. They will also be exercised in the double quick step.

54. The instruction of officers will include all the Titles in this system of drill, and such regulations as prescribe their duties in peace and war.

55. Every officer will make himself perfectly acquainted with the bugle signals, and should, by practice, be enabled, if necessary, to sound them. This knowledge, so necessary in general instruction, becomes of vital importance on actual service in the field.

Instruction of Sergeants.

56. As the discipline and efficiency of a company materially depend on the conduct and character of its sergeants, they should be selected with care, and properly instructed in all the duties appertaining to their rank.

57. Their theoretical instruction should include the School of the Soldier, the School of the Company, and the Drill for Skirmishers. They should likewise know all the details of service, and the regulations prescribing their duties in garrison and in campaign.

58. The captain selects from the corporals in his company those whom he judges fit to be admitted to the theoretical instruction of the sergeants.

Instruction of Corporals.

59. Their theoretical instruction should include the School of the Soldier, and such regulations as prescribe their duties in garrison and in campaign.

60. The captain selects from his company a few

privates, who may be admitted to the theoretical instruction of the corporals.

61. As the instruction of sergeants and corporals is intended principally to qualify them for the instruction of the privates, they should be taught not only to execute, but to explain intelligibly every thing they may be required to teach.

Commands.

There are three kinds.

62. The command of *caution*, which is *attention*.

63. The *preparatory command*, which indicates the movement which is to be executed.

64. The command of *execution*, such as march or halt, or, in the manual of arms, the part of command which causes an execution.

65. The tone of command should be animated, distinct, and of a loudness proportioned to the number of men under instruction.

66. The command *attention* is pronounced at the top of the voice, dwelling on the last syllable.

67. The command of *execution* will be pronounced in a tone firm and brief.

68. The commands of caution and the preparatory commands are herein distinguished by *italics*, those of execution by CAPITALS.

69. Those preparatory commands which, from their length, are difficult to be pronounced at once, must be divided into two or three parts, with an ascending progression in the tone of command, but always in such a manner that the tone of execution may be more energetic and elevated; the divisions are indicated by a hyphen. The parts of commands which are placed in a parenthesis are not pronounced.

TITLE SECOND.

SCHOOL OF THE SOLDIER.

General Rules and Division of the School of the Soldier.

70. THE object of this school being the individual and progressive instruction of the recruits, the instructor never requires a movement to be executed until he has given an exact explanation of it; and he executes, himself, the movement which he commands, so as to join example to precept. He accustoms the recruit to take, by himself, the position which is explained—teaches him to rectify it only when required by his want of intelligence—and sees that all the movements are performed without precipitation.

71. Each movement should be understood before passing to another. After they have been properly executed in the order laid down in each lesson, the instructor no longer confines himself to that order; on the contrary, he should change it, that he may judge of the intelligence of the men.

72. The instructor allows the men to rest at the end of each part of the lessons, and oftener, if he thinks proper, especially at the commencement; for this purpose he commands REST.

73. At the command REST, the soldier is no longer required to preserve immobility, or to remain in his place. If the instructor wishes merely to relieve the attention of the recruit, he commands, *in place*—REST; the soldier is then not required to preserve his immobility, but he always keeps one of his feet in its place.

74. When the instructor wishes to commence the

instruction, he commands—ATTENTION; at this command, the soldier takes his position, remains motionless, and fixes his attention.

75. The *School of the Soldier* will be divided into three parts: the first, comprehending what ought to be taught to recruits without arms; the second, the manual of arms, the loadings and firings; the third, the principles of alignment, the march by the front, the different steps, the march by the flank, the principles of wheeling, and those of change of direction; also, long marches in double quick time and the run.

76. Each part will be divided into lessons, as follows:—

PART FIRST.

Lesson 1.   Position of the soldier without arms: Eyes right, left and front.

Lesson 2.   Facings.

Lesson 3.   Principles of the direct step in common and quick time.

Lesson 4.   Principles of the direct step in double quick time and the run.

PART SECOND.

Lesson 1.   Principles of shouldered arms.

Lesson 2.   Manual of arms.

Lesson 3.   To load in four times, and at will.

Lesson 4.   Firings, direct, oblique, by file, and by rank.

Lesson 5.   To fire and load, kneeling and lying.

Lesson 6.   Bayonet exercise.

PART THIRD.

Lesson 1.   Union of eight or twelve men for instruction in the principles of alignment.

Lesson 2.   The direct march, the oblique march, and the different steps.

Lesson 3. The march by the flank.

Lesson 4. Principles of wheeling and change of direction.

Lesson 5. Long marches in double quick time, and the run, with arms and knapsacks.

PART FIRST.

77. This will be taught, if practicable, to one recruit at a time; but three or four may be united, when the number be great, compared with that of the instructors. In this case, the recruits will be placed in a single rank, at one pace from each other. In this part, the recruits will be without arms.

Lesson I.

Position of the Soldier.

78. Heels on the same line, as near each other as the conformation of the man will permit;

The feet turned out equally, and forming with each other something less than a right angle;

The knees straight without stiffness;

The body erect on the hips, inclining a little forward;

The shoulders square and falling equally;

The arms hanging naturally;

The elbows near the body;

The palm of the hand turned a little to the front, the little finger behind the seam of the pantaloons;

The head erect and square to the front, without constraint;

The chin near the stock, without covering it;

The eyes fixed straight to the front, and striking the ground about the distance of fifteen paces.

Remarks on the position of the Soldier.

Heels on the same line;

79. Because, if one were in rear of the other, the shoulder on that side would be thrown back, or the position of the soldier would be constrained.

Heels more or less closed;

Because, men who are knock-kneed, or who have legs with large calves, cannot, without constraint, make their heels touch while standing.

The feet equally turned out, and not forming too large an angle;

Because, if one foot were turned out more than the other, a shoulder would be deranged, and if both feet be too much turned out, it would not be practicable to incline the upper part of the body forward without rendering the whole position unsteady.

Knees extended without stiffness;

Because, if stiffened, constraint and fatigue would be unavoidable.

The body erect on the hips;

Because, it gives equilibrium to the position. The instructor will observe that many recruits have the bad habit of dropping a shoulder, of drawing in a side, or of advancing a hip, particularly the right, when under arms. These are defects he will labor to correct.

The upper part of the body inclining forward;

Because, commonly, recruits are disposed to do the reverse, to project the belly, and to throw back the shoulders, when they wish to hold themselves erect, from which result great inconveniences in marching. The habit of inclining forward the upper part of the body, is so important to contract, that the instructor must enforce it at the beginning, particularly with recruits who have naturally the opposite habit.

Shoulders square;

Because, if the shoulders be advanced beyond the line of the breast, and the back arched (the defect called *round-shouldered*, not uncommon among recruits), the man cannot align himself, nor use his piece with address. It is important, then, to correct this defect, and necessary to that end that the coat should set easy about the shoulders and armpits; but in correcting this defect, the instructor will take care that the shoulders be not thrown too much to the rear, which would cause the belly to project, and the small of the back to be curved.

The arms hanging naturally, elbows near the body, the palm of the hand a little turned to the front, the little finger behind the seam of the pantaloons;

Because, these positions are equally important to the *shoulder-arms,* and to prevent the man from occupying more space in a rank than is necessary to a free use of the piece; they have, moreover, the advantage of keeping in the shoulders.

The face straight to the front, and without constraint;

Because, if there be stiffness in the latter position, it would communicate itself to the whole of the upper part of the body, embarrass its movements, and give pain and fatigue.

Eyes direct to the front;

Because, this is the surest means of maintaining the shoulders in line—an essential object, to be insisted on and attained.

80. The instructor having given the recruit the

position of the soldier without arms, will now teach him the turning of the head and eyes. He will command:

1. *Eyes*—Right. 2. Front.

81. At the word *right*, the recruit will turn the head gently, so as to bring the inner corner of the left eye in a line with the buttons of the coat, the eyes fixed on the line of the eyes of the men in, or supposed to be in, the same rank.

82. At the second command, the head will resume the direct or habitual position.

83. The movement of *Eyes*—Left will be executed by inverse means.

84. The instructor will take particular care that the movement of the head does not derange the squareness of the shoulders, which will happen if the movement of the former be too sudden.

85. When the instructor shall wish the recruit to pass from the state of attention to that of ease, he will command:

Rest.

86. To cause a resumption of the habitual position, the instructor will command:

1. *Attention.* 2. Squad.

87. At the first word, the recruit will fix his attention; at the second, he will resume the prescribed position and steadiness.

Lesson II.

Facings.

88. Facing to the right and left will be executed in one *time*, or pause. The instructor will command:

1. *Squad.* 2. *Right* (or *left*)—Face.

89. At the second command, raise the right foot

slightly, turn on the left heel, raising the toes a little, and then replace the right heel by the side of the left, and on the same line.

90. The full face to the rear (or front) will be executed in two *times*, or pauses. The instructor will command:

1. *Squad.* 2. ABOUT—FACE.

91. (*First time.*) At the word *about*, the recruit will turn on the left heel, bring the left toe to the front, carry the right foot to the rear, the hollow opposite to, and full three inches from, the left heel, the feet square to each other.

92. (*Second time.*) At the word *face*, the recruit will turn on both heels, raise the toes a little, extend the hams, face to the rear, bringing, at the same time, the right heel by the side of the left.

93. The instructor will take care that these motions do not derange the position of the body.

LESSON III.

Principles of the Direct Step.

94. The length of the direct step, or pace, in common time, will be twenty-eight inches, reckoning from heel to heel, and in swiftness, at the rate of ninety in a minute.

95. The instructor, seeing the recruit confirmed in his position, will explain to him the principle and mechanism of this step—placing himself six or seven paces from, and facing to, the recruit. He will himself execute slowly the step in the way of illustration, and then command:

1. *Squad, forward.* 2. *Common time.*
3. MARCH.

96. At the first command, the recruit will throw the

weight of the body on the right leg, without bending the left knee.

97. At the third command, he will smartly, but without a jerk, carry straight forward the left foot twenty-eight inches from the right, the sole near the ground, the ham extended, the toe a little depressed, and, as also the knee, slightly turned out; he will, at the same time, throw the weight of the body forward, and plant flat the left foot, without shock, precisely at the distance where it finds itself from the right when the weight of the body is brought forward, the whole of which will now rest on the advanced foot. The recruit will next, in like manner, advance the right foot and plant it as above, the heel twenty-eight inches from the heel of the left foot, and thus continue to march without crossing the legs, or striking the one against the other, without turning the shoulders, and preserving always the face direct to the front.

98. When the instructor shall wish to arrest the march, he will command:

1. *Squad.* 2. HALT.

99. At the second command, which will be given at the instant when either foot is coming to the ground, the foot in the rear will be brought up, and planted by the side of the other, without shock.

100. The instructor will indicate, from time to time, to the recruit, the cadence of the step by giving the command *one* at the instant of raising a foot, and *two* at the instant it ought to be planted, observing the cadence of ninety steps in a minute. This method will contribute greatly to impress upon the mind the two motions into which the step is naturally divided.

101. Common time will be employed only in the first and second parts of the School of the Soldier. As soon as the recruit has acquired steadiness, has become established in the principles of shouldered arms and in the

mechanism, length and swiftness of the step in common time, he will be practised only in quick time, the double quick time, and the run.

102. The principles of the step in quick time are the same as for common time, but its swiftness is at the rate of one hundred and ten steps per minute.

103. The instructor wishing the squad to march in quick time, will command:

1. *Squad, forward.* 2. March.

Lesson IV.

Principles of the Double Quick Step.

104. The length of the double quick step is thirty-three inches, and its swiftness at the rate of one hundred and sixty-five steps per minute.

105. The instructor wishing to teach the recruits the principles and mechanism of the double quick step, will command:

1. *Double quick step.* 2. March.

106. At the first command, the recruit will raise his hands to a level with his hips, the hands closed, the nails towards the body, the elbows to the rear.

107. At the second command, he will raise to the front his left leg bent, in order to give to the knee the greatest elevation, the part of the leg between the knee and the instep vertical, the toe depressed; he will then replace his foot in its former position; with the right leg he will execute what has just been prescribed for the left, and the alternate movement of the legs will be continued until the command:

1. *Squad.* 2. Halt.

108. At the second command, the recruit will bring the foot which is raised by the side of the other, and dropping at the same time his hands by his side, will resume the position of the soldier without arms.

109. The instructor placing himself seven or eight paces from, and facing the recruit, will indicate the cadence by the commands, *one* and *two*, given alternately at the instant each foot should be brought to the ground, which at first will be in common time, but its rapidity will be gradually augmented.

110. The recruit being sufficiently established in the principles of this step, the instructor will command:

1. *Squad, forward.* 2. *Double quick.*
3. MARCH.

111. At the first command, the recruit will throw the weight of his body on the right leg.

112. At the second command, he will place his arms as indicated No. 106.

113. At the third command, he will carry forward the left foot, the leg slightly bent, the knee somewhat raised—will plant his left foot, the toe first, thirty-three inches from the right, and with the right foot will then execute what has just been prescribed for the left. This alternate movement of the legs will take place by throwing the weight of the body on the foot that is planted, and by allowing a natural, oscillatory motion to the arms.

114. The double quick step may be executed with different degrees of swiftness. Under urgent circumstances the cadence of this step may be increased to one hundred and eighty per minute. At this rate a distance of four thousand yards would be passed over in about twenty-five minutes.

115. The recruits will be exercised also in running.

116. The principles are the same as for the double quick step, the only difference consisting in a greater degree of swiftness.

117. It is recommended in marching at double quick time, or the run, that the men should breathe as much as possible through the nose, keeping the month closed. Experience has proved that, by conforming to

this principle, a man can pass over a much longer distance, and with less fatigue.

———

PART SECOND.

GENERAL RULES.

118. The instructor will not pass the men to this second part until they shall be well established in the position of the body, and in the manner of marching at the different steps.

119. He will then unite four men, whom he will place in the same rank, elbow to elbow, and instruct them in the position of shouldered arms, as follows:

LESSON I.

Principles of Shouldered Arms.

120. The recruit being placed as explained in the first lesson of the first part, the instructor will cause him to bend the right arm slightly, and place the piece in it, in the following manner:

121. The piece in the right hand—the barrel nearly vertical and resting in the hollow of the shoulder—the guard to the front, the arm hanging nearly at its full length near the body; the thumb and fore-finger embracing the guard, the remaining fingers closed together, and grasping the swell of the stock just under the cock, which rests on the little finger.

122. Recruits are frequently seen with natural defects in the conformation of the shoulders, breast and hips. These the instructor will labor to correct in the lessons without arms, and afterwards, by steady endeavors, so that the appearance of the pieces, in the same line, may be uniform, and this without constraint to the men in their positions.

123. The instructor will have occasion to remark that

Pl. 1.

SHOULDER ARMS (No. 120).

recruits, on first bearing arms, are liable to derange their position by lowering the right shoulder and the right hand, or by sinking the hip and spreading out the elbows.

124. He will be careful to correct all these faults by continually rectifying the position; he will sometimes take away the piece to replace it the better; he will avoid fatiguing the recruits too much in the beginning, but labor by degrees to render this position so natural and easy that they may remain in it a long time without fatigue.

125. Finally, the instructor will take great care that the piece, at a shoulder, be not carried too high nor too low: if too high, the right elbow would spread out, the soldier would occupy too much space in his rank, and the piece be made to waver; if too low, the files would be too much closed, the soldier would not have the necessary space to handle his piece with facility, the right arm would become too much fatigued, and would draw down the shoulder.

126. The instructor, before passing to the second lesson, will cause to be repeated the movements of *eyes right*, *left*, and *front*, and the *facings*.

LESSON II.

Manual of Arms.

127. The manual of arms will be taught to four men, placed, at first, in one rank, elbow to elbow, and afterwards in two ranks.

128. Each command will be executed in one *time* (or pause), but this time will be divided into motions, the better to make known the mechanism.

129. The rate (or swiftness) of each motion, in the manual of arms, with the exceptions herein indicated, is fixed at the ninetieth part of a minute; but, in order not to fatigue the attention, the instructor will, at first, look more particularly to the execution of the motions, without

requiring a nice observance of the cadence, to which he will bring the recruits progressively, and after they shall have become a little familiarized with the handling of the piece.

130. As the motions relative to the cartridge, to the rammer, and to the fixing and unfixing of the bayonet, cannot be executed at the rate prescribed, nor even with a uniform swiftness, they will not be subjected to that cadence. The instructor will, however, labor to cause these motions to be executed with promptness, and, above all, with regularity.

131. The last syllable of the command will decide the brisk execution of the first motion of each time (or pause). The commands *two*, *three*, and *four*, will decide the brisk execution of the other motions. As soon as the recruits shall well comprehend the positions of the several motions of a time, they will be taught to execute the time without resting on its different motions; the mechanism of the time will nevertheless be observed, as well to give a perfect use of the piece, as to avoid the sinking of, or slurring over, either of the motions.

132. The manual of arms will be taught in the following progression: The instructor will command:

Support—ARMS.

One time and three motions.

133. (*First motion.*) Bring the piece, with the right hand, perpendicularly to the front and between the eyes, the barrel to the rear; seize the piece with the left hand at the lower band, raise this hand as high as the chin, and seize the piece at the same time with the right hand four inches below the cock.

134. (*Second motion.*) Turn the piece with the right hand, the barrel to the front; carry the piece to the left shoulder, and pass the fore-arm extended on the breast

Pl. 2.

SUPPORT ARMS (No. 133).

between the right hand and the cock; support the cock against the left fore-arm, the left hand resting on the right breast.

135. (*Third motion.*) Drop the right hand by the side.

136. When the instructor may wish to give repose in this position, he will command:

REST.

137. At this command, the recruits will bring up smartly the right hand to the handle of the piece (small of the stock), when they will not be required to preserve silence, or steadiness of position.

138. When the instructor may wish the recruits to pass from this position to that of silence and steadiness, he will command:

1. *Attention.*   2. SQUAD.

139. At the second word, the recruits will resume the position of the third motion of *support arms.*

Shoulder—ARMS.

One time and three motions.

140. (*First motion.*) Grasp the piece with the right hand under and against the left fore-arm; seize it with the left hand at the lower band, the thumb extended; detach the piece slightly from the shoulder, the left fore-arm along the stock.

141. (*Second motion.*) Carry the piece vertically to the right shoulder with both hands, the rammer to the front, change the position of the right hand so as to embrace the guard with the thumb and forefinger, slip the left hand to the height of the shoulder, the fingers extended and joined, the right arm nearly straight.

142. (*Third motion.*) Drop the left hand quickly by the side.

Present—ARMS.

One time and two motions.

143. (*First motion.*) With the right hand bring the piece erect before the centre of the body, the rammer to the front; at the same time seize the piece with the left hand half-way between the guide sight and lower band, the thumb extended along the barrel and against the stock, the fore-arm horizontal and resting against the body, the hand as high as the elbow.

144. (*Second motion.*) Grasp the small of the stock with the right hand below and against the guard.

Shoulder—ARMS.

One time and two motions.

145. (*First motion.*) Bring the piece to the right shoulder, at the same time change the position of the right hand so as to embrace the guard with the thumb and forefinger, slip up the left hand to the height of the shoulder, the fingers extended and joined, the right arm nearly straight.

146. (*Second motion.*) Drop the left hand quickly by the side.

Order—ARMS.

One time and two motions.

147. (*First motion.*) Seize the piece briskly with the left hand near the upper band, and detach it slightly from the shoulder with the right hand: loosen the grasp of the right hand, lower the piece with the left, reseize the piece with the right hand above the lower band, the little finger in rear of the barrel, the butt about four inches from the ground, the right hand supported against the hip.

148. (*Second motion.*) Let the piece slip through the

PRESENT ARMS (No. 143).

ORDER ARMS (No. 147).

right hand to the ground by opening slightly the fingers, drop the left hand by the side, and take the position about to be described.

Position of Order Arms.

149. The hand low, the barrel between the thumb and fore-finger extended along the stock; the other fingers extended and joined; the muzzle about two inches from the right shoulder; the rammer in front; the toe (or beak) of the butt, against, and in a line with, the toe of the right foot, the barrel perpendicular.

150. When the instructor may wish to give repose in this position, he will command:

Rest.

151. At this command, the recruits will not be required to preserve silence or steadiness.

152. When the instructor may wish the recruits to pass from this position to that of silence and steadiness, he will command:

1. *Attention.* 2. Squad.

153. At the second word, the recruits will resume the position of *order arms.*

Shoulder—Arms.

One time and two motions.

154. (*First motion.*) Raise the piece vertically with the right hand to the height of the right breast, and opposite the shoulder, the elbow close to the body; seize the piece with the left hand below the right, and drop quickly the right hand to grasp the piece at the swell of the stock, the thumb and fore-finger embracing the guard; press the piece against the shoulder with the left hand, the hand at the height of the shoulder, the right arm nearly straight.

155. (*Second motion.*) Drop the left hand quickly by the side.

Load in nine times.

1. LOAD.*
One time and one motion.

156. Grasp the piece with the left hand as high as the right elbow, and bring it vertically opposite the middle of the body, shift the right hand to the upper band, place the butt between the feet, the barrel to the front; seize it with the left hand near the muzzle, which should be three inches from the body; carry the right hand to the cartridge box.

2. *Handle*—CARTRIDGE.
One time and one motion.

157. Seize the cartridge with the thumb and next two fingers, and place it between the teeth.

3. *Tear*—CARTRIDGE.
One time and one motion.

158. Tear the paper to the powder, hold the cartridge upright between the thumb and first two fingers, near the top; in this position place it in front of and near the muzzle—the back of the hand to the front.

4. *Charge*—CARTRIDGE.
One time and one motion.

159. Empty the powder into the barrel: disengage the ball from the paper with the right hand and the thumb and first two fingers of the left; insert it into the bore, the pointed end uppermost, and press it down with the right

---

*Whenever the loadings and firings are to be executed, the instructor will cause the cartridge boxes to be brought to the front.

LOAD (No. 156).

thumb; seize the head of the rammer with the thumb and fore-finger of the right hand, the other fingers closed, the elbows near the body.

5. Draw—RAMMER.

One time and three motions.

160. (*First motion.*) Half draw the rammer by extending the right arm; steady it in this position with the left thumb; grasp the rammer near the muzzle with the right hand, the little finger uppermost, the nails to the front, the thumb extended along the rammer.

161. (*Second motion.*) Clear the rammer from the pipes by again extending the arm; the rammer in the prolongation of the pipes.

162. (*Third motion.*) Turn the rammer, the little end of the rammer passing near the left shoulder; place the head of the rammer on the ball, the back of the hand to the front.

6. Ram—CARTRIDGE.

One time and one motion.

163. Insert the rammer as far as the right, and steady it in this position with the thumb of the left hand; seize the rammer at the small end with the thumb and fore-finger of the right hand, the back of the hand to the front; press the ball home, the elbows near the body.

7. Return—RAMMER.

One time and three motions.

164. (*First motion.*) Draw the rammer half-way out, and steady it in this position with the left thumb; grasp it near the muzzle with the right hand, the little finger uppermost, the nails to the front, the thumb along the rammer; clear the rammer from the bore by extending the

arm, the nails to the front, the rammer in the prolongation of the bore.

165. (*Second motion.*) Turn the rammer, the head of the rammer passing near the left shoulder, and insert it in the pipes until the right hand reaches the muzzle, the nails to the front.

166. (*Third motion.*) Force the rammer home by placing the little finger of the right hand on the head of the rammer; pass the left hand down the barrel to the extent of the arm, without depressing the shoulder.

8. PRIME.*

One time and two motions.

167. (*First motion.*) With the left hand raise the piece till the hand is as high as the eye, grasp the small of the stock with the right hand; half face to the right; place, at the same time, the right foot behind and at right angles with the left; the hollow of the right foot against the left heel. Slip the left hand down to the lower band, the thumb along the stock, the left elbow against the body; bring the piece to the right side, the butt below the right fore-arm—the small of the stock against the body and two inches below the right breast, the barrel upwards, the muzzle on a level with the eye.

168. (*Second motion.*) Half cock with the thumb of the right hand, the fingers supported against the guard and the small of the stock—remove the old cap with one of the fingers of the right hand, and with the thumb and fore-finger of the same hand take a cap from the pouch, place it on the nipple, and press it

---

*If Maynard's primer be used, the command will be, *load in eight times*, and the eighth command will be, *shoulder arms* and executed from *return rammer*, in one time and two motions, as follows:

(*First motion.*) Raise the piece with the left hand, and take the position of shoulder arms, as indicated No. 145.

(*Second motion.*) Drop the left hand quickly by the side.

Pl. 6.

PRIME (No. 167).

down with the thumb; seize the small of the stock with
the right hand.

9 *Shoulder*—ARMS.

One time and two motions.

169. (*First motion.*) Bring the piece to the right shoulder and support it there with the left hand, face to the
front; bring the right heel to the side of and on a line with
the left; grasp the piece with the right hand as indicated in
the position of *shoulder arms*.

170. (*Second motion.*) Drop the left hand quickly by
the side.

READY.

171. (*First motion.*) Raise the piece slightly with the
right hand, making a half face to the right on the left heel;
carry the right foot to the rear, and place it at right angles
to the left, the hollow of it opposite to, and against the left
heel; grasp the piece with the left hand at the lower band
and detach it slightly from the shoulder.

172. (*Second motion.*) Bring down the piece with both
hands, the barrel upwards, the left thumb extended along
the stock, the butt below the right forearm, the small of
the stock against the body and two inches below the right
breast, the muzzle as high as the eye, the left elbow
against the side; place at the same time the right thumb on
the head of the cock, the other fingers under and against
the guard.

173. (*Third motion.*) Cock, and seize the piece at the
small of the stock without deranging the position of the
butt.

AIM.

One time and one motion.

174. Raise the piece with both hands, and support the butt against the right shoulder; the left elbow down, the right as high as the shoulder; incline the head upon the butt, so that the right eye may perceive quickly the notch of the hausse, the front sight, and the object aimed at; the left eye closed, the right thumb extended along the stock, the fore-finger on the trigger.

175. When recruits are formed in two ranks to execute the firings, the front rank men will raise a little less the right elbow, in order to facilitate the aim of the rear rank men.

176. The rear rank men, in aiming, will each carry the right foot about eight inches to the right, and towards the left heel of the man next on the right, inclining the upper part of the body forward.

FIRE.

One time and one motion.

177. Press the fore-finger against the trigger, fire, without lowering or turning the head, and remain in this position.

178. Instructors will be careful to observe when the men fire, that they aim at some distinct object, and that the barrel be so directed that the line of fire and the line of sight be in the same vertical plane. They will often cause the firing to be executed on ground of different inclinations, in order to accustom the men to fire at objects either above or below them.

LOAD.

One time and one motion.

179. Bring down the piece with both hands, at the same time face to the front and take the position of *load*

AIM (No. 174).

Pl. 8.

AS REAR RANK, AIM (No. 176).

as indicated No. 156. Each rear rank man will bring his right foot by the side of the left.

180. The men being in this position, the instructor will cause the loading to be continued by the commands and means prescribed No. 156 and following.

181. If, after firing, the instructor should not wish the recruits to reload, he will command:

*Shoulder—*ARMS.

One time and one motion.

182. Throw up the piece briskly with the left hand, and resume the position of *shoulder arms*, at the same time face to the front. turning on the left heel, and bring the right heel on a line with the left.

183. To accustom the recruits to wait for the command *fire*, the instructor, when they are in the position of *aim*, will command:

*Recover—*ARMS.

One time and one motion.

184. At the first part of the command, withdraw the finger from the trigger; at the command *arms*, retake the position of the third motion of *ready*.

185. The recruits being in the position of the third motion of *ready*, if the instructor should wish to bring them to a shoulder, he will command:

*Shoulder—*ARMS.

One time and one motion.

186. At the command *shoulder*, place the thumb upon the cock, the fore-finger on the trigger, half-cock, and seize the small of the stock with the right hand. At the command *arms*, bring up the piece briskly to the right shoulder, and retake the position of shoulder arms.

187. The recruits being at shoulder arms, when the instructor shall wish to fix bayonets, he will command:

Fix—BAYONET.

One time and three motions.

188. (*First motion.*) Grasp the piece with the left hand at the height of the shoulder, and detach it slightly from the shoulder with the right hand.

189. (*Second motion.*) Quit the piece with the right hand, lower it with the left hand, opposite the middle of the body, and place the butt between the feet without shock; the rammer to the rear, the barrel vertical, the muzzle three inches from the body; seize it with the right hand at the upper band, and carry the left hand reversed to the handle of the sabre-bayonet.

190. (*Third motion.*) Draw the sabre-bayonet from the scabbard and fix it on the extremity of the barrel; seize the piece with the left hand, the arm extended, the right hand at the upper band.

Shoulder—ARMS.

One time and two motions.

191. (*First motion.*) Raise the piece with the left hand and place it against the right shoulder, the rammer to the front; seize the piece at the same time with the right hand at the swell of the stock, the thumb and fore-finger embracing the guard, the right arm nearly extended.

192. (*Second motion.*) Drop briskly the left hand by the side.

Charge—BAYONET.

One time and two motions.

193. (*First motion.*) Raise the piece slightly with the right hand and make a half face to the right on the left

CHARGE BAYONET (No. 193).

heel; place the hollow of the right foot opposite to, and three inches from the left heel, the feet square; seize the piece at the same time with the left hand a little above the lower band.

194. (*Second motion.*) Bring down the piece with both hands, the barrel uppermost, the left elbow against the body; seize the small of the stock, at the same time, with the right hand, which will be supported against the hip; the point of the sabre-bayonet as high as the eye.

Shoulder—ARMS.

One time and two motions.

195. (*First motion.*) Throw up the piece briskly with the left hand to facing to the front, place it against the right shoulder, the rammer to the front; turn the right hand so as to embrace the guard, slide the left hand to the height of the shoulder, the right hand nearly extended.

196. (*Second motion.*) Drop the left hand smartly by the side.

Trail—ARMS.

One time and two motions.

197. (*First motion.*) The same as the first motion of *order arms.*

198. (*Second motion.*) Incline the muzzle slightly to the front, the butt to the rear and about four inches from the ground. The right hand supported at the hip, will so hold the piece that the rear rank men may not touch with their bayonets the men in the front rank.

Shoulder—ARMS.

199. At the command *shoulder*, raise the piece perpendicularly in the right hand, the little finger in rear of the barrel; at the command *arms*, execute what has been

prescribed for the *shoulder* from the position of *order
arms.*

Unfix—BAYONET.

One time and three motions.

200. (*First and second motions.*) The same as the first
and second motions of *fix bayonet,* except that, at the end
of the second command, the thumb of the right hand will
be placed on the spring of the sabre-bayonet, and the left
hand will embrace the handle of the sabre-bayonet and the
barrel, the thumb extended along the blade.

201. (*Third motion.*) Press the thumb of the right
hand on the spring, wrest off the sabre-bayonet, turn it to
the right, the edge to the front, lower the guard until it
touches the right hand, which will seize the back and the
edge of the blade between the thumb and first two fingers,
the other fingers holding the piece; change the position of
the hand without quitting the handle, return the sabre-
bayonet to the scabbard, and seize the piece with the left
hand, the arm extended.

Shoulder—ARMS.

One time and two motions.

202. (*First motion.*) The same as the first motion from
fix bayonet, No. 191.

203. (*Second motion.*) The same as the second motion
from *fix bayonet,* No. 192.

Secure—ARMS.

One time and three motions.

204. (*First motion.*) The same as the first motion of
support arms, No. 133, except with the right hand seize
the piece at the small of the stock.

205. (*Second motion.*) Turn the piece with both hands,

UNFIX BAYONET (No. 200).

SECURE ARMS (No. 204).

the barrel to the front; bring it opposite the left shoulder, the butt against the hip, the left hand at the lower band, the thumb as high as the chin and extended on the rammer; the piece erect and detached from the shoulder, the left fore-arm against the piece.

206. (*Third motion.*) Reverse the piece, pass it under the left arm, the left hand remaining at the lower band, the thumb on the rammer to prevent it from sliding out, the little finger resting against the hip, the right hand falling at the same time by the side.

Shoulder—ARMS.

One time and three motions.

207. (*First motion.*) Raise the piece with the left hand, and seize it with the right hand at the small of the stock. The piece erect and detached from the shoulder, the butt against the hip, the left fore-arm along the piece.

208. (*Second motion.*) The same as the second motion of *shoulder arms from a support.*

209. (*Third motion.*) The same as the third motion of *shoulder arms from a support.*

Right shoulder shift—ARMS.

One time and two motions.

210. (*First motion.*) Detach the piece perpendicularly from the shoulder with the right hand, and seize it with the left between the lower band and guide sight, raise the piece, the left hand at the height of the shoulder and four inches from it; place, at the same time, the right hand on the butt, the beak between the first two fingers, the other two fingers under the butt plate.

211. (*Second motion.*) Quit the piece with the left hand, raise and place the piece on the right shoulder with

the right hand, the lock plate upwards; let fall, at the same time, the left hand by the side.

Shoulder—ARMS.

One time and two motions.

212. (*First motion.*) Raise the piece perpendicularly by extending the right arm to its full length, the rammer to the front, at the same time seize the piece with the left hand at the height of the shoulders.

213. (*Second motion.*) Quit the butt with the right hand, which will immediately embrace the guard, lower the piece to the position of shoulder arms, slide up the left hand to the height of the shoulder, the fingers extended and closed. (*Third motion.*) Drop the left hand by the side.

214. The men being at support arms, the instructor will sometimes cause pieces to be brought to the right shoulder. To this effect, he, will command:

Right shoulder shift—ARMS.

One time and two motions.

215. (*First motion.*) Seize the piece with the right hand, below and near the left fore-arm, place the left hand under the butt, the heel of the butt between the first two fingers.

216. (*Second motion.*) Turn the piece with the left hand, the lock plate upward, carry it to the right shoulder, the left hand still holding the butt, the muzzle elevated; hold the piece in this position and place the right hand upon the butt as is prescribed No. 210, and let fall the left hand by the side.

Support—ARMS.

One time and two motions.

217. (*First motion.*) The same as the first motion of *shoulder arms*, No. 212.

RIGHT SHOULDER SHIFT ARMS (No. 210).

GROUND ARMS (No. 222).

218. (*Second motion.*) Turn the piece with both hands, the barrel to the front, carry it opposite the left shoulder, slip the right hand to the small of the stock, place the left fore-arm extended on the breast as is prescribed No. 134, and let fall, the right hand by the side.

Arms—AT WILL.

One time and one motion.

219. At this command, carry the piece at pleasure on either shoulder, with one or both hands, the muzzle elevated.

Shoulder—ARMS.

One time and one motion.

220. At this command, retake quickly the position of shoulder arms.

221. The recruits being at ordered arms, when the instructor shall wish to cause the pieces to be placed on the ground, he will command:

Ground—ARMS.

One time and two motions.

222. (*First motion.*) Turn the piece with the right hand, the barrel to the left, at the same time seize the cartridge box with the left hand, bend the body, advance the left foot, the heel opposite the lower band; lay the piece on the ground with the right hand, the toe of the butt on a line with the right toe, the knees slightly bent, the right heel raised.

223. (*Second motion.*) Rise up, bring the left foot by the side of the right, quit the cartridge box with the left hand, and drop the hands by the side.

Raise—ARMS.

One time and two motions.

224. (*First motion.*) Seize the cartridge box with the

left hand, bend the body, advance the left foot opposite the lower band, and seize the piece with the right hand.

225. (*Second motion.*) Raise the piece, bringing the left foot by the side of the right; turn the piece with the right hand, the rammer to the front; at the same lime quit the cartridge box with the left hand, and drop this hand by the side.

Inspection of Arms.

226. The recruits being at *ordered arms*, and having the sabre-bayonet in the scabbard, if the instructor wishes to cause an inspection of arms, he will command:

Inspection—ARMS.

One time and two motions.

227. (*First motion.*) Seize the piece with the left hand below and near the upper band, carry it with both hands opposite the middle of the body, the butt between the feet, the rammer to the rear, the barrel vertical, the muzzle about three inches from the body; carry the left hand reversed to the sabre-bayonet, draw it from the scabbard and fix it on the barrel; grasp the piece with the left hand below and near the upper band, seize the rammer with the thumb and fore-finger of the right hand bent, the other fingers closed.

228. (*Second motion.*) Draw the rammer as has been explained in *loading*, and let it glide to the bottom of the bore, replace the piece with the left hand opposite the right shoulder, and retake the position of *ordered arms*.

229. The instructor will then inspect in succession the piece of each recruit, in passing along the front of the rank. Each, as the instructor reaches him, will raise smartly his piece with his right hand, seize it with the left between the lower band and guide sight, the lock to the

front, the left hand at the height of the chin, the piece opposite to the left eye; the instructor will take it with the right hand at the handle, and, after inspecting it, will return it to the recruit, who will receive it back with the right hand, and replace it in the position of *ordered arms*.

230. When the instructor shall have passed him, each recruit will retake the position prescribed at the command *inspection arms*, return the rammer, and resume the position of *ordered arms*.

231. If, instead of *inspection of arms*, the instructor should merely wish to cause bayonets to be fixed, he will command:

Fix—BAYONET.

232. Take the position indicated No. 227, fix bayonets as has been explained, and immediately resume the position of *ordered arms*.

233. If it be the wish of the instructor, after firing, to ascertain whether the pieces have been discharged, he will command:

Spring—RAMMERS.

234. Put the rammer in the barrel as has been explained above, and immediately retake the position of *ordered arms*.

235. The instructor, for the purpose stated, can take the rammer by the small end, and spring it in the barrel, or cause each recruit to make it ring in the barrel.

236. Each recruit, after the instructor passes him, will return rammer, and resume the position of *ordered arms*.

Remarks on the Manual of Arms.

237. The manual of arms frequently distorts the persons of recruits before they acquire ease and confidence

in the several positions. The instructor will therefore frequently recur to elementary principles in the course of the
lessons.

238. Recruits are also extremely liable to curve
the sides and back, and to derange the shoulders,
especially in loading. Consequently, the instructor
will not cause them to dwell too long, at a time, in
one position.

239. When, after some days of exercise in the
manual of arms, the four men shall be well established in their use, the instructor will always terminate
the lesson by marching the men for some time in one
rank, and at one pace apart, in common and quick time, in
order to confirm them more and more in the mechanism
of the step; he will also teach them to mark time and
to change step, which will be executed in the following
manner:

To mark time.

240. The four men marching in the direct step, the
instructor will command:

1. *Mark time.* 2. MARCH.

241. At the second command, which will be given
at the instant a foot is coming to the ground, the recruits
will make a semblance of marching, by bringing the heels
by the side of each other, and observing the cadence
of the step, by raising each foot alternately without
advancing.

242. The instructor wishing the direct step to be
resumed, will command:

1. *Forward.* 2. MARCH.

243. At the second command, which will be given as
prescribed above, the recruits will retake the step of
twenty-eight inches.

To change step.

244. The squad being in march, the instructor will command:

1. *Change step.* 2. MARCH.

245. At the second command, which will be given at the instant either foot is coming to the ground, bring the foot which is in rear by the side of that which is in front, and step off again with the foot which was in front.

To march backwards.

246. The instructor wishing the squad to march backwards, will command:

1. *Squad backward.* 2. MARCH.

247. At the second command, the recruits will step off smartly with the left foot fourteen inches to the rear, reckoning from heel to heel, and so on with the feet in succession till the command *halt*, which will always be preceded by the caution *squad*. The men will halt at this command, and bring back the foot in front by the side of the other.

248. This step will always be executed in quick time.

249. The instructor will be watchful that the recruits march straight to the rear, and that the erect position of the body and the piece be not deranged.

LESSON III.

To load in four times.

250. The object of this lesson is to prepare the recruits to load at will, and to cause them to distinguish the times which require the greatest regularity and attention, such as *charge cartridge, ram cartridge,* and *prime*. It will be divided as follows:

251. The first time will be executed at the end of the command; the three others at the commands, *two*, *three* and *four*.

The instructor will command:

1. *Load in four times.*   2. LOAD.

252. Execute the times to include charge cartridge.

TWO.

253. Execute the times to include ram cartridge.

THREE.

254. Execute the times to include prime.

FOUR.

255. Execute the time of *shoulder arms.*

To load at will.

256. The instructor will next teach loading at will, which will be executed as loading in four times, but continued, and without resting on either of the times. He will command:

1. *Load at will.*   2. LOAD.

257. The instructor will habituate the recruits, by degrees, to load with the greatest possible promptitude, each without regulating himself by his neighbor, and above all without waiting for him.

258. The cadence prescribed No. 129, is not applicable to loading in four times, or at will.

LESSON IV.

Firings.

259. The firings are direct or oblique, and will be executed as follows:

The direct fire.

260. The instructor will give the following commands:

1. *Fire by Squad.* 2. *Squad.* 3. READY. 4. AIM.
5. FIRE. 6. LOAD.

261. These several commands will be executed as has been prescribed in the *Manual of Arms.* At the third command, the men will come to the position of *ready* as heretofore explained. At the fourth they will aim according to the rank in which each may find himself placed, the rear rank men inclining forward a little the upper part of the body, in order that their pieces may reach as much beyond the front rank as possible.

262. At the sixth command, they will load their pieces and return immediately to the position of *ready.*

263. The instructor will recommence the firing by the commands:

1. *Squad.* 2. AIM. 3. FIRE. 4. LOAD.

264. When the instructor wishes the firing to cease, he will command:

Cease firing.

265. At this command, the men will cease firing, but will load their pieces if unloaded, and afterwards bring them to a shoulder.

Oblique Firings.

266. The oblique firings will be executed to the right and left, and by the same commands as the direct fire, with this single difference—the command *aim* will always be preceded by the caution, *right* or *left oblique.*

Position of the two ranks in the Oblique Fire to the right.

267. At the command *ready*, the two ranks will execute what has been prescribed for the direct fire.

268. At the cautionary command, *right oblique*, the two ranks will throw back the right shoulder and look steadily at the object to be hit.

269. At the command *aim*, each front rank man will aim to the right without deranging the feet; each rear rank man will advance the left foot about eight inches towards the right heel of the man next on the right of his file leader, and aim to the right, inclining the upper part of the body forward and bending a little the left knee.

Position of the two ranks in the Oblique Fire to the left.

270. At the cautionary command *left oblique*, the two ranks will throw back the left shoulder and look steadily at the object to be hit.

271. At the command *aim*, the front rank will take aim to the left without deranging the feet; each man in the rear rank will advance the right foot about eight inches towards the right heel of the man next on the right of his file leader, and aim to the left, inclining the upper part of the body forward and bending a little the right knee.

272. In both cases, at the command *load*, the men of each rank will come to the position of load as prescribed in the direct fire; the rear rank men bringing back the foot which is to the right and front by the side of the other. Each man will continue to load as if isolated.

To fire by file.

273. The fire by file will be executed by the two ranks, the files of which will fire successively, and without regulating on each other, except for the first fire.

274. The instructor will command:

1. *Fire by file.*   2. *Squad.*   3. READY.
4. COMMENCE FIRING.

275. At the third command, the two ranks will take the position prescribed in the direct fire.

276. At the fourth command, the file on the right will aim and fire; the rear rank man in aiming will take the position indicated No. 176.

277. The men of this file will load their pieces briskly and fire a second time; reload and fire again, and so on in continuation.

278. The second file will aim, at the instant the first brings down pieces to reload, and will conform in all respects to that which has just been prescribed for the first file.

279. After the first fire, the front and rear rank men will not be required to fire at the same time.

280. Each man, after loading, will return to the position of ready and continue the fire.

281. When the instructor wishes the fire to cease, he will command:

Cease—FIRING.

282. At this command, the men will cease firing. If they have fired they will load their pieces and bring them to a shoulder; if at the position of *ready*, they will half-cock and shoulder arms. If in the position of *aim*, they will bring down their pieces, half-cock, and shoulder arms.

To fire by rank.

283. The fire by rank will be executed by each entire rank, alternately

284. The instructor will command:

1. *Fire by rank.* 2. *Squad.* 3. Ready. 4. *Rear rank.*
  5. Aim. 6. Fire. 7. Load.

285. At the third command, the two ranks will take the position of *ready*, as prescribed in the direct fire.

286. At the seventh command, the rear rank will execute that which has been prescribed in the direct fire, and afterwards take the position of *ready*.

287. As soon as the instructor sees several men of the rear rank in the position of *ready*, he will command:

1. *Front rank.* 2. Aim. 3. Fire. 4. Load.

288. At these commands, the men in the front rank will execute what has been prescribed for the rear rank, but they will not step off with the right foot.

289. The instructor will recommence the firing by the rear rank, and will thus continue to alternate from rank to rank, until he shall wish the firing to cease, when he will command, *cease firing*, which will be executed as heretofore prescribed.

Lesson V.

To fire and load kneeling.

290. In this exercise the squad will be supposed loaded and drawn up in one rank. The instruction will be given to each man individually, without times or motions, and in the following manner.

291. The instructor will command:

FIRE AND LOAD KNEELING.

292. At this command, the man on the right of the squad will move forward three paces and halt; then carry the right foot to the rear and to the right of the left heel, and in a position convenient for placing the right knee upon the ground in bending the left leg; place the right

Pl. 14.

FIRE AND LOAD KNEELING (No. 292).

knee upon the ground; lower the piece, the left fore-arm supported upon the thigh on the same side, the right hand on the small of the stock, the butt resting on the right thigh, the left hand supporting the piece near the lower band.

293. He will next move the right leg to the left around the knee supported on the ground, until this leg is nearly perpendicular to the direction of the left foot, and thus seat himself comfortably on the right heel.

294. Raise the piece with the right hand and support it with the left, holding it near the lower band, the left elbow resting on the left thigh near the knee; seize the hammer with the thumb, the fore-finger under the guard, cock and seize the piece at the small of the stock; bring the piece to the shoulder, *aim* and *fire*.

295. Bring the piece down as soon as it is fired, and support it with the left hand, the butt resting against the right thigh; carry the piece to the rear rising on the knee, the barrel downwards, the butt resting on the ground; in this position support the piece with the left hand at the upper band, draw cartridge with the right and load the piece, ramming the ball, if necessary, with both hands.

296. When loaded bring the piece to the front with the left hand, which holds it at the upper band; seize it at the same time with the right hand at the small of the stock; turn the piece, the barrel uppermost and nearly horizontal, the left elbow resting on the left thigh; half-cock, remove the old cap and prime, rise, and return to the ranks.

297. The second man will then be taught what has just been prescribed for the first, and so on through the remainder of the squad.

To fire and load lying.

298. In this exercise the squad will be in one rank and

loaded; the instruction will be given individually and without times or motions.

299. The instructor will command:

FIRE AND LOAD LYING.

300. At this command, the man on the right of the squad will move forward three spaces and halt; he will then bring his piece to an order, drop on both knees, and place himself on the ground flat on his belly. In this position he will support the piece nearly horizontal with the left hand, holding it near the lower band, the butt end of the piece and the left elbow resting on the ground, the barrel uppermost; cock the piece with the right hand, and carry this hand to the small of the stock; raise the piece with both hands, press the butt against the shoulder, and resting on both elbows, *aim* and *fire*.

301. As soon as he has fired, bring the piece down and turn upon his left side, still resting on his left elbow; bring back the piece until the cock is opposite his breast, the butt end resting on the ground; take out a cartridge with the right hand; seize the small of the stock with this hand, holding the cartridge with the thumb and two first fingers; he will then throw himself on his back, still holding the piece with both hands; carry the piece to the rear, place the butt between the heels, the barrel up, the muzzle elevated. In this position, charge cartridge, draw rammer, ram cartridge, and return rammer.

302. When finished loading, the man will turn again upon his left side, remove the old cap and prime, then raise the piece vertically, rise, turn about, and resume his position in the ranks.

303. The second man will be taught what has just been prescribed for the first, and so on throughout the squad.

GUARD AGAINST INFANTRY (No. 305).

Pl. 16.

GUARD AGAINST CAVALRY (No. 308).

Lesson VI.

Bayonet Exercise.

304. The bayonet exercise in this book will be confined to two movements, the *guard against infantry*, and the *guard against cavalry*. The men will be placed in one rank, with two paces interval, and being at shoulder arms, the instructor will command:

1. *Guard against Infantry.*   2. GUARD.

One time and two motions.

305. (*First motion.*) Make a half face to the right, turning on both heels, the feet square to each other; at the same time raise the piece slightly, and seize it with the left hand above and near the lower band.

306. (*Second motion.*) Carry the right foot twenty inches perpendicularly to the rear, the right heel on the prolongation of the left, the knees slightly bent, the weight of the body resting equally on both legs; lower the piece with both hands, the barrel uppermost, the left elbow against the body; seize the piece at the same time with the right hand at the small of the stock, the arms falling naturally, the point of the bayonet slightly elevated.

*Shoulder—*ARMS.

One time and one motion.

307. Throw up the piece with the left hand, and place it against the right shoulder, at the same time bring the right heel by the side of the left and face to the front.

1. *Guard against Cavalry.*   2. GUARD.

One time and two motions.

308. Both motions the same as for *guard against infantry*, except that the right hand will be supported

against the hip, and the bayonet held at the height of the eye, as in *charge bayonet*.

Shoulder—ARMS.

One time and one motion.

309. Spring up the piece with the left hand and place it against the right shoulder, at the same time bring the right heel by the side of the left, and face to the front.

PART THIRD.

310. When the recruits are well established in the *principles and mechanism of the step, the position of the body*, and *the manual of arms*, the instructor will unite eight men, at least, and twelve men, at most, in order to teach them the principles of alignment, the principles of the touch of elbows in marching to the front, the principles of the march by the flank, wheeling from a halt, wheeling in marching, and the change of direction to the side of the guide. He will place the squad in one rank, elbow to elbow, and number the men from right to left.

LESSON I.
Alignments.

311. The instructor will at first teach the recruits to align themselves man by man, in order the better to make them comprehend the principles of alignment; to this end, he will command the two men on the right flank to march two paces to the front, and having aligned them, he will caution the remainder of the squad to move up, as they may be successively called, each by his number, and align themselves successively on the line of the first two men.

312. Each recruit, as designated by his number, will turn the head and eyes to the right as prescribed in the first lesson of the first part, and will march in *quick time two paces forward*, shortening the last, so as to find himself about six inches behind the new alignment, which he ought never to pass: he will next move up steadily by steps of two or three inches, the hams extended, to the side of the man next to him on the alignment, so that, without deranging the head, the line of the eyes, or that of the shoulders, he may find himself in the exact line of his neighbor, whose elbow he will lightly touch without opening his own.

313. The instructor seeing the rank well aligned, will command:

FRONT.

314. At this, the recruits will turn eyes to the front, and remain firm.

315. Alignments to the left will be executed on the same principles.

316. When the recruits shall have thus learned to align themselves man by man, correctly, and without groping or jostling, the instructor will cause the entire rank to align itself at once by the command:

Right (or *left*)—DRESS.

317. At this, the rank, except the two men placed to advance as a basis of alignment, will move up in *quick time*, and place themselves on the new line, according to the principles prescribed No. 312.

318. The instructor, placed five or six paces in front, and facing the rank, will carefully observe that the principles are followed, and then pass to the flank that has served as the basis, to verify the alignment.

319. The instructor seeing the greater number of the rank aligned, will command:

FRONT.

320. The instructor may afterwards order *this* or *that* file *forward* or *back*, designating each by its number. The file or files designated, only, will slightly turn the head towards the basis, to judge how much they ought to move up or back, steadily place themselves on the line, and then turn eyes to the front, without a particular command to that effect.

321. Alignments to the rear will be executed on the same principles, the recruits stepping back a little beyond the line, and then dressing up according to the principles prescribed No. 312, the instructor commanding:

Right (or *left*) *backward*—DRESS.

322. After each alignment, the instructor will examine the position of the men, and cause the rank to come to *ordered arms*, to prevent too much fatigue, and also the danger of negligence at *shouldered arms*.

LESSON II.

323. The men having learned, in the first and second parts, to march with steadiness in common time, and to take steps equal in length and swiftness, will be exercised in the third part only in *quick time*, *double quick time*, and the *run*; the instructor will cause them to execute successively, at these different gaits, the march to the front, the facing about in marching, the march by the flank, the wheels at a halt and in marching, and the changes of direction to the side of the guide.

324. The instructor will inform the recruits that at the command *march*, they will always move off in *quick time*, unless this command should be preceded by that of *double quick*.

To march to the front.

325. The rank being correctly aligned, when the instructor shall wish to cause it to march by the front, he will place a well-instructed man on the right or the left, according to the side on which he may wish the guide to be, and command:

1. *Squad, forward.* 2. *Guide right* (or *left*). 3. MARCH.

326. At the command *march*, the rank will step off smartly with the left foot; the guide will take care to march straight to the front, keeping his shoulders always in a square with that line.

327. The instructor will observe, in marching to the front, that the men touch lightly the elbow towards the side of the guide; that they do not open out the left elbow, nor the right arm; that they yield to pressure coming from the side of the guide, and resist that coming from the opposite side; that they recover by insensible degrees the slight touch of the elbow, if lost; that they maintain the head direct to the front, no matter on which side the guide may be; and if found before or behind the alignment, that the man in fault corrects himself by shortening or lengthening the step, by degrees, almost insensible.

328. The instructor will labor to cause recruits to comprehend that the alignment can only be preserved, in marching, by the regularity of the step, the touch of the elbow, and the maintenance of the shoulders in a square with the line of direction; that if, for example, the step of some be longer than that of others, or if some march faster than others, a separation of elbows, and a loss of the alignment, would be inevitable; that if (it being required that the head should be direct to the front) they do not strictly observe the touch of elbows, it would be impossible for an individual to judge whether he marches

abreast with his neighbor, or not, and whether there be not an interval between them.

329. The impulsion of the quick step having a tendency to make men too easy and free in their movements, the instructor will be careful to regulate the cadence of this step, and to habituate them to preserve always the erectness of the body, and the due length of the pace.

330. The men being well established in the principles of the direct march, the instructor will exercise them in marching obliquely. The rank being in march, the instructor will command:

1. *Right* (or *left*) *oblique*.   2. MARCH.

331. At the second command, each man will make a half face to the right (or left), and will then march straight forward in the new direction. As the men no longer touch elbows, they will glance along the shoulders of the nearest files, towards the side to which they are obliquing, and will regulate their steps so that the shoulders shall always be behind that of their next neighbor on that side, and that his head shall conceal the heads of the other men in the rank. Besides this, the men should preserve the same length of pace, and the same degree of obliquity.

332. The instructor wishing to resume the primitive direction, will command:

1. *Forward*.   2. MARCH.

333. At the second command, each man will make a half face to the left (or right), and all will then march straight to the front, conforming to the principles of the direct march.

To march to the front in double quick time.

334. When the several principles, heretofore explained, have become familiar to the recruits, and they

shall be well established in the position of the body, the bearing of arms, and the mechanism, length, and swiftness of the step, the instructor will pass them from *quick* to *double quick* time, and the reverse, observing not to make them march obliquely in double quick time, till they are well established in the cadence of this step.

335. The squad being at a march in quick time, the instructor will command:

1. *Double quick.* 2. MARCH.

336. At the command *march*, which will be given when either foot is coming to the ground, the squad will step off in double quick time. The men will endeavor to follow the principles laid down in the first part of this book, and to preserve the alignment.

337. When the instructor wishes the squad to resume the step in quick time, he will command:

1. *Quick time.* 2. MARCH.

338. At the command *march*, which will be given when either foot is coming to the ground, the squad will retake the step in quick time.

339. The squad being in march, the instructor will halt it by the commands and means prescribed Nos. 98 and 99. The command *halt* will be given an instant before the foot is ready to be placed on the ground.

340. The squad being in march in double quick time, the instructor will occasionally cause it to mark time by the commands prescribed No. 240. The men will then mark double quick time, without altering the cadence of the step. He will also cause them to pass from the direct to the oblique step, and reciprocally, conforming to what has been prescribed No. 330, and following.

341. The squad being at a halt, the instructor will cause it to march in double quick time, by preceding the command *march*, by *double quick*.

342. The instructor will endeavor to regulate well the cadence of this step.

To face about in marching.

343. If the squad be marching in quick, or double quick time, and the instructor should wish to march it in retreat, he will command:

1. *Squad right about.*　2. MARCH.

344. At the command *march*, which will be given at the instant the left foot is coming to the ground, the recruit will bring this foot to the ground, and, turning on it, will face to the rear; he will then place the right foot in the new direction, and step off with the left foot.

To march backwards.

345. The squad being at a halt, if the instructor should wish to march it in the back step, he will command:

1. *Squad backward.*　2. *Guide left* (or *right*).　3. MARCH.

346. The back step will be executed by the means prescribed No. 247.

347. The instructor, in this step, will be watchful that the men do not lean on each other.

348. As the march to the front in quick time should only be executed at shouldered arms, the instructor, in order not to fatigue the men too much, and also to prevent negligence in gait and position, will halt the squad from time to time, and cause arms to be ordered.

349. In marching at *double quick time*, the men will always carry their pieces on the *right shoulder*, or at a *trail. This rule is general.*

350. If the instructor shall wish the pieces carried at a trail, he will give the command *trail arms*, before the command *double quick*. If, on the contrary, this command be not given, the men will shift their pieces to the right

shoulder at the command *double quick*. In either case, at
the command *halt*, the men will bring their pieces to the
position of *shoulder arms*. *This rule is general.*

LESSON III.

The march by the flank.

351. The rank being at a halt, and correctly aligned,
the instructor will command:

1. *Squad, right*—FACE. 2. *Forward.* 3. MARCH.

352. At the last part of the first command, the rank
will face to the right; the even numbered men, after facing
to the right, will step quickly to the right side of the odd
numbered men, the latter standing fast, so that when the
movement is executed, the men will be formed into files
of two men abreast.

353. At the third command, the squad will step off
smartly with the left foot; the files keeping aligned, and
preserving their intervals.

354. The march by the left flank will be executed by
the same commands, substituting the word *left* for *right*,
and by inverse means; in this case, the even numbered
men, after facing to the left, will stand fast, and the odd
numbered will place themselves on their left.

355. The instructor will place a well-instructed soldier
by the side of the recruit who is at the head of the rank, to
regulate the step, and to conduct him; and it will be
enjoined on this recruit to march always elbow to elbow
with the soldier.

356. The instructor will cause to be observed in the
march, by the flank, the following rules:

*That the step be executed according to the principles pre-
scribed for the direct step;*

Because these principles, without which men, placed

elbow to elbow, in the same rank, cannot preserve unity and harmony of movement, are of a more necessary observance in marching in file.

That the head of the man who immediately precedes, covers the heads of all who are in front;

Because it is the most certain rule by which each man may maintain himself in the exact line of the file.

357. The instructor will place himself habitually five or six paces on the flank of the rank marching in file, to watch over the execution of the principles prescribed above. He will also place himself sometimes in its rear, halt, and suffer it to pass fifteen or twenty paces, the better to see whether the men cover each other accurately.

358. When he shall wish to halt the rank, marching by the flank, and to cause it to face to the front, he will command:

1. *Squad.* 2. HALT. 3. FRONT.

359. At the second command, the rank will halt, and afterwards no man will stir, although he may have lost his distance. This prohibition is necessary, to habituate the men to a constant preservation of their distances.

360. At the third command, each man will front by facing to the left, if marching by the right flank, and by a face to the right, if marching by the left flank. The rear rank men will at the same time move quickly into their places, so as to form the squad again into one rank.

361. When the men have become accustomed to marching by the flank, the instructor will cause them to change direction by file; for this purpose, he will command:

1. *By file left* (or *right*). 2. MARCH.

362. At the command *march*, the first file will change direction to the left (or right) in describing a small arc of a circle, and will then march straight forward; the two men of this file, in wheeling, will keep up the touch of the elbows, and the man on the side to which the wheel is made, will shorten the first three or four steps. Each file will come successively to wheel on the same spot where that which preceded it wheeled.

363. The instructor will also cause the squad to face by the right or left flank in marching, and for this purpose will command:

1. *Squad by the right* (or *left*) *flank.* 2. MARCH.

364. At the second command, which will be given a little before either foot comes to the ground, the recruits will turn the body, plant the foot that is raised in the new direction, and step off with the other foot without altering the cadence of the step; the men will double or undouble rapidly.

365. If, in facing by the right or the left flank, the squad should face to the rear, the men will come into one rank, agreeably to the principles indicated No. 360. It is to be remarked that it is the men who are in rear who always move up to form into single rank, and in such manner as never to invert the order of the numbers in the rank.

366. If, when the squad has been faced to the rear, the instructor should cause it to face by the left flank, it is the even numbers who will double by moving to the left of the odd numbers; but if by the right flank, it is the odd numbers who will double to the right of the even numbers.

367. This lesson, like the preceding one, will be practised with pieces at a shoulder; but the instructor may, to give relief by change, occasionally order *support arms*,

and he will require of the recruits marching in this position, as much regularity as in the former.

The march by the flank in double quick time.

368. The principles of the march by the flank in double quick time, are the same as in quick time. The instructor will give the commands prescribed No. 351, taking
care always to give the command *double quick* before that
of *march*.

369. He will pay the greatest attention to the cadence
of the step.

370. The instructor will cause the change of direction,
and the march by the flank, to be executed in double
quick time, by the same commands, and according to the
same principles, as in quick time.

371. The instructor will cause the pieces to be carried
either on the *right shoulder* or at a *trail*.

372. The instructor will sometimes march the squad
by the flank, without doubling the files.

373. The principles of this march are the same as in
two ranks, and it will always be executed in quick time.

374. The instructor will give the commands prescribed
No. 351, but he will be careful to caution the squad not to
double files.

375. The instructor will be watchful that the men do
not bend their knees unequally, which would cause them
to tread on the heels of the men in front, and also to lose
the cadence of the step and their distances.

376. The various movements in this lesson will be executed in single rank. In the changes of direction, the leading man will change direction without altering the length
or the cadence of the step. The instructor will recall to the
attention of the men, that in facing by the right or left
flank in marching, they will not double, but march in one
rank.

Lesson IV.

WHEELINGS.

General principles of Wheeling.

377. Wheelings are of two kinds: from halts, or on fixed pivots, and in march, or on movable pivots.

378. Wheeling on a fixed pivot takes place in passing a corps from the order in battle to the order in column, or from the latter to the former.

379. Wheels in marching take place in changes of direction in column, as often as this movement is executed to the side opposite to the guide.

380. In wheels from a halt, the pivot-man only turns in his place, without advancing or receding.

381. In the wheels in marching, the pivot takes steps of nine or eleven inches, according as the squad is marching in quick or double quick time, so as to clear the wheeling point, which is necessary, in order that the subdivisions of a column may change direction without losing their distances, as will be explained in the school of the company.

382. The man on the wheeling flank will take the full step of twenty-eight inches, or thirty-three inches, according to the gait.

Wheeling from a halt, or on a fixed pivot.

383. The rank being at a halt, the instructor will place a well-instructed man on the wheeling flank to conduct it, and then command:

1. *By squad, right wheel.* 2. MARCH.

384. At the second command, the rank will step off with the left foot, turning at the same time the head a little to the left, the eyes fixed on the line of the eyes of the men to their left; the pivot-man will merely mark time in gradually turning his body, in order to conform himself to

the movement of the marching flank; the man who conducts this flank will take steps of twenty-eight inches, and
from the first step advance a little the left shoulder, cast
his eyes from time to time along the rank, and feel constantly the elbow of the next man lightly, but never push
him.

385. The other men will feel lightly the elbow of the
next man towards the pivot, resist pressure coming from
the opposite side, and each will conform himself to the
marching flank—shortening his step according to his
approximation to the pivot.

386. The instructor will make the rank wheel round
the circle once or twice before halting, in order to cause
the principles to be the better understood, and he will be
watchful that the centre does not break.

387. He will cause the wheel to the left to be executed
according to the same principles.

388. When the instructor shall wish to arrest the
wheel, he will command:

1. *Squad.* 2. Halt.

389. At the second command, the rank will halt, and
no man stir. The instructor, going to the flank opposite the
pivot, will place the two outer men of that flank in the
direction he may wish to give to the rank, without however displacing the pivot, who will conform the line of his
shoulders to this direction. The instructor will take care
to have between these two men, and the pivot, only the
space necessary to contain the other men. He will then
command:

Left (or *right*)—Dress.

390. At this, the rank will place itself on the alignment
of the two men established as the basis, in conformity
with the principles prescribed.

391. The instructor will next command FRONT which will be executed as prescribed No. 314.

Remarks on the principles of the wheel from a halt.

392. *Turn a little the head towards the marching flank, and fix the eyes on the line of the eyes of the men who are on that side;*

Because, otherwise, it would be impossible for each man to regulate the length of his step so as to conform his own movement to that of the marching flank.

Touch lightly the elbow of the next man towards the pivot;

In order that the files may not open out in the wheel.

Resist pressure that comes from the side of the marching flank;

Because, if this principle be neglected, the pivot, which ought to be a fixed point, in wheels from a halt, might be pushed out of its place by pressure.

Wheeling in marching, or on a movable pivot.

393. When the recruits have been brought to execute well the wheel from a halt, they will be taught to wheel in marching.

394. To this end, the rank being in march, when the instructor shall wish to cause it to change direction to the reverse flank (to the side opposite to the guide or pivot flank), he will command:

1. *Right* (or *left*) *wheel.* 2. MARCH.

395. The first command will be given when the rank is yet *four* paces from the wheeling point.

396. At the second command, the wheel will be executed in the same manner as from a halt, except that the touch of the elbow will remain towards the marching flank (or side of the guide) instead of the side of the

actual pivot; that the pivot-man, instead of merely turning to his place, will conform himself to the movement of the marching flank, feel lightly the elbow of the next man, take steps of full nine inches, and thus gain ground forward in describing a small curve so as to clear the point of the wheel. The middle of the rank will bend slightly to the rear. As soon as the movement shall commence, the man who conducts the marching flank will cast his eyes on the ground over which he will have to pass.

397. The wheel being ended, the instructor will command:

1. *Forward.*   2. MARCH.

398. The first command will be pronounced when *four* paces are yet required to complete the change of direction.

399. At the command *march*, which will be given at the instant of completing the wheel, the man who conducts the marching flank will direct himself straight forward; the pivot-man and all the rank will retake the step of twenty-eight inches, and bring the head direct to the front.

Turning, or change of direction to the side of the guide.

400. The change of direction to the side of the guide, in marching, will be executed as follows: The instructor will command:

1. *Left* (or *right*) *turn.*   2. MARCH.

401. The first command will be given when the rank is yet *four* paces from the turning point.

402. At the command *march*, to be pronounced at the instant the rank ought to turn, the guide will face to the left (or right) in marching, and move forward in the new direction without slackening or quickening the cadence, and without shortening or lengthening the step. The whole rank will promptly conform itself to the new

direction: to effect which, each man will advance the shoulder opposite to the guide, take the double quick step, to carry himself in the new direction, turn the head and eyes to the side of the guide, and retake the touch of the elbow on that side, in placing himself on the alignment of the guide, from whom he will take the step, and then resume the direct position of the head. Each man will thus arrive successively on the alignment.

Wheeling and changing direction to the side of the guide, in double quick time.

403. When the recruits comprehend and execute well, in quick time, the wheels at a halt and in marching, and the change of direction to the side of the guide, the instructor will cause the same movements to be repeated in double quick time.

404. These various movements will be executed by the same commands and according to the same principles as in quick time, except that the command *double quick* will precede that of *march*. In wheeling while marching, the pivot-man will take steps of eleven inches, and in the changes of direction to the side of the guide, the men on the side opposite the guide must increase the gait in order to bring themselves into line.

405. The instructor, in order not to fatigue the recruits, and not to divide their attention, will cause them to execute the several movements of which this lesson is composed, first without arms, and next, after the mechanism be well comprehended, with arms.

LESSON V.

Long marches in double quick time and the run.

406. The instructor will cause to be resumed the exercises in double quick time and the run, with arms and knapsacks.

407. He will cause long marches to be executed in double quick time, both by the front and by the flank, and by constant practice will lead the men to pass over a distance of five miles in sixty minutes. The pieces will be carried on either shoulder, and sometimes at a trail.

408. He will also exercise them in long marches at a run, the pieces carried at will; the men will be instructed to keep as united as possible, without however exacting much regularity, which is impracticable.

409. The run, in actual service, will only be resorted to when it may be highly important to reach a given point with great promptitude.

To stack arms.

The men being at order arms, the instructor will command:

Stack—ARMS.

410. At this command, the front rank man of every even numbered file will pass his piece before him, seizing it with the left hand near the upper band; will place the butt a little in advance of his left toe, the barrel turned towards the body, and draw the rammer slightly from its place; the front rank man of every odd numbered file will also draw the rammer slightly, and pass his piece to the man next on his left, who will seize it with the right hand near the upper band, and place the butt a little in advance of the right toe of the man next on his right, the barrel turned to the front; he will then cross the rammers of the two pieces, the rammer of the piece of the odd numbered man being inside; the rear rank man of every even file will also draw his rammer, lean his piece forward, the lock-plate downwards, advance the right foot about six inches, and insert the rammer between the rammer and barrel of the piece of his front rank man; with his left hand he will

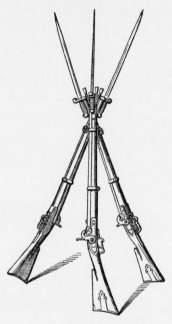

STACK ARMS (No. 410).

place the butt of his piece on the ground, thirty-two inches in rear of, and perpendicular to, the front rank, bringing back his right foot by the side of the left; the front rank man of every even file will at the same time lean the stack to the rear, quit it with his right hand, and force all the rammers down. The stack being thus formed, the rear rank man of every odd file will pass his piece into his left hand, the barrel to the front, and inclining it forward, will rest it on the stack.

411. The men of both ranks having taken the position of the soldier without arms, the instructor will command:

1. *Break ranks.*   2. MARCH.

To resume arms.

412. Both ranks being re-formed in rear of their stacks, the instructor will command:

Take—ARMS.

413. At this command, the rear rank man of every odd numbered file will withdraw his piece from the stack; the front rank man of every even file will seize his own piece with the left hand and that of the man on his right with his right hand, both above the lower band; the rear rank man of the even file will seize his piece with the right hand below the lower band; these two men will raise up the stack to loosen the rammers; the front rank man of every odd file will facilitate the disengagement of the rammers, if necessary, by drawing them out slightly with the left hand, and will receive his piece from the hand of the man next on his left; the four men will retake the position of the soldier at order arms.

MANUAL OF ARMS FOR THE MUSKET.

414. This manual differs in so many respects from that of the rifle and rifle musket that it becomes necessary to specify it for the use of infantry troops armed with the percussion-lock musket.

Shoulder—ARMS.

415. The piece is held in the left hand, the arm being a very little bent, the elbow close to the body, the butt of the musket grasped in the palm of the hand, the heel of the butt between the fore-finger and the middle finger; the thumb on the front screw of the butt-plate, the butt kept well back, so that the piece shall appear perpendicular when seen from the front, and not to be moved from its position by the movement of the thighs in marching; the stock, below the tail band, lying in the hollow of the shoulder; the right arm hanging naturally at the right side.

416. Care should be taken by the instructor that the recruit acquires this position of the musket correctly and maintains it in marching, as it is the position from which most others are taken and to which the soldier must constantly return.

Support—ARMS.

One time and three motions.

417. (*First motion.*) With the right hand seize the small of the stock four inches below the lock, slightly raising but not turning the piece.

SHOULDER ARMS (No. 415).   Shoulder Arms, side view.

SUPPORT ARMS
(No. 417).

PRESENT ARMS
(No. 424).

418. (*Second motion.*) Take the left hand from the butt, extend the left fore-arm under the cock upwards across the breast, the hand flat on the right breast.

419. (*Third motion.*) Drop the right arm to its place at the side.

420. The movement to return to the position of shouldered arms from that of support arms is always:

Carry—ARMS.

One time and three motions.

421. (*First motion.*) Carry the right hand to the small of the stock.

(*Second motion.*) Place the left hand under the butt as before.

(*Third motion.*) Let the right hand fall to the side, and lower the piece slightly to the position of shouldered arms.

422. *Note.*—The command *Carry arms* is only given when coming from the *support* to the position of *shouldered arms*. In every other case the command is *Shoulder arms*.

423. The piece being at the shoulder, the next command of the instructor is:

Present—ARMS.

One time and two motions.

424. (*First motion.*) Turn the piece with the left hand, the lock out, and seize the small of the stock with the right hand, the piece kept vertical and detached from the body, the left hand remaining under the butt.

425. (*Second motion.*) Bring the piece erect before the centre of the body, turning it inwards, the rammer being brought to the front, the right hand close under the guard. Seize the piece at the same time with the left hand above the lock, the thumb extended along the barrel, the left fore-arm resting on the body, and the hand as high as the elbow.

426. To return to the position of shouldered arms, the instructor will command:

Shoulder—ARMS.

One time and two motions.

427. (*First motion.*) Turn the piece with the right hand, the barrel to the front, raise and keep it against the left shoulder with the right hand; place the left under the butt, the right hand simply resting on the small of the stock without grasping it.

428. (*Second motion.*) Drop the right hand to the side.

Order—ARMS.

One time and two motions.

429. (*First motion.*) Extend the left arm so as to lower the piece, and seize it with the right hand just above the tail band. Let go with the left hand, and carry the piece, kept vertical, to the right side, the rammer to the front, the little finger behind the barrel, the right hand against the hip, the butt of the piece three inches from the ground, the piece vertical, the left hand hanging by the side.

430. (*Second motion.*) Let the piece slip through the right hand without shock to the ground, so that the butt will be on a line with the toes; at once drop the arm so that the barrel may be held by the thumb and extended fore-finger, the muzzle of the piece being about two inches from the right shoulder.

431. To resume the position of shouldered arms, the command of the instructor will be:

Shoulder—ARMS.

One time and two motions.

432. (*First motion.*) Raise the piece with the right hand, and carry it up, kept vertical, to the left shoulder, turning it in the passage so as to bring the barrel to the front; place the left hand under the butt, and slip the right hand down to the lock.

433. (*Second motion.*) Let the right hand fall to the side.

CHARGE BAYONET (No. 434).   ORDER ARMS (No. 429).

Charge—Bayonet.

One time and two motions.

434. (*First motion.*) Make a half face to the right, and take the position of the first motion in *about face*. Turn the piece with the left hand, the lock outwards, and seize the small of the stock with the right hand, the piece being kept vertical and slightly detached from the shoulder; the left hand remaining under the butt.

435. (*Second motion.*) Detach the left hand, bringing down the piece with the right, so that the left hand may seize it a little above the tail band, the barrel up, the left elbow near the body, the right hand against the hip, the point of the bayonet as high as the eye.

436. To resume the position of shouldered arms, the command is:

Shoulder—Arms.

One time and two motions.

437. (*First motion.*) Face to the front by turning on the left heel and bringing the right foot alongside; spring the piece up to the left shoulder with the right hand, and place the left under the butt as heretofore prescribed.

438. (*Second motion*). Drop the right hand to the side.

Loading and Firing.

439. In order to instruct recruits in the details of loading and firing their pieces, the first command of the instructor is:

Load in ten times—Load.

One time and two motions.

440. (*First motion.*) Extend the left arm to its full length, seize the piece with the right hand just above the lower band, carry the right foot forward, placing its

heel against the hollow of the left, but without altering the position of the body.

441. (*Second motion.*) With the right hand carry the piece directly downwards along the left thigh, seizing it with the left hand above the right, and letting the butt come to the ground without shock, so that the piece shall touch the left thigh; the muzzle opposite the centre of the body. Then carry the right hand quickly to the cartridge box and open it.

2. Handle—CARTRIDGE.

One time and one motion.

442. Take the cartridge in the thumb and first two fingers, and place the end of it in the teeth.

3. Tear—CARTRIDGE.

One time and one motion.

443. Tear the end of the cartridge down to the powder, then hold it upright, and place it in front of and near the muzzle, the back of the hand to the front.

4. Charge—CARTRIDGE.

One time and one motion.

444. Turn the back of the right hand towards the body, in order to discharge the powder into the barrel, raise the elbow as high as the wrist, shake the cartridge and insert it fully into the muzzle; leave the hand reversed, the fingers closed, but the hand extended.

5. Draw—RAMMER.

One time and three motions.

445. (*First motion.*) Drop the right elbow, and seize the rammer between the thumb and fore-finger bent, the other fingers being closed; draw the rammer, extending the arm; seize it again at the middle between the thumb

LOAD (No. 441).   CHARGE CARTRIDGE
(No. 444).

and fore-finger, the hand reversed, the palm to the front, the nails up; then clear the rammer entirely by again extending the arm.

446. (*Second motion.*) Turn the rammer between the bayonet and the face, the rammer parallel to the bayonet, the arm extended, the butt of the rammer near the muzzle, but not inserted.

447. (*Third motion.*) Insert the rammer, and force it down as low as the hand.

6. *Ram*—CARTRIDGE.

One time and one motion.

448. Extend the arm to its full length, seizing the rammer between the right thumb extended and the fore-finger bent, the other fingers closed; ram the cartridge home twice with force, then seize the rammer at the little end, between the thumb and forefinger bent, the other fingers being closed, and the right elbow touching the body.

7. *Return*—RAMMER.

One time and three motions.

449. (*First motion.*) Draw the rammer, re-seize it at the middle between the thumb and fore-finger, the palm of the hand to the front, the nails up, then clear the rammer from the barrel by extending the arm.

450. (*Second motion.*) Turn the rammer between the bayonet and the face, closing the fingers, the rammer parallel to the bayonet, the arm extended, the little end of the rammer near the first pipe, but not inserted.

451. (*Third motion.*) Insert the rammer, and, with the thumb, which will follow the movement, force it as low as the middle band. Then raise the hand, place the little finger on the butt of the rammer and force it down, at the same time lowering the left hand on the barrel to the extent of the arm, without depressing the shoulder.

8. *Cast*—ABOUT.

One time and two motions.

452. (*First motion.*) Bring up the piece vertically to the left shoulder with the left hand, seize it with the right hand at the small of the stock, and slide the left hand down as low as the chin.

453. (*Second motion.*) Make a half face to the right as in *about face*, except that the hollow of the right foot is close against the left heel, instead of three inches to the rear; carry the piece opposite the right shoulder; with the right hand bring it down into the left, seize it with the left at the tail band, the thumb extended on the stock, the butt under the right forearm, the small of the stock against the body, the right hand grasping the small of the stock, the muzzle as high as the eye.

9. PRIME.

One time and one motion.

454. Half-cock the piece with the thumb of the right hand, keeping the piece in its place with the left; displace the old cap, and, with the thumb and first two fingers of the right hand, take a cap from the pouch, place it upon the cone, push it down with the thumb, and then seize the piece by the small of the stock.

10. *Shoulder*—ARMS.

One time and two motions.

455. This command is executed precisely as in coming to *shouldered arms* from *charge bayonet.* (437–8.)

The loading being thus accomplished, to proceed to firing the command of the instructor is:

READY.

One time and four motions.

456. (*First motion.*) Turn the piece with the left hand,

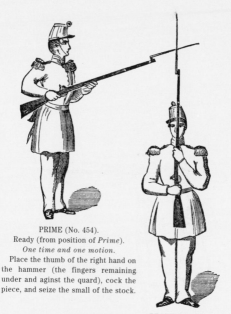

PRIME (No. 454).
Ready (from position of *Prime*).
One time and one motion.
Place the thumb of the right hand on
the hammer (the fingers remaining
under and aginst the quard), cock the
piece, and seize the small of the stock.

READY (No. 456).
SHOULDER—ARMS (from this position of *Ready*).
At the command *shoulder*, support the piece firmly with the left
hand, half-cock the piece, and seize it at the handle with the right
hand. At the word *arms*, face to the front and complete the time.

Pl. 22.

AIM. FRONT AND REAR RANK (No. 460).

bringing the lock to the front, and seize it with the right at the small of the stock. At the same time make a half face to the right, turning on the left heel, bringing the left toe to the front and placing the right foot behind, at right angles to the left, the hollow of the right against the heel of the left.

457. (*Second motion.*) With the right hand bring the piece, kept vertical, to the centre of the body, the left hand placed just above the lock, the thumb extended along the stock, and at the height of the chin, the rammer being turned obliquely to the left and front.

458. (*Third motion.*) Place the thumb on the head of the hammer, the fore-finger under and on the guard, the elbow at the height of the hand.

459. (*Fourth motion.*) Close the right elbow to the body in cocking, seize the piece by the small of the stock with the right hand; let it descend along the body in the left hand to the tail band, which should remain at the height of the shoulder.

AIM.

One time and one motion.

460. Raise the butt of the piece to the right shoulder, at the same time dropping the muzzle, the left hand remaining at the tail band, the left elbow a little down: direct the right eye along the barrel, by dropping the head upon the butt, shut the left eye, and place the forefinger upon the trigger.

461. At the command *aim*, the *rear rank* man will also carry his right foot about eight inches to the right, to enable him to disengage his piece in firing over the shoulder of the front rank man.

FIRE.

One time and one motion.

462. Without any other movement, pull the trigger

firmly and without jerking, and remain in that position.

463. After the piece is discharged, the instructor may desire at once to re-load; or, without loading, to resume the position of shouldered arms. If the latter be his wish, the command is:

Shoulder—ARMS.

One time and two motions.

464. (*First motion.*) Bring back the piece with both hands to its vertical position, face to the front, the piece at the left shoulder, and place the left hand under the butt.

465. (*Second motion.*) Drop the right hand to its place.

466. If it be desired to re-load after firing, while in the position of aim, the instructor will command:

LOAD.

One time and two motions.

467. (*First motion.*) Bring the piece back with both hands, depress the butt strongly by extending the right arm, carry it thus to the left side, the barrel to the front and opposite the left shoulder, the left hand with the back turned to the front, and as high as the chin, the left forearm touching the stock. At the same time, face to the front, and carry the heel of the right foot against the hollow of the left.

468. (*Second motion.*) Let go the small of the stock with the right hand, let the piece descend to the ground without shock through the left, and take the *second* motion of *load*.

The loading may then proceed by the numbers as before.

469. While in the position of *aim*, before firing, the

instructor may desire to exercise his men by bringing them back to the position of *ready*.

To do this the command will be:

*Recover—*ARMS.

470. This is executed precisely as in the manual for the rifle. (184.)

471. The men being in the position of ready or recover arms, if the instructor desire to bring them to that of shouldered arms, the command is:

*Shoulder—*ARMS.

472. At the word *shoulder*, the recruit will face to the front, and bring his piece, kept vertical, to the centre of the body, the left thumb as high as the chin, the little finger just above the lock. Next, with his right thumb on the head of the hammer and the forefinger on the trigger, he will carefully half-cock the piece, and seize the small of the stock with the right hand. At the command *arms*, the piece is carried to the right shoulder in the position of shouldered arms.

473. When a squad has been found to execute the *loading in ten times* well, they may be caused to execute the movement with fewer numbers, by the command:

*Load in four times—*LOAD.

474. (*First motion.*) At the command *load*, the recruit will execute *the first time of loading* (in ten times), *handle cartridge*, *tear cartridge*, and *charge cartridge*.

475. (*Second motion.*) At the command *two*, *draw rammer*, *enter it as far as the hand*, and *ram twice*.

476. (*Third motion.*) At the command *three*, *return rammer*, *cast about*, and *prime*.

477. (*Fourth motion.*) At the command *four*, *shoulder arms*.

478. If the wish of the instructor be to remove the

bayonet while in the position of *shouldered arms*, he gives the command:

Unfix—BAYONET.

One time and three motions.

479. (*First motion.*) Extend the left arm, seize the piece with the right hand, just above the tail band.

480. (*Second motion.*) Drop the piece with the right hand along the left thigh, seize it with the left hand above the right, lengthen out the left arm, rest the butt on the ground without shock; carry the right hand to the bayonet, with the thumb lower the clasp against the stop, and seize the bayonet at the socket and shank.

481. (*Third motion.*) Wrest off the bayonet, place it in the scabbard, and then rest the right little finger upon the butt of the rammer, lower the left hand along the barrel, extending the arm, without depressing the shoulder.

Shoulder—ARMS.

One time and three motions.

482. (*First motion.*) Raise the piece with the left hand along the left side, the hand as high as the chin, the forearm touching the piece, the barrel to the front; drop the right hand to seize the piece a little above the handle, the fore-finger touching the hammer, and the thumb on the counter-plate.

483. (*Second motion.*) Raise the piece with the right hand, place the left under the butt. Bring back the right heel to the side of the left on the same line; support the piece with the right hand against the shoulder, as at *shouldered arms*, the right hand resting on, without grasping, the piece.

484. (*Third motion.*) Let the right hand fall to its place.

SECURE ARMS (No. 485).   TRAIL ARMS (No. 493).

Secure—ARMS.

One time and two motions.

485. (*First motion.*) Seize the piece with the right hand, the thumb on the counter-plate, the fore-finger against the cock; detach the piece from the shoulder, the barrel to the front; seize it at the tail band with the left hand, the thumb extended on the rammer, the rammer erect, opposite the shoulder, the left elbow on the piece.

486. (*Second motion.*) Reverse the piece, pass it under the left arm, the left hand remaining at the tail band, the thumb on the rammer to prevent it from sliding out; the little finger on the hip, the right hand resuming its position at the side.

Shoulder—ARMS.

One time and two motions.

487. (*First motion.*) Raise the piece carefully with the left hand, seize the small of the stock with the right, to support it against the shoulder; quit the hold of the left hand and place it under the butt.

488. (*Second motion.*) Let the right hand drop to its place, at the same time dropping the piece slightly in the left, so as to take the position of shouldered arms.

Fix—BAYONET.

One time and three motions.

489. (*First motion.*) The same as in *unfix bayonet*.

490. (*Second motion.*) The same as in *unfix bayonet*, except that instead of carrying the right hand to the place where the bayonet would be, if fixed, it is carried to the bayonet-scabbard, so as to seize the bayonet by the socket and shank, so that the lower (now upper) end of the socket shall extend about an inch above the heel of the palm.

491. (*Third motion.*) Draw the bayonet from the scabbard, carry and fix it on the muzzle, turning the clasp

towards the body with the right thumb; then lower the left
hand along the barrel, in extending the arm.

Shoulder—ARMS.

492. The same as from *unfix bayonet.* (482.)

Trail—ARMS.

One time and two motions.

493. (*First motion.*) As the first motion of *order
arms.* (429.)

494. (*Second motion.*) Incline the muzzle slightly to the
front, and the butt to the rear, the butt being kept about
three inches from the ground; the right hand, supported at
the hip, will sustain the piece so that the rear rank men
may not touch the front rank men with their bayonets.

Shoulder—ARMS.

495. At the word *shoulder*, bring back the muzzle so as
to make the piece vertical. At the word *arms*, bring the
piece to the shoulder as prescribed in coming from the
position of *order arms.* (432.)

Right shoulder shift—ARMS.

One time and one motion.

496. Turn the piece with the left hand, the lock to the
front, seize it at the same time with the right hand at the
handle, place it on the right shoulder, the left hand not
quitting the butt, the muzzle up, the lock-plate upwards.
Keep the piece in this position by placing the right hand
on the flat of the butt. Let the left hand fall to the side.

Shoulder—ARMS.

One time and one motion.

497. Raise the piece by extending the right arm;
seize it with the left hand above the lock, carry it
against the left shoulder, turning the barrel to the
front; the right hand at the small of the stock; place

RIGHT SHOULDER
SHIFT ARMS (No. 496).

INSPECTION OF
ARMS (No. 501).

the left under the butt, and then let the right fall to its place.

Inspection of—ARMS.

498. From the position of ordered arms, the bayonet being in the scabbard.

One time and three motions.

499. (*First motion.*) Face to the right once and a half on the left heel, carrying the right foot perpendicularly to the rear, at right angles with the left and about six inches from it; seize the piece with the left hand just above the middle band, incline the muzzle to the rear without displacing the heel of the butt, the rammer turned towards the body. Carry the right band to the bayonet and seize it, as in the second motion of *fix bayonet.* (490.)

500. (*Second motion.*) Draw the bayonet from the scabbard, carry and fix it on the muzzle; then seize the rammer, draw it as has been explained in loading *in ten times*, and let it glide to the bottom of the bore.

501. (*Third motion.*) Face to the front, seize the piece with the right hand and retake the position of ordered arms.

502. The instructor will then inspect as in the manual for the rifle. (229.)

503. If, instead of *inspection of arms*, the instructor simply desires that bayonets should be fixed, he will command:

Fix—BAYONET.

504. Take the position as in the first motion of *inspection of arms*, fix the bayonet as explained in part of the second motion, and face to the front.

505. If the instructor wish, after firing, to know whether pieces remain undischarged, he will command:

Spring—RAMMERS.

506. Which will be executed as in the manual for the rifle. (234.)

Arms—PORT.

One time and one motion.

507. Throw the piece diagonally across the body, the lock to the front, seizing it at once with both hands, the right at the small of the stock, the left at the tail band, the two thumbs pointing towards the muzzle, the barrel sloping upwards, and crossing opposite to the point of the left shoulder, the butt proportionally lowered; the palm of the right hand above, and that of the left under the piece, the nails of both hands next to the body, to which the elbows will be closed.

Shoulder—ARMS.

One time and two motions.

508. (*First motion.*) Bring the piece to the left shoulder, placing the left hand under the butt.

509. (*Second motion.*) Drop the right hand to its place at the side.

510. In order to relieve the soldier from the constraint of any fixed position, the instructor will command:

Arms—AT WILL.

One time and one motion.

511. Carry the piece at pleasure on either shoulder, or with one or both hands, the muzzle being up.

Shoulder—ARMS.

512. Resume at once the position of shouldered arms.

513. In going through the manual of arms, the instructor will see that the recruit constantly retains the position of the soldier, which, under the pressure of his arms, he is liable to lose.

END OF THE SCHOOL OF THE SOLDIER.

Pl. 25.

ARMS PORT (No. 507).

TITLE THIRD.

SCHOOL OF THE COMPANY.

General Rules and Division of the School of the Company.

1. INSTRUCTION by company will always precede that by battalion, and the object being to prepare the soldiers for the higher school, the exercises of detail by company will be strictly adhered to, as well in respect to principles, as the order of progression herein prescribed.

2. There will be attached to a company undergoing elementary instruction, a captain, a covering sergeant, and a certain number of file closers, the whole posted in the manner indicated, Title First, and, according to the same Title, the officer charged with the exercise of such company will herein be denominated the *instructor*.

3. The School of the Company will he divided into six lessons, and each lesson will comprehend five articles, as follows:

Lesson I.

(1.) To open ranks.
(2.) Alignments in open ranks.
(3.) Manual of arms.
(4.) To close ranks.
(5.) Alignments, and manual of arms in closed ranks.

Lesson II.

(1.) To load in four times and at will.
(2.) To fire by company.

(3.) To fire by file.
(4.) To fire by rank.
(5.) To fire by the rear rank.

Lesson III.

(1.) To march in line of battle.
(2.) To halt the company marching in line of battle, and to align it.
(3.) Oblique march in line of battle.
(4.) To mark time, to march in double quick time, and the back step.
(5.) To march in retreat in line of battle.

Lesson IV.

(1.) To march by the flank.
(2.) To change direction by file.
(3.) To halt the company marching by the flank, and to face it to the front.
(4.) The company being in march by the flank, to form it on the right or left by file into line of battle.
(5.) The company marching by the flank, to form it by company or platoon into line, and cause it to face to the right and left in marching.

Lesson V.

(1.) To break into column by platoon either at a halt, or while marching.
(2.) To march in column.
(3.) To change direction.
(4.) To halt the column.
(5.) Being in column by platoon, to form to the right or left into line of battle, either at a halt or marching.

Lesson VI.

(1.) To break into platoons, and to re-form the company.

(2.) To break files to the rear, and to cause them to re-enter into line.

(3.) To march in column *in route*, and to execute the movements incident thereto.

(4.) Countermarch.

(5.) Being in column by platoon, to form on the right or left into line of battle.

4. The company will always be formed in two ranks. The instructor will then cause the files to be numbered, and for this purpose will command:

In each rank—Count TWOS.

5. At this command, the men count in each rank, from right to left, pronouncing in a loud and distinct voice, in the same tone, without hurry and without turning the head, *one, two*, according to the place which each one occupies. He will also cause the company to be divided into platoons and sections, taking care that the first platoon is always composed of an even number of files.

6. The instructor will be as clear and concise as possible in his explanations; he will cause faults of detail to be rectified by the captain, to whom he will indicate them, if the captain should not have himself observed them; and the instructor will not otherwise interfere, unless the captain should not well comprehend, or should badly execute his intentions.

7. Composure, or presence of mind, in him who commands, and in those who obey, being the first means of order in a body of troops, the instructor will labor to habituate the company to this essential quality, and will himself give the example.

LESSON FIRST.

ARTICLE FIRST.

To open ranks.

8. The company being at ordered arms, the ranks and file closers well aligned, when the instructor shall wish to cause the ranks to be opened, he will direct the left guide to place himself on the left of the front rank, which being executed, he will command:

1. *Attention.* 2. *Company.* 3. *Shoulder*—ARMS.
4. *To the rear open order.*

9. At the fourth command, the covering sergeant, and the left guide, will step off smartly to the rear, four paces from the front rank, in order to mark the alignment of the rear rank. They will judge this distance by the eye, without counting the steps.

10. The instructor will place himself at the same time on the right flank, in order to observe if these two non-commissioned officers are on a line parallel to the front rank, and if necessary, to correct their position, which being executed, he will command:

5. MARCH.

11. At this command, the front rank will stand fast.

12. The rear rank will step to the rear, without counting the steps, and will place themselves on the alignment marked for this rank, conforming to what is prescribed in the school of the soldier, No. 321.

13. The covering sergeant will align the rear rank on the left guide placed to mark the left of this rank.

14. The file closers will march to the rear at the same

time with the rear rank, and will place themselves two paces from this rank when it is aligned.

15. The instructor seeing the rear rank aligned, will command:

6. Front.

16. At this command, the sergeant on the left of the rear rank will return to his place as a file closer.

17. The rear rank being aligned, the instructor will direct the captain and the covering sergeant to observe the men in their respective ranks, and to correct, if necessary, the positions of persons and pieces.

Article Second.
Alignments in open ranks.

18. The ranks being open, the instructor will, in the first exercises, align the ranks, man by man, the better to inculcate the principles.

19. To effect this, he will cause two or four men on the right or left of each rank to march two or three paces forward, and, after having aligned them, command:

By file right (or *left*)—Dress.

20. At this, the men of each rank will move up successively on the alignment, each man being preceded by his neighbor in the same rank, towards the basis, by two paces, and having correctly aligned himself, will cast his eyes to the front.

21. Successive alignments having habituated the soldiers to dress correctly, the instructor will cause the ranks to align themselves at once, forward and backward, sometimes in a direction parallel, and sometimes in one oblique, to the original direction, giving, in each case, two or four men to serve as a basis of alignment to each rank. To effect which, he will command:

1. *Right* (or *left*)—DRESS.   2. FRONT.

or

1. *Right* (or *left*) *backward*—DRESS.   2. FRONT.

22. In oblique alignments, in *opened* ranks, the men of the rear rank will not seek to cover their file leaders, as the sole object of the exercise is to teach them to align themselves correctly in their respective ranks, in the different directions.

23. In the several alignments, the captain will superintend the front rank, and the covering sergeant the rear rank. For this purpose, they will place themselves on the side by which the ranks are dressed.

24. In oblique alignments, the men will conform the line of their shoulders to the new direction of their rank, and will place themselves on the alignment as has been prescribed in the school of the soldier, No. 317 or No. 321, according as the new direction shall be in front or rear of the original one.

25. At the end of each alignment, the captain and the covering sergeant will pass along the front of the ranks to correct the positions of persons and arms.

ARTICLE THIRD.
Manual of Arms.

26. The ranks being open, the instructor will place himself in a position to see the ranks, and will command the manual of arms in the following order:

Present arms.	*Shoulder arms.*
Order arms.	
Ground arms.	
Raise arms.	*Shoulder arms.*
Support arms.	*Shoulder arms.*
Fix bayonet.	*Shoulder arms.*
Charge bayonet.	*Shoulder arms.*

Trail arms.	*Shoulder arms.*
Unfix bayonet.	*Shoulder arms.*
Secure arms.	*Shoulder arms.*

Load in nine times.

27. The instructor will take care that the position of the body, of the feet, and of the piece, be always exact, and that the times be briskly executed and close to the person.

ARTICLE FOURTH.

To close ranks.

28. The manual of arms being ended, the instructor will command:

1. *Close order.*   2. MARCH.

29. At the command *march*, the rear rank will close up in quick time, each man directing himself on his file leader.

ARTICLE FIFTH.

Alignments, and manual of arms in closed ranks.

30. The ranks being closed, the instructor will cause to be executed parallel and oblique alignments by the right and left, forward and backward, observing to place always two or four files to serve as a basis of alignment. He will give the commands prescribed, No. 21.

31. In alignments in closed ranks, the captain will superintend the front rank, and the covering sergeant the rear rank. They will habituate themselves to judge the alignment by the lines of the eyes and shoulders, in casting a glance of the eye along the front and rear of the ranks.

32. The moment the captain perceives the greater number of the front rank aligned, he will command

FRONT, and rectify, afterwards, if necessary, the alignment of the other men by the means prescribed in the school of the soldier, No. 320. The rear rank will conform to the alignment of the front rank, superintended by the covering sergeant.

33. The ranks being steady, the instructor will place himself on the flank to verify their alignment. He will also see that each rear rank man covers accurately his file leader.

34. In oblique alignments, the instructor will observe what is prescribed, No. 24.

35. In all alignments, the file closers will preserve the distance of two paces from the rear rank.

36. The alignments being ended, the instructor will cause to be executed the manual of arms.

37. The instructor, wishing to rest the men, without deranging the alignment, will first cause arms to be supported, or ordered, and then command:

In place—REST.

38. At this command, the men will no longer be constrained to preserve silence or steadiness of position; but they will always keep one or other heel on the alignment.

39. If, on the contrary, the instructor should wish to rest the men without constraining them to preserve the alignment, he will command:

REST.

40. At which command, the men will not be required to preserve immobility, or to remain in their places.

41. The instructor may, also, when be shall judge proper, cause arms to be stacked, which will be executed as prescribed, school of the soldier.

LESSON SECOND.

42. The instructor, wishing to pass to the second lesson, will cause the company to take arms, if stacks have been formed, and command:

1. *Attention.*   2. *Company.*   3. *Shoulder*—ARMS.

43. The instructor will then cause loadings and firings to be executed in the following order:

ARTICLE FIRST.
To load in four times and at will.

44. Loading in four *times* will be commanded and executed as prescribed in the school of the soldier, No. 251, and following. The instructor will cause this exercise to be often repeated, in succession, before passing to loading at will.

45. Loading at will will be commanded and executed as prescribed in the school of the soldier, No. 256. In priming when loading in four *times*, and also at will, the captain and covering sergeant will half face to the right with the men, and face to the front when the man next to them, respectively, brings his piece to the shoulder.

46. The instructor will labor to the utmost to cause the men, in the different loadings, to execute what has been prescribed in the school of the soldier, Nos. 257 and 258.

47. Loading at will, being that of battle, and consequently the one with which it is most important to render the men familiar, it will claim preference in the exercises the moment the men be well established in the principles. To these they will be brought by degrees, so that every man may be able to load with cartridges, and to fire at least three rounds in a minute with ease and regularity.

ARTICLE SECOND.
To fire by company.

48. The instructor, wishing to cause the fire by company to be executed will command:

> 1. *Fire by company.*   2. *Commence firing.*

49. At the first command, the captain will promptly place himself opposite the centre of his company, and four paces in rear of the line of file closers: the covering sergeant will retire to that line, and place himself opposite to his interval. *This rule is general, for both the captain and covering sergeant, in all the different firings.*

50. At the second command, the captain will add: 1. *Company;* 2. READY; 3. AIM; 4. FIRE; 5. LOAD.

51. At the command *load*, the men will load their pieces, and then take the position of *ready*, as prescribed in the school of the soldier.

52. The captain will immediately recommence the firing, by the commands:

> 1. *Company.*   2. AIM.   3. FIRE.   4. LOAD.

53. The firing will be thus continued until the signal to cease firing is sounded.

54. The captain will sometimes cause aim to be taken to the right and left, simply observing to pronounce *right* (or *left*) *oblique*, before the command *aim.*

ARTICLE THIRD.
The Fire by file.

55. The instructor wishing to cause the fire by file to be executed will command:

> 1. *Fire by file.*   2. *Company.*   3. READY.   4. *Commence firing.*

56. The third and fourth commands will be executed

as prescribed in the school of the soldier, No. 275 and following.

57. The fire will be commenced by the right file of the company; the next file will take aim at the instant the first brings down pieces to re-load, and so on to the left; but this progression will only be observed in the first discharge, after which each man will re-load and fire without regulating himself by others, conforming himself to what is prescribed in the school of the soldier, No. 280.

ARTICLE FOURTH.
The Fire by rank.

58. The instructor wishing the fire by rank to be executed, will command:

1. *Fire by rank.* 2. *Company.* 3. READY.
4. *Rear rank*—AIM. 5. FIRE. 6. LOAD.

59. The fifth and sixth commands will be executed as is prescribed in the school of the soldier, No. 285 and following.

60. When the instructor sees one or two pieces in the rear rank at a ready, he will command:

1. *Front rank.* 2. AIM. 3. FIRE. 4. LOAD.

61. The firing will be continued thus by alternate ranks, until the signal is given to cease firing.

62. The instructor will sometimes cause aim to be taken to the right and left, conforming to what is prescribed No. 54.

63. The instructor will cause the firing to cease, whether by company, by file, or by rank, by sounding the signal *to cease firing*, and at the instant this sound commences, the men will cease to fire, conforming to what is prescribed in the school of the soldier, No. 282.

64. The signal to cease firing will be always followed

by a bugle note; at which sound, the captain and
covering sergeant will promptly resume their places in
line, and will rectify, if necessary, the alignment of
the ranks.

65. In this school, except when powder is used,
the signal to cease firing will be indicated by the command, *cease firing*, which will be pronounced by the
instructor when he wishes the semblance of firing to
cease.

66. The command *posts* will be likewise substituted,
under similar circumstances, for the bugle note employed
as the signal for the return of the captain and covering
sergeant to their places in line, which command will be
given when the instructor sees the men have brought their
pieces to a shoulder.

67. The fire by file being that which is most frequently used against an enemy, it is highly important that
it be rendered perfectly familiar to the troops. The
instructor will, therefore, give it almost exclusive preference, and labor to cause the men to aim with care, and
always, if possible, at some particular object. As it is of
the utmost importance that the men should aim with precision in battle, this principle will be rigidly enforced in
the exercises for purposes of instruction.

ARTICLE FIFTH.

To Fire by the rear rank.

68. The instructor will cause the several fires to be
executed to the rear, that is, by the rear rank. To effect
this, he will command:

1. Face by the rear rank.   2. *Company.*   3. *About—*
FACE.

69. At the first command, the captain will step out
and place himself near to, and facing the right file
of his company; the covering sergeant, and file

closers, will pass quickly through the captain's interval, and place themselves faced to the rear, the covering sergeant a pace behind the captain, and the file closers two paces from the front rank opposite to their places in line, each passing behind the covering sergeant.

70. At the third command, which will be given at the instant the last file closer shall have passed through the interval, the company will face about; the captain will place himself in his interval in the rear rank, now become the front, and the covering sergeant will cover him in the front rank, now become the rear.

71. The company having faced by the rear rank, the instructor will cause it to execute the fire by company, both direct and oblique, the fire by file, and the fire by rank, by the commands and means prescribed in the three preceding articles; the captain, covering sergeant, and the men will conform themselves, in like manner, to what is therein prescribed.

72. The fire by file will commence on the left of the company, now become the right. In the fire by rank, the firing will commence with the front rank, now become the rear.

73. To resume the proper front, the instructor will command:

1. *Face by the front rank.* 2. *Company.* 3. *About—*
FACE.

74. At the first command, the captain, covering sergeant and file closers will conform to what is prescribed Nos. 69 and 70.

75. At the third command, the company having faced about, the captain and covering sergeant will resume their places in line.

76. In this lesson, the instructor will impress on the men the importance of aiming always at some particular

object, and of holding the piece as prescribed in the school of the soldier, No. 178.

77. The instructor will recommend to the captain to make a short pause between the commands *aim* and *fire*, to give the men time to aim with accuracy.

78. The instructor will place himself in position to see the two ranks, in order to detect faults; he will charge the captain and file closers to be equally watchful, and to report to him when the ranks are at rest. He will remand, for individual instruction, the men who may be observed to load badly.

79. The instructor will recommend to the soldiers, in the firings, the highest degree of composure or presence of mind; he will neglect nothing that may contribute to this end.

80. He will give to the men, *as a general principle*, to maintain, in the direct fire, the left heel in its place, in order that the alignment of the ranks and files may not be deranged; and he will verify, by examination, after each exercise in firing, the observance of this principle.

81. The instructor will observe, in addition to these remarks, all those which follow.

82. When the firing is executed with cartridges, it is particularly recommended that the men observe, in uncocking, whether smoke escapes from the tube, which is a certain indication that the piece has been discharged; but if, on the contrary, no smoke escapes, the soldier, in such case, instead of re-loading, will pick and prime again. If, believing the load to be discharged, the soldier should put a second cartridge in his piece, he ought, at least, to perceive it in ramming, by the height of the load; and he would be very culpable, should he put in a third. The instructor will always cause arms to be inspected after firing with cartridges, in order to observe if the fault has been committed, of putting three cartridges, without a

discharge, in the same piece, in which case the ball screw will be applied.

83. It sometimes happens, when a cap has missed fire, that the tube is found stopped up with a hard, white, and compact powder; in this case, picking will be dispensed with, and a new cap substituted for the old one.

LESSON THIRD.

ARTICLE FIRST.

To advance in line of battle.

84. The company being in line of battle, and correctly aligned, when the instructor shall wish to exercise it in marching by the front, he will assure himself that the shoulders of the captain and covering sergeant are perfectly in the direction of their respective ranks, and that the sergeant accurately covers the captain; the instructor will then place himself twenty-five or thirty paces in front of them, face to the rear, and place himself exactly on the prolongation of the line passing between their heels.

85. The instructor, being aligned on the directing file, will command:

1. *Company, forward.*

86. At this, a sergeant, previously designated, will move six paces in advance of the captain: the instructor, from the position prescribed, will correctly align this sergeant on the prolongation of the directing file.

87. This advanced sergeant, who is to be charged with the direction, will, the moment his position is assured, take two points on the ground in the straight line which would pass between his own and the heels of the instructor.

88. These dispositions being made, the instructor will step aside, and command:

2. March.

89. At this, the company will step off with life. The directing sergeant will observe, with the greatest precision, the length and cadence of the step, marching on the two points he has chosen; he will take in succession, and always a little before arriving at the point nearest to him, new points in advance, exactly in the same line with the first two, and at the distance of some fifteen or twenty paces from each other. The captain will march steadily in the trace of the directing sergeant, keeping always six paces from him; the men will each maintain the head direct to the front, feel lightly the elbow of his neighbor on the side of direction, and conform himself to the principles prescribed, school of the soldier, for the march by the front.

90. The man next to the captain will take special care not to pass him; to this end, he will keep the line of his shoulders a little in the rear, but in the same direction with those of the captain.

91. The file closers will march at the habitual distance of two paces behind the rear rank.

92. If the men lose the step, the instructor will command:

*To the—*Step.

93. At this command, the men will glance towards the directing sergeant, retake the step from him, and again direct their eyes to the front.

94. The instructor will cause the captain and covering sergeant to be posted sometimes on the right, and sometimes on the left of the company.

95. The directing sergeant, in advance, having the greatest influence on the march of the company, he will be selected for the precision of his step, his habit of maintaining his shoulders in a square with a given

line of direction, and of prolonging that line without variation.

96. If this sergeant should fail to observe these principles, undulations in the front of the company must necessarily follow; the men will be unable to contract the habit of taking steps equal in length and swiftness, and of maintaining their shoulders in a square with the line of direction—the only means of attaining perfection in the march in line.

97. The instructor, with a view the better to establish the men in the length and cadence of the step, and in the principles of the march in line, will cause the company to advance three or four hundred paces, at once, without halting, if the ground will permit. In the first exercises, he will march the company with open ranks, the better to observe the two ranks.

98. The instructor will see, with care, that all the principles of the march in line are strictly observed; he will generally be on the directing flank, in a position to observe the two ranks, and the faults they may commit; he will sometimes halt behind the directing file during some thirty successive steps, in order to judge whether the directing sergeant, or the directing file, deviate from the perpendicular.

ARTICLE SECOND.

To halt the company, marching in line of battle, and to align it.

99. The instructor, wishing to halt the company, will command:

1. *Company.* 2. HALT.

100. At the second command, the company will halt; the directing sergeant will remain in advance, unless ordered to return to the line of file closers. The company being at a halt, the instructor may advance the first three

or four files on the side of direction, and align the company on that basis, or he may confine himself to causing the alignment to be rectified. In this last case, he will command: *Captain, rectify the alignment.* The captain will direct the covering sergeant to attend to the rear rank, when each, glancing his eyes along his rank, will promptly rectify it, conforming to what is prescribed in the school of the soldier, No. 320.

ARTICLE THIRD.

Oblique march in line of battle.

101. The company being in the direct march, when the instructor shall wish to cause it to march obliquely, he will command:

1. *Right* (or *left*) *oblique.* 2. MARCH.

102. At the command *march*, the company will take the oblique step. The men will accurately observe the principles prescribed in the school of the soldier, No. 331. The rear rank men will preserve their distances, and march in rear of the man next on the right (or left) of their habitual file leaders.

103. When the instructor wishes the direct march to be resumed, he will command:

1. *Forward.* 2. MARCH.

104. At the command *march*, the company will resume the direct march. The instructor will move briskly twenty paces in front of the captain, and facing the company, will place himself exactly in the prolongation of the captain and covering sergeant; and then, by a sign, will move the directing sergeant on the same line, if he be not already on it; the latter will immediately take two points on the ground between himself and the instructor, and as he

advances, will take new points of direction, as is explained No. 89.

105. In the oblique march, the men not having the touch of elbows, the guide will always be on the side towards which the oblique is made, without any indication to that effect being given; and when the direct march is resumed, the guide will be, equally without indication, on the side where it was previous to the oblique.

106. The instructor will, at first, cause the oblique to be made towards the side of the guide. He will also direct the captain to have an eye on the directing sergeant, in order to keep on the same perpendicular line to the front with him, while following a parallel direction.

107. During the continuance of the march, the instructor will be watchful that the men follow parallel directions, in conforming to the principles prescribed in the school of the soldier, for preserving the general alignment; whenever the men lose the alignment, he will be careful that they regain it by lengthening or shortening the step, without altering the cadence, or changing the direction.

108. The instructor will place himself in front of the company and face to it, in order to regulate the march of the directing sergeant, or the man who is on the flank towards which the oblique is made, and to see that the principles of the march are properly observed, and that the files do not crowd.

ARTICLE FOURTH.

To mark time, to march in double quick time, and the back step.

109. The company being in the direct march and in quick time, the instructor, to cause it to mark time, will command:

1. *Mark time.* 2. MARCH.

110. To resume the march, he will command:

1. *Forward.* 2. MARCH.

111. To cause the march in double quick time, the instructor will command:

1. *Double quick.* 2. MARCH.

112. The command *march* will be pronounced at the instant either foot is coming to the ground.

113. To resume quick time, the instructor will command:

1. *Quick time.* 2. MARCH.

114. The command march will be pronounced at the instant either foot is coming to the ground.

115. The company being at a halt, the instructor may cause it to march in the back step; to this effect, he will command:

1. *Company backward.* 2. MARCH.

116. The back step will be executed according to the principles prescribed in the school of the soldier No. 247, but the use of it being rare, the instructor will not cause more than fifteen or twenty steps to be taken in succession, and to that extent but seldom.

117. The instructor ought not to exercise the company in marching in double quick time till the men are well established in the length and swiftness of the pace in quick time: he will then endeavor to render the march of one hundred and sixty-five steps in the minute equally easy and familiar, and also cause them to observe the same erectness of body and composure of mind as if marching in quick time.

118. When marching in double quick time, if a subdivision (in a column) has to change direction by *turning*, or has to form into line, the men will quicken the pace to one

hundred and eighty steps in a minute. The same swiftness of step will be observed under all circumstances where great rapidity of movement is required. But, as ranks of men cannot march any length of time at so swift a rate, without breaking or confusion, this acceleration will not be considered a prescribed exercise, and accordingly companies or battalions will only be habitually exercised in the double quick time of one hundred and sixty-five steps in the minute.

ARTICLE FIFTH.

To march in retreat.

119. The company being halted and correctly aligned, when the instructor shall wish to cause it to march in retreat, he will command:

1. *Company.* 2. *About*—FACE.

120. The company having faced to the rear, the instructor will place himself in front of the directing file, conforming to what is prescribed, No. 84.

121. The instructor, being correctly established on the prolongation of the directing file, will command:

3. *Company, forward.*

122. At this, the directing sergeant will conform himself to what is prescribed, Nos. 86 and 87, with this difference—he will place himself six paces in front of the line of file closers, now leading.

123. The covering sergeant will step into the line of file closers, opposite to his interval, and the captain will place himself in the rear rank, now become the front.

124. This disposition being promptly made, the instructor will command:

4. MARCH.

125. At this, the directing sergeant, the captain, and the men, will conform themselves to what is prescribed No. 89, and following.

126. The instructor will cause to be executed, marching in retreat, all that is prescribed for marching in advance; the commands and the means of execution will be the same.

127. The instructor having halted the company, will, when he may wish, cause it to face to the front by the commands prescribed No. 119. The captain, the covering sergeant, and the directing sergeant, will resume their habitual places in line, the moment they shall have faced about.

128. The company being in march by the front rank, if the instructor should wish it to march in retreat, he will cause the right about to be executed while marching, and to this effect will command:

1. *Company.* 2. *Right about.* 3. MARCH.

129. At the third command, the company will promptly face about, and recommence the march by the rear rank.

130. The directing sergeant will face about with the company, and will move rapidly six paces in front of the file closers, and upon the prolongation of the guide. The instructor will place him in the proper direction by the means prescribed No. 104. The captain, the covering sergeant, and the men, will conform to the principles prescribed for the march in retreat.

131. When the instructor wishes the company to march by the front rank, he will give the same commands, and will regulate the direction of the march by the same means.

132. The instructor will cause to be executed in double quick time, all the movements prescribed in the 3d, 4th, 5th, and 6th lessons of this school, with the exception of the march backwards, which will be executed only in

Pl. 26.

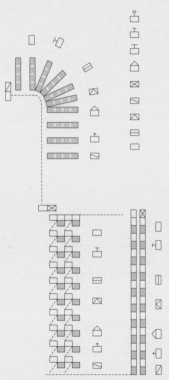

Marching by a flank doubling the files, and filing to the left or right (No. 135).

quick time. He will give the same commands, observing to add *double quick* before the command *march*.

133. When the pieces are carried on the right shoulder, in quick time, the distance between the ranks will be sixteen inches. Whenever, therefore, the instructor brings the company from a shoulder to this position, the rear rank must shorten a little the first steps in order to gain the prescribed distance, and will lengthen the steps, on the contrary, in order to close up when the pieces are again brought to a shoulder. In marching in double quick time, the distance between the ranks will be twenty-six inches, and the pieces will be carried habitually on the right shoulder.

134. Whenever a company is halted, the men will bring their pieces at once to a shoulder at the command *halt*. The rear rank will close to its proper distance. *These rules are general.*

LESSON FOURTH.

Article First.

To march by the flank.

135. The company being in line of battle, and at a halt, when the instructor shall wish to cause it to march by the right flank, he will command:

1. *Company, right*—FACE.　2. *Forward.*
3. MARCH.

136. At the first command, the company will face to the right, the covering sergeant will place himself at the head of the front rank, the captain having stepped out for the purpose, so far as to find himself by the side of the sergeant, and on his left; the front rank will double as is prescribed in the school of the soldier, No. 352; the rear

rank will, at the same time, side-step to the right one pace, and double in the same manner; so that when the movement is completed, the files will be formed of four men aligned, and elbow to elbow. The intervals will be preserved.

137. The file closers will also move by side step to the right, so that when the ranks are formed, they will be two paces from the rearmost rank.

138. At the command *march*, the company will move off briskly in quick time; the covering sergeant at the head of the front rank, and the captain on his left, will march straight forward. The men of each file will march abreast of their respective front rank men, heads direct to the front; the file closers will march opposite their places in line of battle.

139. The instructor will cause the principles of the march by the flank to be observed, in placing himself, pending the march, as prescribed to the school of the soldier, No. 357.

140. The instructor will cause the march by the left flank to be executed by the same commands, substituting *left* for *right;* the ranks will double as has been prescribed in the school of the soldier, No. 354; the rear rank will side-step to the left one pace before doubling.

141. At the instant the company faces to the left, the left guide will place himself at the head of the front rank; the captain will pass rapidly to the left, and place himself by the right side of this guide; the covering sergeant will replace the captain in the front rank, the moment the latter quits it to go to the left.

ARTICLE SECOND.

To change direction by file.

142. The company being faced by the flank, and either in march, or at a halt, when the instructor

shall wish to cause it to wheel by file, he will command:

1. *By file, left* (or *right*).   2. MARCH.

143. At the command *march*, the first file will wheel; if to the side of the front rank man, the latter will take care not to turn at once, but to describe a short arc of a circle, shortening a little the first five or six steps in order to give time to the fourth man of this file to conform himself to the movement. If the wheel be to the side of the rear rank, the front rank man will wheel in the step of twenty-eight inches, and the fourth man will conform himself to the movement by describing a short arc of a circle as has been explained. Each file will come to wheel on the same ground where that which preceded it wheeled.

144. The instructor will see that the wheel be executed according to these principles, in order that the distance between the files may always be preserved, and that there be no check or hinderance at the wheeling point.

ARTICLE THIRD.

To halt the company marching by the flank, and to face to the front.

145. To effect these objects, the instructor will command:

1. *Company.*   2. HALT.   3. FRONT.

146. The second and third commands will be executed as prescribed in the school of the soldier, Nos. 359 and 360. As soon as the files have undoubled, the rear rank will close to its proper distance. The captain and covering sergeant, as well as the left guide, if the march be by the left flank, will return to their

habitual places in line at the instant the company faces to
the front.

147. The instructor may then align the company by
one of the means prescribed, No. 100.

Article Fourth.

**The company being in march by the flank, to form
it on the right (or left) by file into line of battle.**

148. If the company be marching by the right flank,
the instructor will command:

1. *On the right, by file into line.* 2. March.

149. At the command *march*, the rear rank men doubled will mark time; the captain and the covering sergeant
will turn to the right, march straight forward, and be
halted by the instructor when they shall have passed at
least six paces beyond the rank of file closers; the captain
will place himself correctly on the line of battle, and will
direct the alignment as the men of the front rank successively arrive; the covering sergeant will place himself
behind the captain at the distance of the rear rank; the
two men on the right of the front rank doubled, will continue to march, and passing beyond the covering sergeant
and the captain, will turn to the right; after turning, they
will continue to march elbow to elbow, and direct themselves towards the line of battle, but when they shall
arrive at two paces from this line, the even number will
shorten the step so that the odd number may precede him
on the line, the odd number placing himself by the side
and on the left of the captain; the even number will afterwards oblique to the left, and place himself on the left of
the odd number; the next two men of the front rank doubled, will pass in the same manner behind the two first,
turn then to the right, and place themselves, according to
the means just explained, to the left, and by the side of,

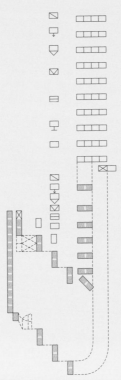

On the right by file into line (No. 148).

the two men already established on the line; the remaining files of this rank will follow in succession, and be formed to the left in the same manner. The rear rank doubled will execute the movement in the manner already explained for the front rank, taking care not to commence the movement until four men of the front rank are established on the line of battle; the rear rank men, as they arrive on the line, will cover accurately their file leaders.

150. If the company be marching by the left flank, the instructor will cause it to form by file on the left into line of battle, according to the same principles and by the same commands, substituting the indication *left* for *right*. In this case, the odd numbers will shorten the step, so that the even numbers may precede them on the line. The captain, placed on the left of the front rank, and the left guide, will return to their places in line of battle, by order of the instructor, after the company shall be formed and aligned.

151. To enable the men the better to comprehend the mechanism of this movement, the instructor will at first cause it to be executed separately by each rank doubled, and afterwards by the two ranks united and doubled.

152. The instructor will place himself on the line of battle, and without the point where the right or left is to rest, in order to establish the base of the alignment, and afterwards he will follow up the movement to assure himself that each file conforms itself to what is prescribed No. 149.

Article Fifth.

The company being in march by the flank, to form it by company, or by platoon, into line, and to cause it to face to the right and left in marching.

153. The company being in march by the right flank, the instructor will order the captain to form it into line; the captain will immediately command:

1. *By company, into line*;   2. MARCH.

154. At the command *march*, the covering sergeant will continue to march straight forward; the men will advance the right shoulder, take the double quick step, and move into line, by the shortest route, taking care to undouble the files, and to come on the line one after the other.

155. As the front rank men successively arrive in line with the covering sergeant, they will take from him the step, and then turn their eyes to the front.

156. The men of the rear rank will conform to the movements of their respective file leaders, but without endeavoring to arrive in line at the same time with the latter.

157. At the instant the movement begins, the captain will face to his company in order to follow up the execution; and, as soon as the company is formed, he will command, *guide left*, place himself two paces before the centre, face to the front, and take the step of the company.

158. At the command *guide left*, the second sergeant will promptly place himself in the front rank, on the left, to serve as guide, and the covering sergeant who is on the opposite flank will remain there.

159. When the company marches by the left flank, this movement will be executed by the same commands, and according to the same principles; the company being formed, the captain will command *guide right*, and place himself in front of his company as above; the covering

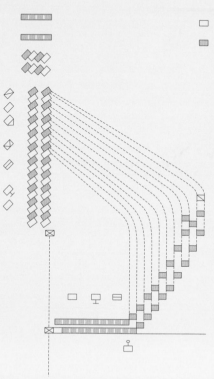

By company into line (No. 153).

sergeant who is on the right of the front rank will serve as guide, and the second sergeant placed on the left flank will remain there.

160. Thus, in a column by company, right or left in front, the covering sergeant and the second sergeant of each company will always be placed on the right and left, respectively, of the front rank; they will be denominated *right guide* and *left guide*, and the one or the other charged with the direction.

161. The company being in march by the flank, if it be the wish of the instructor to cause it to form platoons, he will give an order to that effect to the captain, who will command:

1. *By platoon, into line.*   2. MARCH.

162. The movement will be executed by each platoon according to the above principles. The captain will place himself before the centre of the first platoon, and the first lieutenant before the centre of the second, passing through the opening made in the centre of the company, if the march be by the right flank, and around the left of his platoon, if the march be by the left: in this last case, the captain will also pass around the left of the second platoon in order to place himself in front of the first. Both the captain and lieutenant, without waiting for each other, will command *guide left* (or *right*) at the instant their respective platoons are formed.

163. At the command *guide left* (or *right*), the guide of each platoon will pass rapidly to the indicated flank of the platoon, if not already there.

164. The right guide of the company will always serve as the guide of the right or left of the first platoon, and the left guide of the company will serve, in like manner, as the guide of the second platoon.

165. Thus, in a column by platoon, there will be but one guide to each platoon; he will always be placed on its left flank, if the right be in front, and on the right flank, if the left be in front.

166. In these movements, the file closers will follow the platoons to which they are attached.

167. The instructor may cause the company, marching by the flank, to form by company, or by platoon, into line, by his own direct commands, using those prescribed for the captain, No. 153 or 161.

168. The instructor will exercise the company in passing, without a halt, from the march by the front, to the march by the flank, and reciprocally. In either case, he will employ the commands prescribed in the school of the soldier, No. 363, substituting *company* for *squad*. The company will face to the right or left, in marching, and the captain, the guides, and file closers will conform themselves to what is prescribed for each in the march by the flank, or in the march by the front of a company supposed to be a subdivision of a column.

169. If, after facing to the right or left, in marching, the company find itself faced by the rear rank, the captain will place himself two paces behind the centre of the front rank, now in the rear, the guides will pass to the rear rank, now leading, and the file closers will march in front of this rank.

170. The instructor, in order to avoid fatiguing the men, and to prevent them from being negligent in the position of shoulder arms, will sometimes order support arms in marching by the flank, and arms on the right shoulder, when marching in line.

LESSON FIFTH.

ARTICLE FIRST.

To break into column by platoon, either at a halt or in march.

171. The company being at a halt, in line of battle, the

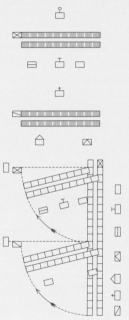

To break into column by platoons (No. 171).

instructor, wishing to break it into column, by platoon to the right, will command:

1. *By platoon, right wheel.* 2. MARCH.

172. At the first command, the chiefs of platoon will rapidly place themselves two paces before the centres of their respective platoons, the lieutenant passing around the left of the company. They need not occupy themselves with dressing, one upon the other. The covering sergeant will replace the captain in the front rank.

173. At the command *march*, the right front rank man of each platoon will face to the right, the covering sergeant standing fast; the chief of each platoon will move quickly by the shortest line, a little beyond the point at which the marching flank will rest when the wheel shall be completed, face to the late rear, and place himself so that the line which he forms with the man on the right (who had faced) shall be perpendicular to that occupied by the company in line of battle; each platoon will wheel according to the principles prescribed for the wheel on a fixed pivot, and when the man who conducts the marching flank shall approach near to the perpendicular, its chief will command:

1. *Platoon.* 2. HALT.

174. At the command *halt*, which will be given at the instant the man who conducts the marching flank shall have arrived at three paces from the perpendicular, the platoon will halt; the covering sergeant will move to the point where the left of the first platoon is to rest, passing by the front rank; the second sergeant will place himself, in like manner, in respect to the second platoon. Each will take care to leave between himself and the man on the right of his platoon, a space equal to its front; the captain and first lieutenant will look to this, and each take

care to align the sergeant between himself and the man of
the platoon who had faced to the right.

175. The guide of each platoon, being thus established
on the perpendicular, each chief will place himself two
paces outside of his guide, and, facing towards him, will
command:

Left—DRESS.

176. The alignment being ended, each chief of platoon
will command, FRONT, and place himself two paces before
its centre.

177. The file closers will conform themselves to the
movement of their respective platoons, preserving always
the distance of two paces from the rear rank.

178. The company will break by platoon to the left,
according to the same principles. The instructor will command:

1. *By platoon, left wheel.*   2. MARCH.

179. The first command will be executed in the same
manner as if breaking by platoon to the right.

180. At the command *march*, the left front rank
man of each platoon will face to the left, and the platoons
will wheel to the left, according to the principles prescribed for the wheel on a fixed pivot; the chiefs of
platoon will conform to the principles indicated Nos. 173
and 174.

181. At the command *halt*, given by the chief of each
platoon, the covering sergeant on the right of the front
rank of the first platoon, and the second sergeant *near the
left of the second platoon*, will each move to the points
where the right of his platoon is to rest. The chief of each
platoon should be careful to align the sergeant between
himself and the man of the platoon who had faced to the
left, and will then command:

Right—DRESS.

182. The platoons being aligned, each chief of platoon will command, FRONT, and place himself opposite its centre.

183. The instructor wishing to break the company by platoon to the right, and to move the column forward after the wheel is completed, will caution the company to that effect, and command:

1. *By platoon, right wheel.* 2. MARCH.

184. At the first command, the chiefs of platoon will move rapidly in front of their respective platoons, conforming to what has been prescribed No. 172, and will remain in this position during the continuance of the wheel. The covering sergeant will replace the chief of the first platoon in the front rank.

185. At the command *march*, the platoons will wheel to the right, conforming to the principles herein prescribed; the man on the pivot will not face to the right, but will mark time, conforming himself to the movement of the marching flank; and when the man who is on the left of this flank shall arrive *near* the perpendicular, the instructor will command:

3. *Forward.* 4. MARCH. 5. *Guide left.*

186. At the fourth command, which will be given at the instant the wheel is completed, the platoons will move straight to the front, all the men taking the step of twenty-eight inches. The covering sergeant and the second sergeant will move rapidly to the left of their respective platoons, the former passing before the front rank. The leading guide will immediately take points on the ground in the direction which may be indicated to him by the instructor.

187. At the fifth command, the men will take the touch of elbows lightly to the left.

188. If the guide of the second platoon should lose his distance, or the line of direction, he will

conform to the principles herein prescribed Nos. 202 and 203.

189. If the company be marching in line to the front, the instructor will cause it to break by platoon to the right by the same commands. At the command *march*, the platoons will wheel in the manner already explained; the man on the pivot will take care to mark time in his place, without advancing or receding; the instructor, the chiefs of platoon, and the guides, will conform to what has been prescribed Nos. 184 and following.

190. The company may be broken by platoons to the left, according to the same principles, and by inverse means, the instructor giving the commands prescribed Nos. 183 and 185, substituting *left* for *right*, and reciprocally.

191. The movements explained in Nos. 183 and 189 will only be executed after the company has become well established in the principles of the march in column, Articles Second and Third.

Remarks.

192. The instructor, placed in front of the company, will observe whether the movement be executed according to the principles prescribed above; whether the platoons, after breaking into column, are perpendicular to the line of battle just occupied; and whether the guide, who placed himself where the marching flank of his platoon had to rest, has left, between himself and the front rank man on the right (or left), the space necessary to contain the front of the platoon.

193. After the platoons have broken, if the rearmost guide should not accurately cover the leading one, he will not seek to correct his position till the column be put in march, unless the instructor, wishing to wheel immediately into line, should think it necessary to rectify the direction of the guides,

which would be executed as will be hereinafter explained in Article Fifth of this Lesson.

194. The instructor will observe, that the man on the right (or left) of each platoon, who, at the command *march*, faces to the right (or left), being the true pivot of the wheel, the front rank man next to him ought to gain a little ground to the front in wheeling, so as to clear the pivot-man.

ARTICLE SECOND.

To march in column.

195. The company having broken by platoon, right (or left) in front, the instructor, wishing to cause the column to march, will throw himself twenty-five or thirty paces in front, face to the guides, place himself correctly, on their direction, and caution the leading guide to take points on the ground.

196. The instructor being thus placed, the guide of the leading platoon will take two points on the ground in the straight line passing between his own and the heels of the instructor.

197. These dispositions being made, the instructor will step aside, and command:

1. *Column, forward.*   2. *Guide left* (or *right*).
3. MARCH.

198. At the command *march*, promptly repeated by the chiefs of platoon, they, as well as the guides, will lead off, by a decided step, their respective platoons, in order that the whole may move smartly, and at the same moment.

199. The men will each feel lightly the elbow of his neighbor towards the guide, and conform himself, in marching, to the principles prescribed in the school of the soldier, No. 327. The man next to the guide, in each platoon, will take care never to pass him, and also to march always about six inches to the right (or

left) from him, in order not to push him out of the direction.

200. The leading guide will observe, with the greatest precision, the length and cadence of the step, and maintain the direction of his march by the means prescribed No. 89.

201. The following guide will march exactly in the trace of the leading one, preserving between the latter and himself a distance precisely equal to the front of his platoon, and marching in the same step with the leading guide.

202. If the following guide lose his distance from the one leading (which can only happen by his own fault), he will correct himself by slightly lengthening or shortening a few steps, in order that there may not be sudden quickenings or slackenings in the march of his platoon.

203. If the same guide, having neglected to march exactly in the trace of the preceding one, find himself sensibly out of the direction, he will remedy this fault by advancing more or less the shoulder opposite to the true direction, and thus, in a few steps, insensibly regain it, without the inconvenience of the oblique step, which would cause a loss of distance. In all cases, each chief of platoon will cause it to conform to the movements of its guide.

Remarks on the march in column.

204. If the chiefs and guides of subdivisions neglect to lead off, and to decide the march from the first step, the march will be begun in uncertainty, which will cause waverings, a loss of step, and a loss of distance.

205. If the leading guide take unequal steps, the march of his subdivision, and that which follows, will be uncertain; there will be undulations, quickenings, and slackenings in the march.

206. If the same guide be not habituated to prolong a

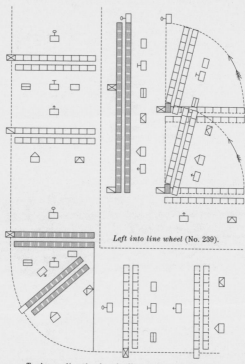

Left into line wheel (No. 239).

To change direction by wheeling to the right (No. 211).

given direction, without deviation, he will describe a crooked line, and the column must wind to conform itself to such line.

207. If the following guide be not habituated to march in the trace of the preceding one, he will lose his distance at every moment in endeavors to regain the trace, the preservation of which is the most important principle in the march in column.

208. The guide of each subdivision in column will be responsible for the direction, distance, and step; the chief of the subdivision, for the order and the conformity of his subdivision with the movements of the guide. Accordingly, the chief will frequently turn, in the march, to observe his subdivision.

209. The instructor, placed on the flank of the guides, will watch over the execution of all the principles prescribed; he will, also, sometimes place himself in the rear, align himself on the guides, and halt, pending some thirty paces together, to verify the accuracy of the guides.

210. In column, chiefs of subdivision will always repeat, with the greatest promptitude, the commands *march* and *halt*, no chief waiting for another, but each repeating the command the moment he catches it from the instructor. They will repeat no other command given by him; but will explain, if necessary, to their subdivisions, in an under-tone of voice, what they will have to execute, as indicated by the commands of caution.

ARTICLE THIRD.

To change direction.

211. The changes of direction of a column while marching, will be executed according to the principles prescribed for wheeling on the march. Whenever, therefore, a column is to change direction, the instructor will change the guide, if not already there,

to the flank opposite the side to which the change is to be made.

212. The column being in march right in front, if it be the wish of the instructor to change direction to the right, he will give the order to the chief of the first platoon, and immediately go himself, or send a marker, to the point at which the change of direction is to be made; the instructor, or marker, will place himself on the direction of the guides, so as to present the breast to that flank of the column.

213. The leading guide will direct his march on that person, so that, in passing, his left arm may just graze his breast. When the leading guide shall have approached near to the marker, the chief of his platoon will command:

1. *Right wheel.*   2. MARCH.

214. The first command will be given when the platoon is at the distance of four paces from the marker.

215. At the command *march*, which will be pronounced at the instant the guide shall have arrived opposite the marker, the platoon will wheel to the right, conforming to what is prescribed in the school of the soldier, No. 396.

216. Four paces before, the wheel being finished, the chief of each platoon will command:

3. *Forward.*   4. MARCH.

217. These commands will be pronounced and executed as is prescribed in the school of the soldier, Nos. 398 and 399. The guide of the first platoon will take points on the ground in the new direction, in order the better to regulate the march.

218. The second platoon will continue to march straight forward till up with the marker, when it will wheel to the right, and re-take the direct march by the

same commands and the same means which governed the first platoon.

219. The column being in march right in front, if the instructor should wish to change direction to the left, he will command, *guide right*. At this command, the two guides will move rapidly to the right of their respective platoons, each passing in front of his subdivision; the men will take the touch of elbows to the right; the instructor will afterwards conform to what is prescribed No. 212.

220. The change of direction to the left will then be executed according to the same principles as the change of direction to the right, but by inverse means.

221. When the change of direction is completed, the instructor will command, *guide left*.

222. The changes of direction in a column, left in front, will be executed according to the same principles.

223. In changes of direction in double quick time, the platoons will wheel according to the principles prescribed in the school of the soldier, No. 404.

224. In order to prepare the men for those formations in line which can be executed only by turning to the right or the left, the instructor will sometimes cause the column to change direction to the side of the guide. In this case, the chief of the leading platoon will command: *Left* (or *right*) *turn*, instead of *left* (or *right*) *wheel*. The subdivisions will each turn, in succession, conforming to what is prescribed in the school of the soldier, No. 402. The leading guide, as soon as he has turned, will take points on the ground, the better to regulate the direction of the march.

225. It is highly important, in order to preserve distances and the direction, that all the subdivisions of the column should change direction precisely at the point where the leading subdivision changed; it is for this reason that that point ought to be marked in advance, and

that it is prescribed that the guides direct their march on the marker, also that each chief of subdivision shall not cause the change to commence till the guide of his subdivision has grazed the breast of this marker.

226. Each chief will take care that his subdivision arrives at the point of change in a square with the line of direction: with this view, he will face to his subdivision when the one which precedes has commenced to turn or to wheel, and he will be watchful that it continues to march squarely until it arrives at the point where the change of direction is to commence.

227. If, in changes of direction, the pivot of the subdivision which wheels should not clear the wheeling point, the next subdivision would be arrested and distances lost; for the guide who conducts the marching flank having to describe an arc, in length about a half greater than the front of the subdivision, the second subdivision would be already up with the wheeling point, whilst the first which wheels has yet the half of its front to execute, and hence would be obliged to mark time until that half be executed. It is therefore prescribed, that the pivot of each subdivision should take steps of nine or eleven inches in length, according to the swiftness of the gait, in order not to arrest the march of the next subdivision. The chiefs of subdivision will look well to the step of the pivot, and cause his step to be lengthened or shortened as may be judged necessary. By the nature of this movement, the centre of each subdivision will bend a little to the rear.

228. The guides will never alter the length or the cadence of the step, whether the change of direction be to the side of the guide or to the opposite side.

229. The marker, placed at the wheeling point, will always present his breast to the flank of the column. The instructor will take the greatest pains in causing the prescribed principles to be observed; he will see that each

subdivision only commences the change of direction when the guide, grazing the breast of the marker, has nearly passed him, and that the marching flank does not describe the arc of too large a circle, in order that it may not be thrown beyond the new direction.

230. In change of direction by wheel, the guide of the wheeling flank will cast his eyes over the ground at the moment of commencing the wheel, and will describe an arc of a circle whose radius is equal to the front of the subdivision.

ARTICLE FOURTH.

To halt the column.

231. The column being in march, when the instructor shall wish to halt it, he will command:

1. *Column.* 2. HALT.

232. At the second command, promptly repeated by the chiefs of platoon, the column will halt; the guides also will stand fast, although they may have lost both distance and direction.

233. If the command *halt*, be not repeated with the greatest vivacity, and executed at the same instant, distances will be lost.

234. If a guide, having lost his distance, seek to recover it after that command, he will only throw his fault on the following guide, who, if he have marched well, will no longer be at his proper distance; and if the latter regain what he has thus lost, the movement will be propagated to the rear of the column.

ARTICLE FIFTH.

Being in column by platoon, to form to the right or left into line of battle, either at a halt or on the march.

235. The instructor having halted the column right in

front, and wishing to form it into line of battle, will place himself at platoon distance in front of the leading guide, face to him, and rectify, if necessary, the position of the guide beyond; which being executed, he will command:

Left—DRESS.

236. At this command, which will not be repeated by the chiefs of platoon, each of them will place himself briskly two paces outside of his guide, and direct the alignment of the platoon perpendicularly to the direction of the column.

237. Each chief having aligned his platoon, will command, FRONT, and return quickly to his place in column.

238. This disposition being made, the instructor will command:

1. *Left into line, wheel.*   2. MARCH.

239. At the command *march*, briskly repeated by the chiefs of platoon, the front rank man on the left of each platoon will face to the left, and place his breast lightly against the arm of the guide by his side, who stands fast; the platoons will wheel to the left on the principle of wheels from a halt, and in conformity to what is prescribed No. 194. Each chief will turn to his platoon to observe its movement, and when the marching flank has approached near the line of battle, he will command:

1. *Platoon.*   2. HALT.

240. The command *halt*, will be given when the marching flank of the platoon is three paces from the line of battle.

241. The chief of the second platoon, having halted it, will return to his place as a file closer, passing around the left of his subdivision.

242. The captain having halted the first platoon,

will move rapidly to the point at which the right of the company will rest in line of battle, and command:

Right—DRESS.

243. At this command, the two platoons will dress up on the alignment; the front rank man on the right of the leading platoon, who finds himself opposite the instructor established on the direction of the guides, will place his breast lightly against the left arm of this officer. The captain will direct the alignment from the right on the man on the opposite flank of the company.

244. The company being aligned, the captain will command:

FRONT.

245. The instructor seeing the company in line of battle, will command:

Guides—POSTS.

246. At this command, the covering sergeant will cover the captain, and the left guide will return to his place as a file closer.

247. If the column be left in front, and the instructor should wish to form it to the right into line of battle, he will place himself at platoon distance in front of the leading guide, face to him, and rectify, if necessary, the position of the guide beyond; which being executed, he will command:

1. *Right into line, wheel.* 2. MARCH.

248. At the command *march*, the front rank man on the right of each platoon will face to the right and place his breast lightly against the left arm of the guide by his side, who stands fast; each platoon will wheel to the right, and will be halted by its chief, when the marching flank has approached near the

line of battle; for this purpose, the chief of each platoon
will command:

1. *Platoon.*   2. HALT.

249. The command *halt*, will be given when the marching flank of the platoon is three paces from the line of battle. The chief of the second platoon having halted his
platoon, will resume his place in the rank of file closers.

250. The captain having halted the first platoon, will
move briskly to the point at which the left of the company
will rest, and command:

Left—DRESS.

251. At this command, the two platoons will dress up
on the alignment; the man on the left of the second platoon, opposite the instructor, will place his breast lightly
against the right arm of this officer, and the captain will
direct the alignment from the left on the man on the opposite flank of the company.

252. The company being aligned, the captain will
command:

FRONT.

253. The instructor will afterwards command:

Guides—POSTS.

254. At this command, the captain will move to the
right of his company, the covering sergeant will cover him,
and the left guide will return to his place as a file closer.

255. The instructor may omit the command *left* or
right dress, previous to commanding *left* or *right into
line, wheel*, unless, after rectifying the position of the
guides, it should become necessary to dress the platoons,
or one of them, laterally to the right or left.

256. The instructor, before the command *left* (or
right) *into line, wheel*, will assure himself that the rearmost platoon is at its exact wheeling distance from the

one in front. This attention is important, in order to detect negligence on the part of guides in this essential point.

257. If the column be marching right in front, and the instructor should wish to form it into line without halting the column, he will give the commands prescribed No. 238, and move rapidly to platoon distance in front of the leading guide.

258. At the command *march*, briskly repeated by the chiefs of platoon, the left guides will halt short, the instructor, the chiefs of platoon, and the platoons, will conform to what is prescribed No. 239 and following.

259. If the column be in march left in front, this formation will be made according to the same principles, and by inverse means.

260. If the column be marching right in front, and the instructor should wish to form it into line without halting the column, and to march the company in line to the front, he will command:

1. *By platoons left wheel.* 2. MARCH.

261. At the command *march*, briskly repeated by the chiefs of platoon, the left guides will halt: the man next to the left guide in each platoon will mark time: the platoons will wheel to the left, conforming to the principles of the wheel on a fixed pivot. When the right of the platoons shall arrive near the line of battle, the instructor will command:

3. *Forward.* 4. MARCH. 5. *Guide right* (or *left*).

262. At the fourth command, given at the instant the wheel is completed, all the men of the company will move off together with the step of twenty-eight inches; the captain, the chief of the second platoon, the covering sergeant, and the left guide will take their positions as in line of battle.

263. At the fifth command, which will be given

immediately after the fourth, the captain and covering sergeant, if not already there, will move briskly to the side on
which the guide is designated. The non-commissioned
officer charged with the direction will move rapidly in
front of the guide, and will be assured in his line of march
by the instructor, as is prescribed No. 104. That non-
commissioned officer will immediately take points on
the ground as indicated in the same number. The men
will take the touch of elbows to the side of the guide,
conforming themselves to the principles of the march in
line.

264. The same principles are applicable to a column
left in front.

LESSON SIXTH.

Article First.

To break the company into platoons, and to re-form the company.

To break the company into platoons.

265. The company marching in the cadenced step, and
supposed to make part of a column, right in front, when
the instructor shall wish to cause it to break by platoon,
he will give the order to the captain, who will command:
1. *Break into platoons,* and immediately place himself
before the centre of the first platoon.

266. At the command *break into platoons,* the first
lieutenant will pass quickly around the left to the centre
of his platoon, and give the caution: *Mark time.*

267. The captain will then command: 2. *March.*

268. The first platoon will continue to march straight
forward; the covering sergeant will move rapidly to the
left flank of this platoon (passing by the front rank) as
soon as the flank shall be disengaged.

Pl. 31.

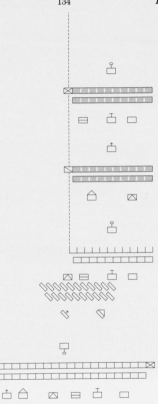

To break the company into platoons, and to re-form company (No. 265).

269. At the command *march*, given by the captain, the second platoon will begin to mark time; its chief will immediately add: 1. *Right oblique*; 2. MARCH. The last command will be given so that this platoon may commence obliquing the instant the rear rank of the first platoon shall have passed. The men will shorten the step in obliquing, so that when the command *forward march* is given, the platoon may have its exact distance.

270. The guide of the second platoon being near the direction of the guide of the first, the chief of the second will command *Forward*, and add MARCH, the instant that the guide of his platoon shall cover the guide of the first.

271. In a column, left in front, the company will break into platoons by inverse means, applying to the first platoon all that has been prescribed for the second, and reciprocally.

272. In this case, the left guide of the company will shift to the right flank of the second platoon, and the covering sergeant will remain on the right of the first.

To re-form the company.

273. The column, by platoon, being in march, right in front, when the instructor shall wish to cause it to form company, he will give the order to the captain, who will command: *Form company*.

274. Having given this command, the captain will immediately add: 1. *First platoon*; 2. *Right oblique*.

275. The chief of the second platoon will caution it to continue to march straight forward.

276. The captain will then command: 3. MARCH.

277. At this command, repeated by the chief of the second, the first platoon will oblique to the right, in order to unmask the second; the covering sergeant, on the left of the first platoon, will return to the right of the company, passing by the front rank.

278. When the first platoon shall have nearly unmasked the second, the captain will command: 1. *Mark time*, and at the instant the unmasking shall be complete, he will add: 2. MARCH. The first platoon will then cease to oblique, and mark time.

279. In the mean time the second platoon will have continued to march straight forward, and when it shall be nearly up with the first, the captain will command *Forward*, and at the instant the two platoons shall unite, add MARCH; the first platoon will then cease to mark time.

280. In a column, left in front, the same movement will be executed by inverse means, the chief of the second platoon giving the command *Forward*, and the captain adding the command MARCH, when the platoons are united.

281. The guide of the second platoon, on its right, will pass to its left flank the moment the platoon begins to oblique; the guide of the first, on its right, remaining on that flank of the platoon.

282. The instructor will also sometimes cause the company to break and re-form, by platoon, by his own direct commands. In this case, he will give the general commands prescribed for the captain above: 1. *Break into platoons*; 2. MARCH; and 1. *Form company*; 2. MARCH.

283. If, in breaking the company into platoons, the subdivision that breaks off should mark time too long, it might, in a column of many subdivisions, arrest the march of the following one, which would cause a lengthening of the column, and a loss of distances.

284. In breaking into platoons, it is necessary that the platoons which oblique should not shorten the step too much, in order not to lose distance in column, and not to arrest the march of the following sub division.

285. If a platoon obliques too far to a flank, it would

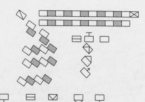
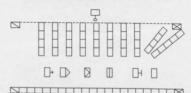

*To break files to the rear, and to cause them to re-enter the
line* (No. 289).

be obliged to oblique again to the opposite flank, to regain the direction, and by the double movement arrest, probably, the march of the following subdivision.

286. The chiefs of those platoons which oblique will face to their platoons, in order to enforce the observance of the foregoing principles.

287. When, in a column of several companies, they break in succession, it is of the greatest importance that each company should continue to march in the same step, without shortening or slackening, whilst that which precedes breaks, although the following company should close up on the preceding one. This attention is essential to guard against an elongation of the column.

288. Faults of but little moment, in a column of a few companies, would be serious inconveniences in a general column of many battalions. Hence the instructor will give the greatest care in causing all the prescribed principles to be strictly observed. To this end, he will hold himself on the directing flank, the better to observe all the movements.

ARTICLE SECOND.

Being in column, to break files to the rear, and to cause them to re-enter into line.

289. The company being in march, and supposed to constitute a subdivision of a column, right (or left) in front, when the instructor shall wish to cause files to break off he will give the order to the captain, who will immediately turn to his company, and command:

1. *Two files from left* (or *right*) *to rear.*   2. MARCH.

290. At the command *march*, the two files on the left (or right) of the company will mark time, the others will continue to march straight forward; the two rear rank

men of these files will, as soon as the rear rank of the
company shall clear them, move to the right by advancing
the outer shoulder; the odd number will place himself
behind the third file from that flank, the even number
behind the fourth, passing for this purpose behind the odd
number; the two front rank men will, in like manner, move
to the right when the rear rank of the company shall clear
them, the odd number will place himself behind the first
file, the even number behind the second file, passing for
this purpose behind the odd number. If the files are
broken from the right, the men will move to the left,
advancing the outer shoulder, the even number of the rear
rank will place himself behind the third file, the odd number of the same rank behind the fourth; the even number
of the front rank behind the first file, the odd number of
the same rank behind the second, the odd numbers for
this purpose passing behind the even numbers. The men
will be careful not to lose their distances, and to keep
aligned.

291. If the instructor should still wish to
break two files from the same side, he will give
the order to the captain, who will proceed as above
directed.

292. At the command *march*, given by the captain,
the files already broken, advancing a little the outer
shoulder, will gain the space of two files to the right,
if the files are broken from the left, and to the left, if
the files are broken from the right, shortening, at the
same time, the step, in order to make room between
themselves and the rear rank of the company for the
files last ordered to the rear; the latter will break
by the same commands and in the same manner
as the first. The men who double should increase the
length of the step in order to prevent distances from
being lost.

293. The instructor may thus diminish the front of a
company by breaking off successive groups of two files,

but the new files must always be broken from the same side.

294. The instructor, wishing to cause files broken off to return into line, will give the order to the captain, who will immediately command:

1. *Two files into line.*   2. MARCH.

295. At the command *march*, the first two files of those marching by the flank will return briskly into line, and the others will gain the space of two files by advancing the inner shoulder towards the flank to which they belong.

296. The captain will turn to his company, to watch the observance of the principles which have just been prescribed.

297. The instructor having caused groups of two files to break one after another, and to return again into line, will afterwards cause two or three groups to break together, and for this purpose will command: *Four or six files from left* (or *right*) *to rear*; MARCH. The files designated will mark time; each rank will advance a little the outer shoulder as soon as the rear rank of the company shall clear it, will oblique at once, and each group will place itself behind the four neighboring files, and in the same manner, as if the movement had been executed group by group, taking care that the distances are preserved.

298. The instructor will next order the captain to cause two or three groups to be brought into line at once, who, turning to the company, will command:

Four or six files into line—MARCH.

299. At the command *march*, the files designated will advance the inner shoulder, move up and form on the flank of the company by the shortest lines.

300. As often as files shall break off to the rear, the guide on that flank will gradually close on the nearest

front rank man remaining in line, and he will also open out to make room for files ordered into line.

301. The files which march in the rear are disposed in the following order: the left files as if the company was marching by the right flank, and the right files as if the company was marching by the left flank. Consequently, whenever there is on the right or left of a subdivision, a file which does not belong to a group, it will be broken singly.

302. It is necessary to the preservation of distances in column that the men should be habituated in the schools of detail to execute the movements of this article with precision.

303. If new files broken off do not step well to the left or right in obliquing; if, when files are ordered into line, they do not move up with promptitude and precision, in either case the following files will be arrested in their march, and thereby cause the column to be lengthened out.

304. The instructor will place himself on the flank from which the files are broken, to assure himself of the exact observance of the principles.

305. Files will only be broken off from the side of direction, in order that the whole company may easily pass from the front to the flank march.

Article Third.

To march the column in route, and to execute the movements incident thereto.

306. The swiftness of the route step will be one hundred and ten steps in a minute; this swiftness will be habitually maintained in columns in route, when the roads and ground may permit.

307. The company being at a halt, and supposed to constitute a subdivision of a column, when the instructor shall wish to cause it to march in the route step, he will command:

1. *Column, forward.*   2. *Guide, left* (or *right*).
3. *Route step.*   4. MARCH.

308. At the command *march*, repeated by the captain, the two ranks will step off together: the rear rank will take, in marching, by shortening a few steps, a distance of one pace (twenty-eight inches) from the rank preceding, which distance will be computed from the breasts of the men in the rear rank, to the knapsacks of the men in the front rank. The men, without further command, will immediately carry their arms *at will*, as indicated in the school of the soldier, No. 219. They will no longer be required to march in the cadenced pace, or with the same foot, or to remain silent. The files will march at ease; but care will be taken to prevent the ranks from intermixing, the front rank from getting in advance of the guide, and the rear rank from opening to too great a distance.

309. The company marching in the route step, the instructor will cause it to change direction, which will be executed without formal commands, on a simple caution from the captain; the rear rank will come up to change direction in the same manner as the front rank. Each rank will conform itself, although in the route step, to the principles which have been prescribed for the change in closed ranks, with this difference only; that the pivot-man, instead of taking steps of nine, will take steps of fourteen inches, in order to clear the wheeling point.

310. The company marching in the route step, to cause it to pass to the cadenced step, the instructor will first order pieces to be brought to the right shoulder, and then command:

1. *Quick time.*   2. MARCH.

311. At the command *march*, the men will resume the cadenced step, and will close so as to leave a distance of sixteen inches between each rank.

312. The company marching in the cadenced pace, the instructor, to cause it to take the route step, will command:

1. *Route step.*   2. MARCH.

313. At the command *march*, the front rank will continue the step of twenty-eight inches, the rear rank will take, by gradually shortening the step, the distance of twenty-eight inches from the front rank; the men will carry their arms at will.

314. If the company be marching in the route step, and the instructor should suppose the necessity of marching by the flank in the same direction, he will command:

1. *Company by the right* (or *left*) *flank.*   2. *By file left*
(or *right*).   3 MARCH.

315. At the command *march*, the company will face to the right (or left) in marching, the captain will place himself by the side of the guide who conducts the leading flank: this guide will wheel immediately to the left or right; all the files will come in succession to wheel on the same spot as the guide; if there be files broken off to the rear, they will, by wheeling, regain their respective places, and follow the movement of the company.

316. The instructor having caused the company to be again formed into line, will exercise it in increasing and diminishing front, by platoon, which will be executed by the same commands, and the same means, as if the company were marching in the cadenced step. When the company breaks into platoons, the chief of each will move to the flank of his platoon, and will take the place of the guide, who will step back into the rear rank.

317. The company being in column, by platoon, and supposed to march in the route step, the instructor can cause the front to be diminished and increased, by

section, if the platoons have a front of twelve files or more.

318. The movements of diminishing and increasing front, by section, will be executed according to the principles indicated for the same movements by platoon. The right sections of platoons will be commanded by the captain and first lieutenant, respectively; the left sections, by the two next subalterns in rank, or, in their absence, by sergeants.

319. The instructor wishing to diminish by section, will give the order to the captain, who will command:

1. *Break into sections.*   2. MARCH.

320. As soon as the platoons shall be broken, each chief of section will place himself on its directing flank in the front rank, the guides who will be thus displaced will fall back into the rear rank: the file closers will close up to within one pace of this rank.

321. Platoons will be broken into sections only in the column in route: the movement will never be executed in the manœuvres, whatever may be the front of the company.

322. When the instructor shall wish to re-form platoons, he will give the order to the captain, who will command:

1. *Form platoons.*   2. MARCH.

323. At the first command, each chief of section will place himself before its centre, and the guides will pass into the front rank. At the command *march*, the movement will be executed as has been prescribed for forming company. The moment the platoons are formed, the chiefs of the left sections will return to their places as file closers.

324. The instructor will also cause to be executed the diminishing and increasing front by files, as prescribed in the preceding article, and in the same manner as if

marching in the cadenced step. When the company is broken into sections, the subdivisions must not be reduced to a front of less than six files, not counting the chief of the section.

325. The company being broken by platoon, or by section, the instructor will cause it, marching in the route step, to march by the flank in the same direction, by the commands and the means indicated Nos. 314 and 315. The moment the subdivisions shall face to the right (or left), the first file of each will wheel to the left (or right), in marching, to prolong the direction, and to unite with the rear file of the subdivision immediately preceding. The file closers will take their habitual places in the march by the flank, before the union of the subdivisions.

326. If the company be marching by the right flank, and the instructor should wish to undouble the files, which might sometimes be found necessary, he will inform the captain, who, after causing the cadenced step to be resumed, and arms to be shouldered or supported, will command:

1. *In two ranks, undouble files.*   2. MARCH.

327. At the second command, the odd numbers will continue to march straight forward, the even numbers will shorten the step, and obliquing to the left will place themselves promptly behind the odd numbers; the rear rank will gain a step to the left so as to retake the touch of elbows on the side of the front rank.

328. If the company be marching by the left flank, it will be the even numbers who will continue to march forward, and the odd numbers who will undouble.

329. If the instructor should wish to double the files, he will give the order to the captain, who will command:

1. *In four ranks, double files.*   2. MARCH.

330. At the command *march*, the files will double in the manner as explained, when the company faces by the right or the left flank. The instructor will afterwards cause the route step to be resumed.

331. The various movements prescribed in this lesson may be executed in double quick time. The men will be brought, by degrees, to pass over at this gait about eleven hundred yards in seven minutes.

332. When the company marching in the route step shall halt, the rear rank will close up at the command *halt*, and the whole will shoulder arms.

333. Marching in the route step, the men will be permitted to carry their pieces in the manner they shall find most convenient, paying attention only to holding the muzzles up, so as to avoid accidents.

ARTICLE FOURTH.
Countermarch.

334. The company being at a halt, and supposed to constitute part of a column, right in front, when the instructor shall wish to cause it to countermarch, he will command:

1. *Countermarch.*   2. *Company, right*—FACE.
3. *By file left.*   4. MARCH.

335. At the second command, the company will face to the right, the two guides to the right about; the captain will go to the right of his company and cause two files to break to the rear, and then place himself by the side of the front rank man, to conduct him.

336. At the command *march*, both guides will stand fast; the company will step off smartly; the first file, conducted by the captain, will wheel around the right guide, and direct its march along the front rank so as to arrive

behind, and two paces from the left guide; each file
will come in succession to wheel on the same ground
around the right guide; the leading file having arrived
at a point opposite to the left guide, the captain will
command:

1. *Company.* 2. HALT. 3. FRONT. 4. *Right—*
DRESS.

337. The first command will be given at *four* paces
from the point where the leading file is to rest.

338. At the second command, the company will halt.

339. At the third, it will face to the front.

340. At the fourth, the company will dress by the right;
the captain will step two paces outside of the left guide,
now on the right, and direct the alignment, so that
the front rank may be enclosed between the two guides;
the company being aligned, he will command FRONT,
and place himself before the centre of the company as
if in column; the guides, passing along the front rank,
will shift to their proper places, on the right and left
of that rank.

341. In a column, by platoon, the countermarch will be
executed by the same commands, and according to the
same principles; the guide of each platoon will face about,
and its chief will place himself by the side of the file on
the right, to conduct it.

342. In a column, left in front, the countermarch will
be executed by inverse commands and means, but according to the same principles. Thus, the movement will be
made by the right flank of subdivisions, if the right be in
front, and by the left flank, if the left be in front; in both
cases the subdivisions will wheel by file to the side of the
front rank.

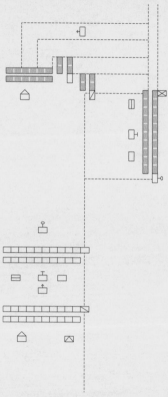

On the right into line (No. 344).

ARTICLE FIFTH.

Being in column by platoon, to form on the right (or left) into line of battle.

343. The column by platoon, right in front, being in march, the instructor, wishing to form it on the right into line of battle, will command:

1. *On the right into line.*   2. *Guide right.*

344. At the second command, the guide of each platoon will shift quickly to its right flank, and the men will touch elbows to the right; the column will continue to march straight forward.

345. The instructor having given the second command, will move briskly to the point at which the right of the company ought to rest in line, and place himself facing the point of direction to the left which he will choose.

346. The line of battle ought to be so chosen that the guide of each platoon, after having turned to the right, may have, at least, ten paces to take before arriving upon that line.

347. The head of the column being nearly opposite to the instructor, the chief of the first platoon will command: 1. *Right turn*; and when exactly opposite to that point, he will add:

2. MARCH.

348. At the command *march*, the first platoon will turn to the right, in conformity with the principles prescribed in the school of the soldier, No. 402. Its guide will so direct his march as to bring the front rank man, next on his left, opposite to the instructor; the chief of the platoon will march before its centre; and when its guide shall be near the line of battle, he will command:

1. *Platoon.*   2. HALT.

349. At the command *halt*, which will be given at the instant the right of the platoon shall arrive at the distance of three paces from the line of battle, the platoon will halt; the files, not yet in line, will come up promptly. The guide will throw himself on the line of battle, opposite to one of the three left files of his platoon; he will face to the instructor, who will align him on the point of direction to the left. The chief of platoon having, at the same time, gone to the point where the right of the company is to rest, will, as soon as he sees all the files of the platoon in line, command:

Right—DRESS.

350. At this, the first platoon will align itself; the front rank man, who finds himself opposite to the guide, will rest his breast lightly against the right arm of this guide, and the chief of the platoon, from the right, will direct the alignment on this man.

351. The second platoon will continue to march straight forward, until its guide shall arrive opposite to the left file of the first; it will then turn to the right at the command of its chief, and march towards the line of battle, its guide directing himself on the left file of the first platoon.

352. The guide having arrived at the distance of three paces from the line of battle, this platoon will be halted, as prescribed for the first; at the instant it halts, its guide will spring on the line of battle, opposite to one of the three left files of his platoon, and will be assured in his position by the instructor.

353. The chief of the second platoon, seeing all its files in line, and its guide established on the direction, will command:

Right—DRESS.

354. Having given this command, he will return to his

place as a file closer, passing around the left; the second platoon will dress up on the alignment of the first, and, when established, the captain will command:

FRONT.

355. The movement ended, the instructor will command:

Guides—POSTS.

356. At this command, the two guides will return to their places in line of battle.

357. A column, by platoon, left in front, will form on the left into line of battle, according to the same principles, and, by inverse means, applying to the second platoon what is prescribed for the first, and reciprocally. The chief of the second platoon having aligned it, from the point of *appui* (the left), will retire to his place as a file closer. The captain having halted the first platoon three paces behind the line of battle, will go to the same point to align this platoon, and then command: FRONT. At the command, *guides— posts*, given by the instructor, the captain will shift to his proper flank, and the guides take their places in line of battle.

358. When the companies of a regiment are to be exercised, at the same time, in the school of the company, the colonel will indicate the lesson or lessons they are severally to execute. The whole will commence by a bugle signal, and terminate in like manner.

Formation of a company from two ranks into single rank, and reciprocally.

359. The company being formed into two ranks in the manner indicated No. 8, school of the soldier, and supposed to make part of a column, right or left in

front, when the instructor shall wish to form it into single rank, he will command:

1. *In one rank, form company.* 2. MARCH.

360. At the first command, the right guide will face to the right.

361. At the command *march*, the right guide will step off and march in the prolongation of the front rank.

362. The first file will step off at the same time with the guide; the front rank man will turn to the right at the first step, follow the guide, and be himself followed by the rear rank man of his file, who will come to turn on the same spot where he had turned. The second file, and successively all the other files, will step off as has been prescribed for the first, the front rank man of each file following immediately the rear rank man of the file next on his right. The captain will superintend the movement, and when the last man shall have stepped off, he will halt the company, and face it to the front.

363. The file closers will take their places in line of battle, two paces in rear of the rank.

364. The company being in single rank, when the instructor shall wish to form it into two ranks, he will command:

1. *In two ranks, form company.* 2. *Company right*—FACE. 3. MARCH.

365. At the second command, the company will face to the right: the right guide and the man on the right will remain faced to the front.

366. At the command *march*, the men who have faced to the right, will step off, and form files in the following manner: the second man in the rank will place himself behind the first to form the first file; the third will place himself by the side of the first in the front rank; the fourth

behind the third in the rear rank. All the others will, in like manner, place themselves, alternately, in the front and rear rank, and will thus form files of two men, on the left of those already formed.

367. The formations above described will be habitually executed by the right of companies; but when the instructor shall wish to have them executed by the left, he will face the company *about*, and post the guides in the rear rank.

368. The formation will then be executed by the same commands, and according to the same principles as by the front rank; the movement commencing with the left file, now become the right, and in each file by the rear rank man, now become the front; the left guide will conform to what has been prescribed for the right.

369. The formation ended, the instructor will face the company to its proper front.

370. When a battalion in line has to execute either of the formations above described, the colonel will cause it to break to the rear by the right or left of companies, and will then give the commands just prescribed for the instructor. Each company will execute the movement as if acting singly.

Formation of a company from two ranks into four, and reciprocally, at a halt, and in march.

371. The company being formed in two ranks, at a halt, and supposed to form part of a column right in front, when the instructor shall wish to form it into four ranks, he will command:

1. *In four ranks, form company.* 2. *Company left*—
    FACE. 3. MARCH (or *double quick*—MARCH).

372. At the second command, the left guide will remain faced to the front, the company will face to the left: the rear rank will gain the distance of one pace from

the front rank by a side step to the left and rear, and the men will form into four ranks as prescribed in the school of the soldier.

373. At the command *march*, the first file of four men will reface to the front without undoubling. All the other files of four will step off, and closing successively to about five inches of the preceding file, will halt, and immediately face to the front, the men remaining doubled.

374. The file closers will take their new places in line of battle, at two paces in rear of the fourth rank.

375. The captain will superintend the movement.

376. The company being in four ranks, when the instructor shall wish to form it into two ranks, he will command:

1. *In two ranks, form company.* 2. *Company right—*
FACE. 3. MARCH (or *double quick—*MARCH).

377. At the second command, the left guide will stand fast, the company will face to the right.

378. At the command *march*, the right guide will step off and march in the prolongation of the front rank. The leading file of four men will step off at the same time, the other files standing fast; the second file will step off when there shall be between it and the first space sufficient to form into two ranks. The following files will execute successively what has been prescribed for the second. As soon as the last file shall have its distance, the instructor will command:

1. *Company.* 2. HALT. 3. FRONT.

379. At the command *front*, the company will face to the front, and the files will undouble.

380. The company being formed in two ranks, and marching to the front, when the instructor shall wish to form it into four ranks, he will command:

1. *In four ranks, form company.* 2. *By the left; double files.* 3. MARCH (or *double quick*—MARCH).

381. At the command *march*, the left guide and the left file of the company will continue to march straight to the front: the company will make a half face to the left, the odd numbers placing themselves behind the even numbers. The even numbers of the rear rank will shorten their steps a little, to permit the odd numbers of the front rank to get between them and the even numbers of that rank. The files thus formed of fours, except the left file, will continue to march obliquely, lengthening their steps slightly, so as to keep constantly abreast of the guide; each file will close successively on the file next on its left, and when at the proper distance from that file, will face to the front by a half face to the right, and take the touch of elbows to the left.

382. The company being in march to the front in four ranks, when the instructor shall wish to form it into two ranks, he will command:

1. *In two ranks, form company.* 2. *By the right, undouble files.* 3. MARCH (or *double quick*—MARCH).

383. At the command *march*, the left guide and the left file of the company will continue to march straight to the front; the company will make a half face to the right and march obliquely, lengthening the step a little, in order to keep, as near as possible, abreast of the guide. As soon as the second file from the left shall have gained to the right the interval necessary for the left file to form into two ranks, the second file will face to the front by a half face to the left, and march straight forward; the left file will immediately form into two ranks, and take the touch of elbows to the left. Each file will execute successively what has just been prescribed for the file next to the left, and each file will form into two ranks when the file next

on its right has obliqued the required distance and faced to the front.

384. If the company be supposed to make part of a column, left in front, these different movements will be executed according to the same principles and by inverse means, substituting the indication *left* for *right*.

END OF THE SCHOOL OF THE COMPANY.

INSTRUCTION FOR SKIRMISHERS.

General principles and division of the instruction.

1. THE movements of skirmishers should be subjected to such rules as will give to the commander the means of moving them in any direction with the greatest promptitude.

2. It is not expected that these movements should be executed with the same precision as in closed ranks, nor is it desirable, as such exactness would materially interfere with their prompt execution.

3. When skirmishers are thrown out to clear the way for, and to protect the advance of, the main corps, their movements should be so regulated by this corps, as to keep it constantly covered.

4. Every body of skirmishers should have a reserve, the strength and composition of which will vary according to circumstances.

5. If the body thrown out be within sustaining distance of the main corps, a very small reserve will be sufficient for each company, whose duty it shall be to fill vacant places, furnish the line with cartridges, relieve the fatigued, and serve as a rallying point for the skirmishers.

6. If the main corps be at a considerable distance, besides the company reserves, another reserve will be required, composed of entire companies, which will be employed to sustain and reinforce such parts of the line as may be warmly attacked: this reserve should be strong enough to relieve at least half the companies deployed as skirmishers.

7. The reserves should be placed behind the center

of the line of skirmishers, the company reserves at one hundred and fifty, and the principal reserve at four hundred paces. This rule, however, is not invariable. The reserves, while holding themselves within sustaining distance of the line, should be, as much as possible, in position to afford each other mutual protection, and must carefully profit by any accidents of the ground to conceal themselves from the view of the enemy, and to shelter themselves from his fire.

8. The movements of skirmishers will be executed in quick, or double quick time. The run will be resorted to only in cases of urgent necessity.

9. Skirmishers will be permitted to carry their pieces in the manner most convenient to them.

10. The movements will be habitually indicated by the sounds of the bugle.

11. The officers, and, if necessary, the non-commissioned officers, will repeat, and cause the commands to be executed, as soon as they are given; but to avoid mistakes, when the signals are employed, they will wait until the last bugle note is sounded before commencing the movement.

12. When skirmishers are ordered to move rapidly, the officers and non-commissioned officers will see that the men economize their strength, keep cool, and profit by all the advantages which the ground may offer for cover. It is only by this continual watchfulness on the part of all grades, that a line of skirmishers can attain success.

13. This instruction will be divided into five articles, and subdivided as follows:

ARTICLE FIRST.

(1.) To deploy forward.
(2.) To deploy by the flank.
(3.) To extend intervals.

(4.) To close intervals.
(5.) To relieve skirmishers.

ARTICLE SECOND.

(1.) To advance in line.
(2.) To retreat in line.
(3.) To change direction.
(4.) To march by the flank.

ARTICLE THIRD.

(1.) To fire at a halt.
(2.) To fire marching.

ARTICLE FOURTH.

(1.) The rally.
(2.) To form column to march in any direction.
(3.) The assembly.

ARTICLE FIFTH.

(1.) To deploy a battalion as skirmishers.
(2.) To rally the battalion deployed as skirmishers.

14. In the first four articles, it is supposed that the movements are executed by a company deployed as skirmishers, on a front equal to that of the battalion in order of battle. In the fifth article, it is supposed that each company of the battalion, being deployed as skirmishers, occupies a front of one hundred paces. From these two examples, rules may be deduced for all cases, whatever may be the numerical strength of the skirmishers, and the extent of ground they ought to occupy.

ARTICLE FIRST.

Deployments.

15. A company may be deployed as skirmishers in two ways: forward, and by the flank.

16. The deployment forward will be adopted when the company is behind the line on which it is to be established as skirmishers: it will be deployed by the flank, when it finds itself already on that line.

17. Whenever a company is to be deployed as skirmishers, it will be divided into two platoons, and each platoon will be subdivided into two sections; the comrades in battle, forming groups of four men, will be careful to know and to sustain each other. The captain will assure himself that the files in the centre of each platoon and section are designated.

18. A company may be deployed as skirmishers on its right, left, or centre file, or on any other named file whatsoever. In this manner, skirmishers may be thrown forward with the greatest possible rapidity on any ground they may be required to occupy.

19. A chain of skirmishers ought generally to preserve their alignment, but no advantages which the ground may present should be sacrificed to attain this regularity.

20. The interval between skirmishers depends on the extent of ground to be covered; but, in general, it is not proper that the groups of four men should be removed more than forty paces from each other. The habitual distance between men of the same group in open grounds will be five paces; in no case will they lose sight of each other.

21. The front to be occupied to cover a battalion comprehends its front and the half of each interval which separates it from the battalion on its right and left. If a line, whose wings are not supported, should be covered by skirmishers, it will be necessary either to protect the flanks with skirmishers, or to extend them in front of the line so far beyond the wings as effectually to oppose any attempt which might be made by the enemy's skirmishers to disturb the flanks.

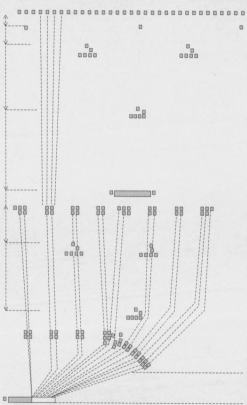

To deploy forward (No. 22).

To deploy forward.

22. A company being at a halt or in march, when the captain shall wish to deploy it forward on the left file of the first platoon, holding the second platoon in reserve, he will command:

(1.) *First platoon—as skirmishers.*

(2.) *On the left file—take intervals.*

(3.) MARCH (or *double quick—*MARCH).

23. At the first command, the second and third lieutenants will place themselves rapidly two paces behind the centres of the right and left sections of the first platoon; the fifth sergeant will move one pace in front of the centre of the first platoon, and will place himself between the two sections in the front rank as soon as the movement begins; the fourth sergeant will place himself on the left of the front rank of the same platoon, as soon as he can pass. The captain will indicate to this sergeant the point on which he wishes him to direct his march. The first lieutenant, placing himself before the centre of the second platoon, will command:

*Second platoon backward—*MARCH.

24. At this command, the second platoon will step three paces to the rear, so as to unmask the flank of the first platoon. It will then be halted by its chief, and the second sergeant will place himself on the left, and the third sergeant on the right flank of this platoon.

25. At the command *march*, the left group of four men, conducted by the fourth sergeant, will direct itself on the point indicated; all the other groups of fours, throwing forward briskly the left shoulder, will move diagonally to the front in double quick time, so as to gain to the right the space of twenty paces, which shall be the

distance between each group and that immediately on its left. When the second group from the left shall arrive on a line with, and twenty paces from, the first, it will march straight to the front, conforming to the gait and direction of the first, keeping constantly on the same alignment and at twenty paces from it. The third group, and all the others, will conform to what has just been prescribed for the second; they will arrive successively on the line. The right guide will arrive with the last group.

26. The left guide having reached the point where the left of the line should rest, the captain will command the skirmishes to halt; the men composing each group of fours will then immediately deploy at five paces from each other, and to the right and left of the front rank man of the even file in each group, the rear rank men placing themselves on the left of their file leaders. If any groups be not in line at the command *halt*, they will move up rapidly, conforming to what has just been prescribed.

27. If, during the deployment, the line should be fired upon by the enemy, the captain may cause the groups of fours to deploy, as they gain their proper distances.

28. The line being formed, the non-commissioned officers on the right, left and centre of the platoon will place themselves ten paces in rear of the line, and opposite the positions they respectively occupied. The chiefs of sections will promptly rectify any irregularities, and then place themselves twenty-five or thirty paces in rear of the centre of their sections, each having with him four men taken from the reserve, and also a bugler, who will repeat, if necessary, the signals sounded by the captain.

29. Skirmishers should be particularly instructed to take advantage of any cover which the ground may offer, and should lie flat on the ground whenever such a movement is necessary to protect them from the fire of the

enemy. Regularity in the alignment should yield to this important advantage.

30. When the movement begins, the first lieutenant will face the second platoon *about*, and march it promptly, and by the shortest line, to about one hundred and fifty paces in rear of the centre of the line. He will hold it always at this distance, unless ordered to the contrary.

31. The reserve will conform itself to all the movements of the line. *This rule is general.*

32. Light troops will carry their bayonets habitually in the scabbard, and this rule applies equally to the skirmishers and the reserve; whenever bayonets are required to be fixed, a particular signal will be given. The captain will give a general superintendence to the whole deployment, and then promptly place himself about eighty paces in rear of the centre of the line. He will have with him a bugler and four men taken from the reserve.

33. The deployment may be made on the right or the centre of the platoon, by the same commands, substituting the indication *right* or *centre*, for that of *left* file.

34. The deployment on the right or the centre will be made according to the principles prescribed above: in this latter case, the centre of the platoon will be marked by the right group of fours in the second section: the fifth sergeant will place himself on the right of this group, and serve as the guide of the platoon during the deployment.

35. In whatever manner the deployment be made, on the right, left, or centre, the men in each group of fours will always deploy at five paces from each other, and upon the front rank man of the even numbered file. The deployments will habitually be made at twenty paces interval; but if a greater interval be required, it will be indicated in the command.

36. If a company be thrown out as skirmishers, so

near the main body as to render a reserve unnecessary, the entire company will be extended in the same manner, and according to the same principles, as for the deployment of a platoon. In this case, the third lieutenant will command the fourth section, and a non-commissioned officer designated for that purpose, the fifth section; the fifth sergeant will act as centre guide; the file closers will place themselves ten paces in rear of the line, and opposite their places in line of battle. The first and second lieutenant will each have a bugler near him.

To deploy by the flank.

37. The company being at a halt, when the captain shall wish to deploy it by the flank, holding the first platoon in reserve, he will command:

1. *Second platoon—as skirmishers.* 2. *By the right flank—take intervals.* 3. MARCH (or *double quick—* MARCH).

38. At the first command, the first and third lieutenants will place themselves, respectively, two paces behind the centres of the first and second sections of the second platoon; the fifth sergeant will place himself one pace in front of the centre of the second platoon; the third sergeant, as soon as he can pass, will place himself on the right of the front rank of the same platoon. The captain will indicate to him the point on which he wishes him to direct his march. The chief of the first platoon will execute what has been prescribed for the chief of the second platoon, Nos. 23 and 24. The fourth sergeant will place himself on the left flank of the reserve, the first sergeant will remain on the right flank.

39. At the second command, the first and third lieutenants will place themselves two paces behind the left group of their respective sections.

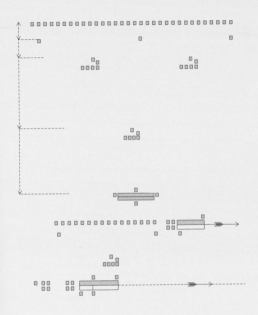

To deploy by the flank (No. 37).

40. At the command *march*, the second platoon will face to the right, and commence the movement; the left group of fours will stand fast, but will deploy as soon as there is room on its right, conforming to what has been prescribed No. 26; the third sergeant will place himself on the left of the right group, to conduct it; the second group will halt at twenty paces from the one on its left, the third group at twenty paces from the second, and so on to the right. As the groups halt, they will face to the enemy, and deploy as has been explained for the left group.

41. The chiefs of sections will pay particular attention to the successive deployments of the groups, keeping near the group about to halt, so as to rectify any errors which may be commited. When the deployment is completed, they will place themselves thirty paces in rear of the centre of their sections, as has been heretofore prescribed. The non-commissioned officers will also place themselves as previously indicated.

42. As soon as the movement commences, the chief of the first platoon, causing it to face about, will move it as indicated No. 30.

43. The deployment may be made by the left flank according to the same principles, substituting *left flank* for *right flank*.

44. If the captain should wish to deploy the company upon the centre of one of the platoons, he will command:

1. *Second platoon—as skirmishers.* 2. *By the right and left flanks—take intervals.* 3. MARCH (or *double quick—*MARCH).

45. At the first command, the officers and non-commissioned officers will conform to what has been prescribed No. 38.

46. At the second command, the first lieutenant will place himself behind the left group of the right section of

the second platoon, the third lieutenant behind the right
group of the left section of the same platoon.

47. At the command *march*, the right section will
face to the right, the left section will face to the left,
the group on the right of this latter section will stand fast.
The two sections will move off in opposite directions:
the third sergeant will place himself on the left of the right
file to conduct it, the second sergeant on the right of
the left file. The two groups nearest that which stands
fast, will each halt at twenty paces from this group,
and each of the other groups will halt at twenty paces
from the group which is in rear of it. Each group will
deploy as heretofore prescribed No. 40.

48. The first and third lieutenants will direct the
movement, holding themselves always abreast of the
group which is about to halt.

49. The captain can cause the deployment to be made
on any named group whatsoever; in this case, the fifth sergeant will place himself before the group indicated, and
the deployment will be made according to the principles
heretofore prescribed.

50. The entire company may be also deployed
according to the same principles.

To extend intervals.

51. This movement, which is employed to extend a
line of skirmishers, will be executed according to the principles prescribed for deployments.

52. If it be supposed that the line of skirmishers is at
a halt, and that the captain wishes to extend it to the left,
he will command:

> 1. *By the left flank* (*so many paces*) *extend intervals.*
> 2. MARCH (or *double quick*—MARCH).

53. At the command *march*, the group on the right
will stand fast, all the other groups will face to the left,

To extend intervals (No. 51).

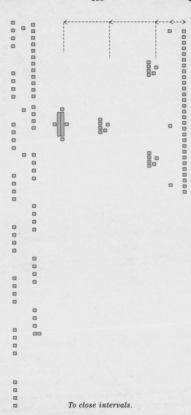

To close intervals.

and each group will extend its interval to the prescribed distance by the means indicated No. 40.

54. The men of the same group will continue to preserve between each other the distance of five paces, unless the nature of the ground should render it necessary that they should close nearer, in order to keep in sight of each other. The intervals refer to the spaces between the groups, and not to the distances between the men in each group. The intervals will be taken from the right or left man of the neighboring group.

55. If the line of skirmishers be marching to the front, and the captain should wish to extend it to the right, he will command:

1. *On the left group (so many paces) extend intervals.*
2. MARCH (or *double quick*—MARCH).

56. The left group, conducted by the guide, will continue to march on the point of direction; the other groups throwing forward the left shoulder, and taking the double quick step, will open their intervals to the prescribed distance, by the means indicated No. 25, conforming also to what is prescribed No. 54.

57. Intervals may be extended on the centre of the line, according to the same principles.

58. If, in extending intervals, it be intended that one company or platoon should occupy a line which had been previously occupied by two, the men of the company or platoon which is to retire, will fall successively to the rear as they are relieved by the extension of the intervals.

To close intervals.

59. This movement, like that of opening intervals, will be executed according to the principles prescribed for the deployments.

60. If the line of skirmishers be halted, and the

captain should wish to close intervals to the left, he will
command:

> 1. *By the left flank (so many paces) close intervals.*
>   2. MARCH (*or double quick*—MARCH).

61. At the command *march*, the left group will stand
fast, the other groups will face to the left and close to the
prescribed distance, each group facing to the enemy as it
attains its proper distance.

62. If the line be marching to the front, the captain
will command:

> 1. *On the left group (so many paces) close intervals.*
>   2. MARCH (*or double quick*—MARCH).

63. The left group, conducted by the guide, will continue to move on in the direction previously indicated; the
other groups, advancing the right shoulder, will close to
the left, until the intervals are reduced to the prescribed
distance.

64. Intervals may be closed on the right, or on the
centre, according to the same principles.

65. When intervals are to be closed up, in order to
reinforce a line of skirmishers, so as to cause two companies to cover the ground which had been previously occupied by one, the new company will deploy so as to finish
its movement at twenty paces in rear of the line it is to
occupy, and the men will successively move upon that
line, as they shall be unmasked by the men of the old
company. The reserves of the two companies will unite
behind the centre of the line.

To relieve a company deployed as skirmishers.

66. When a company of skirmishers is to be relieved,
the captain will be advised of the intention, which he will
immediately communicate to his first and second lieutenants.

67. The new company will execute its deployment

forward, so as to finish the movement at about twenty paces in rear of the line.

68. Arrived at this distance, the men of the new company, by command of their captain, will advance rapidly a few paces beyond the old line and halt; the new line being established, the old company will assemble on its reserve, taking care not to get into groups of fours until they are beyond the fire of the enemy.

69. If the skirmishers to be relieved are marching in retreat, the company thrown out to relieve them will deploy by the flank, as prescribed No. 38 and following. The old skirmishers will continue to retire with order, and having passed the new line, they will form upon the reserve.

ARTICLE SECOND.

To advance.

To advance in line, and to retreat in line.

70. When a platoon or a company deployed as skirmishers is marching by the front, the guide will be habitually in the centre. No particular indication to this effect need be given in the commands, but if on the contrary it be intended that the directing guide should be on the right, or left, the command *guide right*, or *guide left*, will be given immediately after that of forward.

71. The captain, wishing the line of skirmishers to advance, will command:

1. *Forward.* 2. MARCH (or *double quick*—MARCH).

72. This command will be repeated with the greatest rapidity by the chiefs of sections, and, in case of need, by the sergeants. This rule is general, whether the skirmishers march by the front or by the flank.

73. At the first command, three sergeants will move

briskly on the line, the first on the right, the second on the left, and the third in the centre.

74. At the command *march*, the line will move to the front, the guide charged with the direction will move on the point indicated to him, the skirmishers will hold themselves aligned on this guide, and preserve their intervals towards him.

75. The chiefs of sections will march immediately behind their sections, so as to direct their movements.

76. The captain will give a general superintendence to the movement.

77. When he shall wish to halt the skirmishers, he will command:

HALT.

78. At this command, briskly repeated, the line will halt. The chiefs of sections will promptly rectify any irregularity in the alignment and intervals, and after taking every possible advantage which the ground may offer for protecting the men, they, with the three sergeants in the line, will retire to their proper places in rear.

79. The captain, wishing to march the skirmishers in retreat, will command:

1. *In retreat.*   2. MARCH (or *double quick*—MARCH).

80. At the first command, the three sergeants will move on the line as prescribed No. 73.

81. At the command *march*, the skirmishers will face about individually, and march to the rear, conforming to the principles prescribed No. 74.

82. The officers and sergeants will use every exercise to preserve order.

83. To halt the skirmishers, marching in retreat, the captain will command:

HALT.

84. At this command, the skirmishers will halt, and immediately face to the front.

85. The chiefs of sections and the three guides will each conform himself to what is prescribed No. 78.

To change direction.

86. If the commander of a line of skirmishers shall wish to cause it to change direction to the right, he will command:

1. *Right wheel.* 2. MARCH (or *double quick*—MARCH).

87. At the command *march*, the right guide will mark time in his place; the left guide will move in a circle to the right, and, that he may properly regulate his movements, will occasionally cast his eyes to the right, so as to observe the direction of the line, and the nature of the ground to be passed over. The centre guide will also march in a circle to the right, and in order to conform his movements to the general direction, will take care that his steps are only half the length of the steps of the guide on the left.

88. The skirmishers will regulate the length of their steps by their distance from the marching flank, being less as they approach the pivot, and greater as they are removed from it; they will often look to the marching flank, so as to preserve the direction and their intervals.

89. When the commander of the line shall wish to resume the direct march, he will command:

1. *Forward.* 2. MARCH.

90. At the command *march*, the line will cease to wheel, and the skirmishers will move direct to the front; the centre guide will march on the point which will be indicated to him.

91. If the captain should wish to halt the line, in place of moving it to the front, he will command:

HALT.

92. At this command, the line will halt.

93. A change of direction to the left will be made according to the same principles, and by inverse means.

94. A line of skirmishers marching in retreat, will change direction by the same means, and by the same commands, as a line marching in advance; for example, if the captain should wish to refuse his left, now become the right, he will command: 1. *Left wheel*. 2. MARCH. At the command *halt*, the skirmishers will face to the enemy.

95. But if, instead of halting the line, the captain should wish to continue to march it in retreat, he will, when he judges the line has wheeled sufficiently, command:

1. *In retreat.*
2. MARCH.

To march by the flank.

96. The captain, wishing the skirmishers to march by the right flank, will command:

1. *By the right flank.*
2. MARCH (or *double quick*—MARCH).

97. At the first command, the three sergeants will place themselves on the line.

98. At the command *march*, the skirmishers will face to the right and move off; the right guide will place himself by the side of the leading man on the right to conduct him, and will march on the point indicated; each skirmisher will take care to follow exactly in the direction of the one immediately preceding him, and to preserve his distance.

99. The skirmishers may be marched by the left flank, according to the same principles, and by the same commands, substituting *left* for *right*; the left guide will place himself by the side of the leading man to conduct him.

100. If the skirmishers be marching by the flank, and the captain should wish to halt them, he will command:

HALT.

101. At this command, the skirmishers will halt and face to the enemy. The officers and sergeants will conform to what has been prescribed No. 78.

102. The reserve should execute all the movements of the line, and be held always about one hundred and fifty paces from it, so as to be in position to second its operations.

103. When the chief of the reserve shall wish to march it in advance, he will command: 1. *Platoon forward.* 2. *Guide left.* 3. MARCH. If he should wish to march it in retreat, he will command: 1. *In retreat.* 2. MARCH. 3. *Guide right.* At the command *halt*, it will re-face to the enemy.

104. The men should be made to understand that the signals or commands, such as *forward*, mean that the skirmishers shall march on the enemy; *in retreat*, that they shall retire, and to *the right or left flank*, that the men must face to the right or left, whatever may be their position.

105. If the skirmishers be marching by the flank, and the captain should wish to change direction to the right (or left), he will command: 1. *By file right* (or *left*). 2. MARCH. These movements will also be executed by the signals Nos. 14 and 15.

ARTICLE THIRD.

The firings.

106. Skirmishers will fire either at a halt or marching.

To fire at a halt.

107. To cause this fire to be executed, the captain will command:

Commence—FIRING.

108. At this command, briskly repeated, the men of the front rank will commence firing; they will re-load rapidly, and hold themselves in readiness to fire again. During this time the men of the rear rank will come to a ready, and as soon as their respective file leaders have loaded, they will also fire and re-load. The men of each file will thus continue the firing, conforming to this principle, that the one or the other shall always have his piece loaded.

109. Light troops should be always calm, so as to aim with accuracy; they should, moreover, endeavor to estimate correctly the distances between themselves and the enemy to be hit, and thus be enabled to deliver their fire with the greater certainty of success.

110. Skirmishers will not remain in the same place whilst re-loading, unless protected by accidents in the ground.

To fire marching.

111. This fire will be executed by the same commands as the fire at a halt.

112. At the command *commence firing*, if the line be advancing, the front rank man of every file will halt, fire, and re-load before throwing himself forward. The rear rank man of the same file will continue to march, and after passing ten or twelve paces beyond his front rank man, will halt, come to a ready, select his object, and fire when his front rank man has loaded; the fire will thus continue to be executed by each file; the skirmishers will keep united, and endeavor, as much as possible, to preserve the general direction of the alignment.

113. If the line be marching in retreat, at the command *commence firing*, the front rank man of every file will halt, face to the enemy, fire, and then re-load whilst moving to the rear; the rear rank man of the same file will

continue to march, and halt ten or twelve paces beyond his front rank man, face about, come to a ready, and fire, when his front rank man has passed him in retreat and loaded; after which, he will move to the rear and re-load; the front rank man in his turn, after marching briskly to the rear, will halt at ten or twelve paces from the rear rank, face to the enemy, load his piece and fire, conforming to what has just been prescribed; the firing will thus be continued.

114. If the company be marching by the right flank, at the command, *commence firing*, the front rank man of every file will face to the enemy, step one pace forward, halt, and fire; the rear rank man will continue to move forward. As soon as the front rank man has fired, he will place himself briskly behind his rear rank man and re-load whilst marching. When he has loaded, the rear rank man will, in his turn, step one pace forward, halt, and fire, and, returning to the ranks, will place himself behind his front rank man; the latter, in his turn, will act in the same manner, observing the same principles. At the command, *cease firing*, the men of the rear rank will retake their original positions, if not already there.

115. If the company be marching by the left flank, the fire will be executed according to the same principles, but in this case it will be the rear rank men who will fire first.

116. The following rules will be observed in the cases to which they apply.

117. If the line be firing at a halt, or whilst marching by the flank, at the command, *Forward*—MARCH, it will be the men whose pieces are loaded, without regard to the particular rank to which they belong, who will move to the front. Those men whose pieces have been discharged, will remain in their places to load them before moving forward, and the firing will be continued agreeably to the principles prescribed No. 112.

118. If the line be firing either at a halt, advancing, or whilst marching by the flank, at the command, *In retreat*—MARCH, the men whose pieces are loaded will remain faced to the enemy, and will fire in this position; the men whose pieces are discharged will retreat loading them, and the fire will be continued agreeably to the principles prescribed No. 113.

119. If the line of skirmishers be firing either at a halt, advancing, or in retreat, at the command, *By the right* (or *left*) *flank*—MARCH, the men whose pieces are loaded will step one pace out of the general alignment, face to the enemy, and fire in this position; the men whose pieces are unloaded will face to the right (or left) and march in the direction indicated. The men who stepped out of the ranks will place themselves, immediately after firing, upon the general direction, and in rear of their front or rear rank men, as the case may be. The fire will be continued according to the principles prescribed No. 114.

120. Skirmishers will be habituated to load their pieces whilst marching; but they will be enjoined to halt always an instant, when in the act of charging cartridge, and priming.

121. They should be practised to fire and load kneeling, lying down, and sitting, and much liberty should be allowed in these exercises, in order that they may be executed in the manner found to be most convenient. Skirmishers should be cautioned not to forget that, in whatever position they may load, it is important that the piece should be placed upright before ramming, in order that the entire charge of powder may reach the bottom of the bore.

122. In commencing the fire, the men of the same rank should not all fire at once, and the men of the same file should be particular that one or the other of them is always loaded.

123. In retreating, the officer commanding the skirmishers should seize on every advantage which the

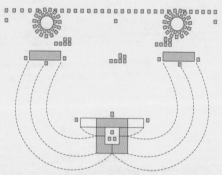

The rally (No. 127): *by sections* (No. 132), *by platoons* (No. 137), *on the reserve* (No. 139).

too weak, but should wish to hold his position by strengthening his line, he will command:

Rally by sections.

132. At this command, the chiefs of sections will move rapidly on the centre group of their respective sections, or on any other interior group whose position might offer a shelter, or other particular advantage; the skirmishers will collect rapidly at a run on this group, and without distinction of numbers. The men composing the group on which the formation is made, will immediately form square, as heretofore explained, and elevate their pieces, the bayonets uppermost, in order to indicate the point on which the rally is to be made. The other skirmishers, as they arrive, will occupy and fill the open angular spaces between these four men, and successively rally around this first nucleus, and in such manner as to form rapidly a compact circle. The skirmishers will take, as they arrive, the position of charge bayonet, the point of the bayonet more elevated, and will cock their pieces in this position. The movement concluded, the two exterior ranks will fire as occasion may offer, and load without moving their feet.

133. The captain will move rapidly with his guard, wherever he may judge his presence most necessary.

134. The officers and sergeants will be particular to observe that the rally is made in silence, and with promptitude and order; that some pieces in each of their subdivisions be at all times loaded, and that the fire is directed on those points only where it will be most effective.

135. If the reserve should be threatened, it will form into a circle around its chief.

136. If the captain, or commander of a line of skirmishers formed of many platoons, should judge that the rally by section does not offer sufficient resistance, he

will cause the rally by platoons to be executed, and for this purpose will command:

Rally by platoons.

137. This movement will be executed according to the same principles, and by the same means, as the rally by sections. The chiefs of platoon will conform to what has been prescribed for the chiefs of section.

138. The captain wishing to rally the skirmishers on the reserve, will command:

Rally on the reserve.

139. At this command, the captain will move briskly on the reserve; the officer who commands it will take immediate steps to form square; for this purpose, he will cause the half sections on the flanks to be thrown perpendicularly to the rear; he will order the men to come to a ready.

140. The skirmishers of each section, taking the run, will form rapidly into groups, and upon that man of each group who is nearest the centre of the section. These groups will direct themselves diagonally towards each other, and in such manner as to form into sections with the greatest possible rapidity while moving to the rear; the officers and sergeants will see that this formation is made in proper order, and the chiefs will direct their sections upon the reserve, taking care to unmask it to the right and left. As the skirmishers arrive, they will continue and complete the formation of the square begun by the reserve, closing in rapidly upon the latter, without regard to their places in line; they will come to a ready without command, and fire upon the enemy; which will also be done by the reserve as soon as it is unmasked by the skirmishers.

141. If a section should be closely pressed by cavalry while retreating, its chief will command *halt*; at this command, the men will form rapidly into a compact circle

around the officer, who will re-form his section and resume the march, the moment he can do so with safety.

142. The formation of the square in a prompt and efficient manner, requires coolness and activity on the part of both officers and sergeants.

143. The captain will also profit by every moment of respite which the enemy's cavalry may leave him; as soon as he can, he will endeavor to place himself beyond the reach of their charges, either by gaining a position where he may defend himself with advantage, or by returning to the corps to which he belongs. For this purpose, being in square, he will cause the company to break into column by platoons at half distance; to this effect, he will command:

1. *Form column.* 2. MARCH.

144. At the command *march*, each platoon will dress on its centre, and the platoon which was facing to the rear will face about without command. The guides will place themselves on the right and left of their respective platoons, those of the second platoon will place themselves at half distance from those of the first, counting from the rear rank. These dispositions being made, the captain can move the column in whatever direction he may judge proper.

145. If he wishes to march it in retreat, he will command:

1. *In retreat.* 2. MARCH (or *double quick*—MARCH).

146. At the command *march*, the column will immediately face by the rear rank, and move off in the opposite direction. As soon as the column is in motion, the captain will command:

3. *Guide right* (or *left*).

147. He will indicate the direction to the leading guide;

the guides will march at their proper distances, and the men will keep aligned.

148. If again threatened by cavalry, the captain will command:

1. *Form column.*   2. MARCH.

149. At the command *march*, the column will halt; the first platoon will face about briskly, and the outer half sections of each platoon will be thrown perpendicularly to the rear, so as to form the second and third fronts of the square. The officers and sergeants will promptly rectify any irregularities which may be committed.

150. If he should wish to march the column in advance, the captain will command:

1. *Form column.*   2. MARCH.

151. Which will be executed as prescribed No. 144:

152. The column being formed, the captain will command:

1. *Forward.*   2. MARCH (or *double quick*—MARCH).
3. *Guide left* (or *right*).

153. At the second command, the column will move forward, and at the third command, the men will take the touch of elbows to the side of the guide.

154. If the captain should wish the column to gain ground to the right or left, he will do so by rapid wheels to the side opposite the guide, and, for this purpose, will change the guide whenever it may be necessary.

155. If a company be in column by platoon, at half distance, right in front, the captain can deploy the first platoon as skirmishers by the means already explained; but if it should be his wish to deploy the second platoon forward on the centre file, leaving the first platoon in reserve, he will command:

1. *Second platoon—as skirmishers.* 2. *On the centre file—take intervals.* 3. MARCH (or *double quick—* MARCH).

156. At the first command, the chief of the first platoon will caution his platoon to stand fast; the chiefs of sections of the second platoon will place themselves before the centre of their sections; the fifth sergeant will place himself one pace in front of the centre of the second platoon.

157. At the second command, the chief of the right section, second platoon, will command: *Section right face*; the chief of the left section: *Section left face.*

158. At the command *march*, these sections will move off briskly in opposite directions, and having unmasked the first platoon, the chiefs of sections will respectively command: *By the left flank*—MARCH, and *By the right flank*—MARCH; and as soon as these sections arrive on the alignment of the first platoon, they will command, *As skirmishers*—MARCH. The groups will then deploy according to prescribed principles, on the right group of the left section, which will be directed by the fifth sergeant on the point indicated.

159. If the captain should wish the deployment made by the flank, the second platoon will be moved to the front by the means above stated, and halted after passing some steps beyond the alignment of the first platoon; the deployment will then be made by the flank according to the principles prescribed.

160. When one or more platoons are deployed as skirmishers, and the captain should wish to rally them on the battalion, he will command:

Rally on the battalion.

161. At this command, the skirmishers and the reserve, no matter what position the company to which they belong may occupy in order of battle, will rapidly

unmask the front of the battalion, directing themselves in a run towards its nearest flank, and then form in its rear.

162. As soon as the skirmishers have passed beyond the line of file closers, the men will take the quick step, and the chief of each platoon or section will re-form his subdivision, and place it in column behind the wing on which it is rallied, and at ten paces from the rank of file closers. These subdivisions will not be moved except by order of the commander of the battalion, who may, if he thinks proper, throw them into line of battle at the extremities of the line, or in the intervals between the battalions.

163. If many platoons should be united behind the same wing of a battalion, or behind any shelter whatsoever, they should be formed always into close column, or into column at half distance.

164. When the battalion, covered by a company of skirmishers, shall be formed into square, the platoons and sections of the covering company will be directed by their chiefs to the rear of the square, which will be opened at the angles to receive the skirmishers, who will be then formed into close column by platoons in rear of the first front of the square.

165. If circumstances should prevent the angles of the square from being opened, the skirmishers will throw themselves at the feet of the front rank men, the right knee on the ground, the butt of the piece resting on the thigh, the bayonet in a threatening position. A part may also place themselves about the angles, where they can render good service by defending the sectors without fire.

166. If the battalion on which the skirmishers are rallied be in column ready to form square, the skirmishers will be formed into close column by platoon, in rear of the centre of the third division, and at the command, *Form*

square—MARCH, they will move forward and close on the buglers.

167. When skirmishers have been rallied by platoon or section behind the wings of a battalion, and it be wished to deploy them again to the front, they will be marched by the flank towards the intervals on the wings, and be then deployed so as to cover the front of the battalion.

168. When platoons or sections, placed in the interior of squares or columns, are to be deployed, they will be marched out by the flanks, and then thrown forward, as is prescribed No. 157; as soon as they shall have unmasked the column or square, they will be deployed, the one on the right, the other on the left file.

The assembly.

169. A company deployed as skirmishers will be assembled when there is no longer danger of its being disturbed; the assembly will be made habitually in quick time.

170. The captain wishing to assemble the skirmishers on the reserve, will command:

Assemble on the reserve.

171. At this command, the skirmishers will assemble by groups of fours; the front rank men will place themselves behind their rear rank men; and each group of fours will direct itself on the reserve, where each will take its proper place in the ranks. When the company is re-formed, it will rejoin the battalion to which it belongs.

172. It may be also proper to assemble the skirmishers on the centre, or on the right or left of the line, either marching or at a halt.

173. If the captain should wish to assemble them on the centre while marching, he will command:

Assemble on the centre.

174. At this command, the centre guide will continue to march directly to the front on the point indicated; the front rank man of the directing file will follow the guide, and be covered by his rear rank man; the other two comrades of this group, and likewise those on their left, will march diagonally, advancing the left shoulder and accelerating the gait, so as to re-form the groups while drawing nearer and nearer the directing file; the men of the right section will unite in the same manner into groups, and then upon the directing file, throwing forward the right shoulder. As they successively unite on the centre, the men will bring their pieces to the right shoulder.

175. To assemble on the right or left file will be executed according to the same principles.

176. The assembly of a line marching in retreat will also be executed according to the same principles, the front rank men marching behind their rear rank men.

177. To assemble the line of skirmishers at a halt, and on the line they occupy, the captain will give the same commands; the skirmishers will face to the right or left, according as they should march by the right or left flank, re-form the groups while marching, and thus arrive on the file which served as the point of formation. As they successively arrive, the skirmishers will support arms.

Article Fifth.

To deploy a battalion as skirmishers, and to rally this battalion.

To deploy the battalion as skirmishers.

178. A battalion being in line of battle, if the commander should wish to deploy it on the right of the sixth company, holding the three right companies in reserve, he

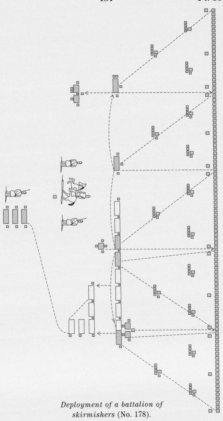

*Deployment of a battalion of
skirmishers* (No. 178).

will signify his intention to the lieutenant colonel and
adjutant, and also to the major, who will be directed to
take charge of the reserve. He will point out to the lieutenant colonel the direction he wishes to give the line, as
well as the point where he wishes the right of the sixth
company to rest, and to the commander of the reserve the
place he may wish it established.

179. The lieutenant colonel will move rapidly in front
of the right of the sixth company, and the adjutant in front
of the left of the same company. The commander of the
reserve will dispose of it in the manner to be hereinafter
indicated.

180. The colonel will command:

1. *First* (or *second*) *platoons—as skirmishers.*
2. *On the right of the sixth company—take intervals.*
3. MARCH (or *double quick*—MARCH).

181. At the second command, the captains of the fifth
and sixth companies will prepare to deploy the first platoons of their respective companies, the sixth on its right,
the fifth on its left file.

182. The captain of the fourth company will face it to
the right, and the captains of the seventh and eighth companies will face their respective companies to the left.

183. At the command *march*, the movement will commence. The platoons of the fifth and sixth companies will
deploy forward; the right guide of the sixth will march on
the point which will be indicated to him by the lieutenant
colonel.

184. The company which has faced to the right, and
also the companies which have faced to the left, will
march straight forward. The fourth company will take an
interval of one hundred paces counting from the left of
the fifth, and its chief will deploy its first platoon on its
left file. The seventh and eighth companies will each take
an interval of one hundred paces, counting from the first

file of the company which is immediately on its right; and the chiefs of these companies will afterwards deploy their first platoons on the right file.

185. The guides who conduct the files on which the deployment is made, should be careful to direct themselves towards the outer man of the neighboring company, already deployed as skirmishers; or, if the company has not finished its deployment, they will judge carefully the distance which may still be required to place all these files in line, and will then march on the point thus marked out. The companies, as they arrive on the line, will align themselves on those already deployed.

186. The lieutenant colonel and adjutant will follow the deployment, the one on the right, the other on the left; the movement concluded, they will place themselves near the colonel.

187. The reserves of the companies will be established in echellon in the following manner: the reserve of the sixth company will be placed one hundred and fifty paces in rear of the right of this company; the reserves of the fourth and fifth companies, united, opposite the centre of their line of skirmishers, and thirty paces in advance of the reserve of the sixth company; the reserves of the seventh and eighth companies, also united, opposite the centre of their line of skirmishers, and thirty paces farther to the rear than the reserve of the sixth company.

188. The major commanding the companies composing the reserve, on receiving an order from the colonel to that effect, will march these companies thirty paces to the rear, and will then ploy them into column by company, at half distance; after which, he will conduct the column to the point which shall have been indicated to him.

189. The colonel will have a general superintendence of the movement; and, when it is finished, will move to a point in rear of the line, whence his view may best embrace all the parts, in order to direct their movements.

190. If, instead of deploying forward, it be desired to deploy by the flank, the sixth and fifth companies will be moved to the front ten or twelve paces, halted, and deployed by the flank, the one on the right, the other on the left file, by the means already indicated. Each of the other companies will be marched by the flank; and as soon as the last file of the company, next towards the direction, shall have taken its interval, it will be moved upon the line established by the fifth and sixth companies, halted, and deployed.

191. In the preceding example, it has been supposed that the battalion was in order of battle; but if in column, it would be deployed as skirmishers by the same commands and according to the same principles.

192. If the deployment is to be made *forward*, the directing company, as soon as it is unmasked, will be moved ten or twelve paces in front of the head of the column, and will be then deployed on the file indicated. Each of the other companies will take its interval to the right or left, and deploy as soon as it is taken.

193. If the deployment is to be made by the flank, the directing company will be moved in the same manner to the front, as soon as it is unmasked, and will then be halted and deployed by the flank on the file indicated. Each of the other companies will be marched by the flank, and, when its interval is taken, will be moved on the line, halted, and deployed as soon as the company next towards the direction shall have finished its deployment.

194. It has been prescribed to place the reserves in echellon, in order that they may, in the event of a rally, be

able to protect themselves without injuring each other; and the reserves of two contiguous companies have been united, in order to diminish the number of the echellons, and to increase their capacity for resisting cavalry.

195. The echellons, in the example given, descend from right to left; but they may, on an indication from the colonel to that effect, be posted on the same principle, so as to descend from left to right.

196. When the color-company is to be deployed as skirmishers, the color, without its guard, will be detached, and remain with the battalion reserve.

The Rally.

197. The colonel may cause all the various movements prescribed for a company, to be executed by the battalion, and by the same commands and the same signals. When he wishes to rally the battalion, he will cause the *rally on the battalion* to be sounded, and will so dispose his reserve as to protect this movement.

198. The companies deployed as skirmishers will be rallied in squares on their respective reserves; each reserve of two contiguous companies will form the first front of the square, throwing to the rear the sections on the flanks; the skirmishers who arrive first will complete the lateral fronts, and the last the fourth front. The officers and sergeants will superintend the rally, and as fast as the men arrive, they will form them into two ranks, without regard to height, and cause them to face outwards.

199. The rally being effected, the commanders of squares will profit by any interval of time the cavalry may allow for putting them in safety, either by marching upon the battalion reserve, or by seizing an advantageous position; to this end, each of the squares will be formed into column, and march in this order; and

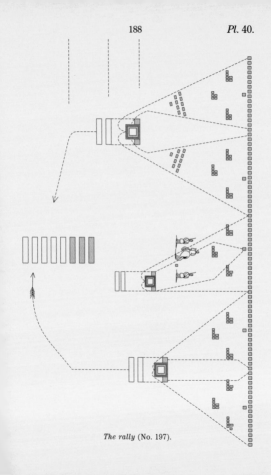

The rally (No. 197).

if threatened anew, it will halt, and again form itself into square.

200. As the companies successively arrive near the battalion reserve, each will re-form as promptly as possible, and, without regard to designation or number, take place in the column next in rear of the companies already in it.

201. The battalion reserve will also form square, if itself threatened by cavalry. In this case, the companies in marching towards it will place themselves promptly in the sectors without fire, and thus march on the squares.

END OF INSTRUCTION FOR SKIRMISHERS.

MANUAL OF THE SWORD OR SABRE, FOR OFFICERS.

POSITION OF THE SWORD OR SABRE, UNDER ARMS

The carry. The gripe is in the right hand, which will be supported against the right hip, the back of the blade against the shoulder.

TO SALUTE WITH THE SWORD OR SABRE.

Three times (or pauses).

One. At the distance of six paces from the person to be saluted, raise the sword or saber perpendicularly, the point up, the flat of the blade opposite to the right eye, the guard at the height of the shoulder, the elbow supported on the body.

Two. Drop the point of the sword or sabre by extending the arm, so that the right hand may be brought to the side of the right thigh, and remain in that position until the person to whom the salute is rendered shall be passed, or shall have passed, six paces.

Three. Raise the sword or sabre smartly, and place the back of the blade against the right shoulder.

COLOR-SALUTE.

In the ranks, the color-bearer, whether at a halt or in march, will always carry the heel of the color-lance supported at the right hip, the right hand generally placed on the lance at the height of the shoulder, to hold it steady. When the color has to render honors, the color-bearer will salute as follows:

At the distance of six paces slip the right hand along the lance to the height of the eye; lower the lance by straightening the arm to its full extent, the heel of the lance remaining at the hip, and bring back the lance to the habitual position when the person saluted shall be passed, or shall have passed, six paces.

MANUAL FOR RELIEVING SENTINELS.

Arms—PORT.

One time and one motion.

Throw the piece diagonally across the body, the lock to the front, seize it smartly at the same instant with both hands, the right at the handle, the left at the lower band, the two thumbs pointing towards the muzzle, the barrel sloping upwards and crossing opposite the point of the left shoulder, the butt proportionally lowered. The palm of the right hand will be above, and that of the left under, the piece, the nails of both hands next to the body, to which the elbows will be closed.

Shoulder—ARMS.

One time and two motions.

(*First motion.*) Bring the piece smartly to the right shoulder, placing the right hand as in the position of shoulder arms, slip the left hand to the height of the shoulder, the fingers extended.

(*Second motion.*) Drop the left hand smartly by the side.

Being on parade and at order arms, if it be wished to give the men rest, the command will be:

Parade—Rest.

At the command *rest*, turn the piece on the heel of the butt, the barrel to the left, the muzzle in front of the centre of the body; seize it at the same time with the left hand just above, and with the right at the upper band; carry the right foot six inches to the rear, the left knee slightly bent.

INSTRUCTION FOR THE CHIEF BUGLER
AND DRUM MAJOR.

The posts of the field music and band have been given Title I., for the order in battle.

In column in manœuvre, the field music and band will march abreast with the left centre company, and on the side opposite the guide.

In column in route, as well as in the passage of defiles to the front or in retreat, they will march at the head of their respective battalions.

GENERAL CALLS.

1. *Attention.*
2. *The general.*
3. *The assembly.*
4. *To the color.*
5. *The recall.*
6. *Quick time.*
7. *Double quick time.*
8. *The charge.*
9. *The reveille.*
10. *Retreat.*
11. *Tattoo.*
12. *To extinguish lights.*
13. *Assembly of the buglers.*

14. *Assembly of the guard.*
15. *Orders for orderly sergeants.*
16. *For officers to take their places in line after firing.*
17. *The disperse.*
18. *Officers' call.*
19. *Breakfast call.*
20. *Dinner call.*
21. *Sick call.*
22. *Fatigue call.*
23. *Church call.*
24. *Drill call.*
25. *School call.*

CALLS FOR SKIRMISHERS.

1. *Fix bayonet.*
2. *Unfix bayonet.*
3. *Quick time.*
4. *Double quick time.*
5. *The run.*
6. *Deploy as skirmishers.*
7. *Forward.*
8. *In retreat.*
9. *Halt.*
10. *By the right flank.*
11. *By the left flank.*
12. *Commence firing.*
13. *Cease firing.*
14. *Change direction to the right.*
15. *Change direction to the left.*
16. *Lie down.*
17. *Rise up.*
18. *Rally by fours.*
19. *Rally by sections.*
20. *Rally by platoons.*

21. *Rally on the reserve.*
22. *Rally on the battalion.*
23. *Assemble on the battalion.*

NOTE.—When the whole of the troops, in the same camp or garrison, are to depart, *the general, the assembly,* and *to the color,* will be beaten or sounded, at the proper intervals, in the order here mentioned. At the first, the troops will prepare for the movement; at the second, they will form by company, and at the third, unite by battalion.

EXPLANATION OF THE SIGNS.

MOVEMENT OF THE MÉTRONOME.

76 = ♩ — 𝄞 4 — or 76 steps to the minute.

80 = ♩. — 𝄞 3 — or 80 steps to the minute.

100 = ♩. — 𝄞 6/8 — or 100 steps to the minute.

120 = ♩ — 𝄞 2 — or 120 steps to the minute.

Silence . . 𝄽 — Demi-silence . . 𝄾

GENERAL CALLS.

1.—ATTENTION.

120 = ♩ *Allegro.*

2.—THE GENERAL.

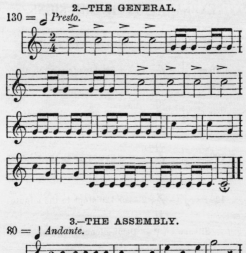

3.—THE ASSEMBLY.

4.—TO THE COLOR.

$80 = $ ♩ *Andante.*

5.—THE RECALL.

$80 = $ ♩ *Andante.*

6.—QUICK TIME.

$110 = $ ♩ *Allegro.*

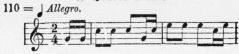

7.—DOUBLE QUICK TIME.

165 = ♩ *Allegro.*

8.—THE CHARGE.

115 = ♩ *Allegro.*

9.—THE REVEILLE.

10.—RETREAT.

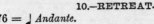

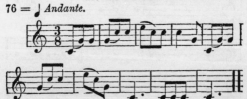

11.—TATTOO.

12.—TO EXTINGUISH LIGHTS.

76 = ♩ *Allegro.*

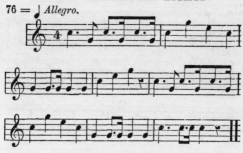

13.—ASSEMBLY OF THE BUGLERS.

160 = ♩ *Presto.*

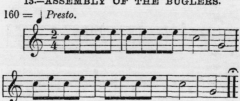

14.—ASSEMBLY OF THE GUARD.

112 = ♩ *Allegro.*

15.—ORDERS FOR ORDERLY SERGEANTS.

72 = ♩ *Allegro.*

16.—FOR OFFICERS TO TAKE THEIR PLACES IN LINE AFTER FIRING.

108 = ♩. *Allegro.*

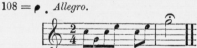

17.—THE DISPERSE.

120 = ♩ *Allegro.*

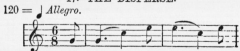

18.—OFFICERS' CALL.

152 = ♩ *Allegro.*

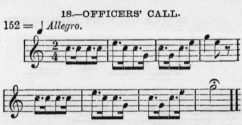

19.—BREAKFAST CALL.

138 = ♩ *Allegro.*

20.—DINNER CALL.

110 := ♩ *Allegro.*

21.—SICK CALL.

110 = ♩ *Allegro.*

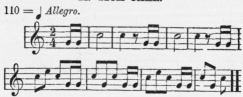

22.—FATIGUE CALL.

92 = ♩ *Allegro.*

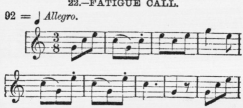

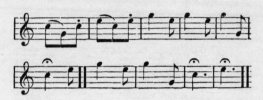

23.—CHURCH CALL.

80 = 𝅗𝅥 *Andante.*

24.—DRILL CALL.

76 = 𝅗𝅥 *Maestoso.*

25.—SCHOOL CALL.

110 = ♩ *Allegro.*

CALLS FOR SKIRMISHERS.

1.—FIX BAYONET.

2.—UNFIX BAYONET.

80 = ♩ *Andante.*

3.—QUICK TIME.

(*Music the same as in "General Calls."*)

4.—DOUBLE QUICK TIME.

5.—THE RUN.

6.—DEPLOY AS SKIRMISHERS.

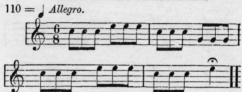

7.—FORWARD.

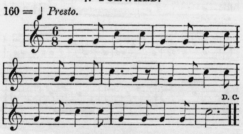

8.—IN RETREAT.

9.—HALT.

10.—BY THE RIGHT FLANK.

11.—BY THE LEFT FLANK.

12.—COMMENCE FIRING,

18

13.—CEASE FIRING.

14.—CHANGE DIRECTION TO THE RIGHT.

15.—CHANGE DIRECTION TO THE LEFT.

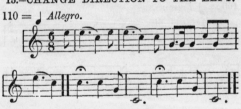

16.—LIE DOWN.

17.—RISE UP.

18.—RALLY BY FOURS.

19.—RALLY BY SECTIONS.

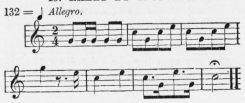

20.—RALLY BY PLATOONS.

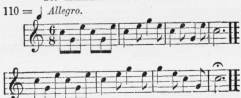

21.—RALLY ON THE RESERVE.

76 = ♩ *Andante.*

22.—RALLY ON THE BATTALION.

76 = ♩ *Andante.*

23.—ASSEMBLE ON THE BATTALION.

80 = ♩ *Andante.*

TITLE FOURTH.

SCHOOL OF THE BATTALION.

Formation of the Battalion.

1. Every colonel will labor to habituate his battalion to form line of battle, by night as well as by day, with the greatest possible promptitude.

2. The color-company will generally be designated as the directing company. That, as soon as formed, will be placed on the direction the colonel may have determined for the line of battle. The other companies will form on it, to the right and left, on the principles of successive formations which will be herein prescribed.

3. The color-bearer may have received the color from the hands of the colonel; but if there be daylight, and time, the color will be produced with due solemnity.

Composition and march of the color-escort.

4. When the battalion turns out under arms and the color is wanted, a company, other than that of the color, will be put in march to receive and escort it.

5. The march will be in the following order, in quick time, and without music: the field music, followed by the band; the escort in column by platoon, right in front, with arms on the right shoulder, and the color-bearer between the platoons.

6. Arrived in front of the tent or quarters of the colonel, the escort will form line, the field music and band on the right, and arms will be brought to a shoulder.

7. The moment the escort is in line, the color-bearer, preceded by the first lieutenant, and followed by a sergeant of the escort, will go to receive the color.

8. When the color-bearer shall come out, followed by the lieutenant and sergeant, he will halt before the entrance; the escort will present arms, and the field music will sound *to the color*.

9. After some twenty seconds, the captain will cause the sound to cease, arms to be shouldered, and then break by platoon into column; the color-bearer will place himself between the platoons, and the lieutenant and sergeant will resume their posts.

10. The escort will march back to the battalion to the sound of music in quick time, and in the same order as above, the guide on the right. The march will be so conducted that when the escort arrives at one hundred and fifty paces in front of the right of the battalion, the direction of the march will be parallel to its front, and when the color arrives nearly opposite its place in line, the column will change direction to the left, and the right guide will direct himself on the centre of the battalion.

Honors paid to the color.

11. Arrived at the distance of twenty paces from the battalion, the escort will halt, and the music cease; the colonel will place himself six paces before the centre of the battalion, the color-bearer will approach the colonel, by the front, in quick time; when at the distance of ten paces, he will halt: the colonel will cause arms to be presented, and *to the color* to be sounded, which being executed, the color-bearer will take his place in the front rank of the color-guard, and the battalion, by command, shoulder arms.

12. The escort, field music, and band, will return in quick time to their several places in line of battle, marching by the rear of the battalion.

13. The color will be escorted back to the colonel's tent or quarters in the above order.

General Rules and Division of the School of the Battalion.

14. This school has for its object the instruction of battalions singly, and thus to prepare them for manœuvres in line. The harmony so indispensable in the movements of many battalions can only be attained by the use of the same commands, the same principles, and the same means of execution. Hence, all colonels and actual commanders of battalions will conform themselves, without addition or curtailment, to what will herein be prescribed.

15. When a battalion instructed in this drill shall manœuvre in line, the colonel will regulate its movements, as prescribed in the third volume of the Tactics for heavy infantry.

16. The school of the battalion will be divided into five parts.

17. The first will comprehend opening and closing ranks, and the execution of the different fires.

18. The second, the different modes of passing from the order in battle, to the order in column.

19. The third, the march in column, and the other movements incident thereto.

20. The fourth, the different modes of passing from the order in column to the order in battle.

21. The fifth will comprehend the march in line of battle, in advance and in retreat; the passage of defiles in retreat; the march by the flank; the formation by file into line of battle; the change of front; the column doubled on the centre; dispositions against cavalry, the rally, and rules for manœuvring by the rear rank.

PART FIRST.

Opening and closing ranks, and the execution of the different fires.

ARTICLE FIRST.

To open and to close ranks.

22. The colonel, wishing the ranks to be opened, will command:

1. *Prepare to open ranks.*

23. At this command, the lieutenant colonel and major will place themselves on the right of the battalion, the first on the flank of the file closers, and the second four paces from the front rank of the battalion.

24. These dispositions being made, the colonel will command:

2. *To the rear, open order.*   3. MARCH.

25. At the second command, the covering sergeants, and the sergeant on the left of the battalion, will place themselves four paces in rear of the front rank, and opposite their places in line of battle, in order to mark the new alignment of the rear rank; they will be aligned by the major on the left sergeant of the battalion, who will be careful to place himself exactly four paces in rear of the front rank, and to hold his piece between the eyes, erect and inverted, the better to indicate to the major the direction to be given to the covering sergeants.

26. At the command *march*, the rear rank and the file closers will step to the rear without counting steps; the men will pass a little in rear of the line traced for this rank, halt, and dress forward on the covering sergeants, who will align correctly the men of their respective companies.

27. The file closers will fall back and preserve the

distance of two paces from the rear rank, glancing eyes to the right; the lieutenant colonel will, from the right, align them on the file closer of the left, who, having placed himself accurately two paces from the rear rank, will invert his piece, and hold it up erect between his eyes, the better to be seen by the lieutenant colonel.

28. The colonel, seeing the ranks aligned, will command:

4. FRONT.

At this command, the lieutenant colonel, major, and the left sergeant, will retake their places in line of battle.

29. The colonel will cause the ranks to be closed by the commands prescribed for the instructor in the school of the company, No. 28.

ARTICLE SECOND.

Manual of arms.

30. The ranks being closed, the colonel will cause the following times and pauses to be executed:

Present arms.	*Shoulder arms.*
Order arms.	*Shoulder arms.*
Support arms.	*Shoulder arms.*
Fix bayonet.	*Shoulder arms.*
Charge bayonet.	*Shoulder arms.*
Unfix bayonet.	*Shoulder arms.*

ARTICLE THIRD.

Loading at will, and the Firings.

31. The colonel will next cause to be executed loading at will, by the commands prescribed in the school of the company, No. 45; the officers and sergeants in the ranks will half face to the right with the men at the eighth

time of loading, and will face to the front when the men next to them come to a shoulder.

32. The colonel will cause to be executed the fire by company, the fire by wing, the fire by battalion, the fire by file, and the fire by rank, by the commands to be herein indicated.

33. The fire by company and the fire by file will always be direct; the fire by battalion, the fire by wing, and the fire by rank, may be either direct or oblique.

34. When the fire ought to be oblique, the colonel will give, at every round, the caution *right* (or *left*) *oblique*, between the commands *ready* and *aim*.

35. The fire by company will be executed alternately by the right and left companies of each division, as if the division were alone. The right company will fire first; the captain of the left will not give his first command till he shall see one or two pieces at a ready in the right company; the captain of the latter, after the first discharge, will observe the same rule in respect to the left company; and the fire will thus be continued alternately.

36. The colonel will observe the same rule in the firing by wing.

37. The fire by file will commence in all the companies at once, and will be executed as has been prescribed in the school of the company, No. 55 and following. The fire by rank will be executed by each rank alternately, as has been prescribed in the school of the company, No. 58 and following.

38. The color-guard will not fire, but reserve itself for the defence of the color.

The fire by company.

39. The colonel, wishing the fire by company to be executed, will command:

1. *Fire by company.*   2. *Commence firing.*

40. At the first command, the captains and covering sergeants will take the positions indicated in the school of the company No. 49.

41. The color and its guard will step back at the same time, so as to bring the front rank of the guard in a line with the rear rank of the battalion. *This rule is general for all the different firings.*

42. At the second command, the odd numbered companies will commence to fire; their captains will each give the commands prescribed in the school of the company No. 50, observing to precede the command *company* by that of *first, third, fifth,* or *seventh,* according to the number of each.

43. The captains of the even numbered companies will give, in their turn, the same commands, observing to precede them by the number of their respective companies.

44. In order that the odd numbered companies may not all fire at once, their captains will observe, but only for the first discharge, to give the command *fire* one after another: thus, the captain of the third company will not give the command *fire* until he has heard the fire of the first company; the captain of the fifth will observe the same rule with respect to the third, and the captain of the seventh the same rule with respect to the fifth.

45. The colonel will cause the fire to cease by the sound to *cease firing*; at this sound, the men will execute what is prescribed in the school of the company No. 63; at the sound for officers to take their places after firing, the captains, covering sergeants, and color-guard, will promptly resume their places in line of battle. *This rule is general for all the firings.*

The fire by wing.

46. When the colonel shall wish this fire to be executed, he will command:

1. *Fire by wing.* 2. *Right wing.* 3. READY.
4. AIM. 5. FIRE. 6. LOAD.

47. The colonel will cause the wings to fire alternately, and he will recommence the fire by the commands: 1. *Right wing*; 2. AIM; 3. FIRE; 4. LOAD. 1. *Left wing*; 2. AIM; 3. FIRE; 4. LOAD; in conforming to what is prescribed No. 35.

The fire by battalion.

48. The colonel will cause this fire to be executed by the commands last prescribed, substituting for the first two, 1. *Fire by battalion*; 2. *Battalion*.

The fire by file.

49. To cause this to be executed, the colonel will command:

1. *Fire by file.* 2. *Battalion.* 3. READY.
4. *Commence firing.*

50. At the fourth command, the fire will commence on the right of each company, as prescribed in the school of the company No. 57. The colonel may, if he thinks proper, cause the fire to commence on the right of each platoon.

The fire by rank.

51. To cause this fire to be executed, the colonel will command:

1. *Fire by rank.* 2. *Battalion.* 3. READY.
4. *Rear rank.* 5. AIM. 6. FIRE.
7. LOAD.

52. This fire will be executed as has been explained in the school of the company No. 59, in following the progression prescribed for the two ranks which should fire alternately.

To fire by the rear rank.

53. When the colonel shall wish the battalion to fire to the rear, he will command:

1. *Face by the rear rank.* 2. *Battalion.*
3. *About*—FACE.

54. At the first command, the captains, covering sergeants, and file closers will execute what has been prescribed in the school of the company No. 69; the color-bearer will pass into the rear rank, and, for this purpose, the corporal of his file will step before the corporal next on his right to let the color-bearer pass, and will then take his place in the front rank; the lieutenant colonel, adjutant, major, sergeant major, and the music will place themselves before the front rank, and face to the rear, each opposite his place in the line of battle—the first two passing around the right, and the others around the left, of the battalion.

55. At the third command, the battalion will face about; the captains and covering sergeants observing what is prescribed in the school of the company No. 70.

56. The battalion facing thus by the rear rank, the colonel will cause it to execute the different fires by the same commands as if it were faced by the front rank.

57. The right and left wings will retain the same designations, although faced about; the companies also will preserve their former designations, as *first, second, third*, &c.

58. The fire by file will commence on the left of each company, now become the right.

59. The fire by rank will commence by the front rank, now become the rear rank. This rank will preserve its denomination.

60. The captains, covering sergeants, and color-guard

will, at the first command given by the colonel, take the places prescribed for them in the fires, with the front rank leading.

61. The colonel, after firing to the rear, wishing to face the battalion to its proper front, will command:

1. *Face by the front rank.*   2. *Battalion.*   3. *About*— FACE.

62. At these commands, the battalion will return to its proper front by the means prescribed Nos. 54 and 55.

63. The fire by file being that most used in war, the colonel will give it the preference in the preparatory exercises, in order that the battalion may be brought to execute it with the greatest possible regularity.

64. When the colonel may wish to give some relaxation to the battalion, without breaking the ranks, he will execute what has been prescribed in the school of the company Nos. 37 and 38 or Nos. 39 and 40.

65. When the colonel shall wish to cause arms to be stacked, he will bring the battalion to ordered arms, and then command:

1. *Stack*—ARMS.   2. *Break ranks.*   3. MARCH.

66. The colonel wishing the men to return to the ranks, will cause *attention* to be sounded, at which the battalion will re-form behind the stacks of arms. The sound being finished, the colonel, after causing the stacks to be broken, will command:

Battalion.

67. At this command, the men will fix their attention, and remain immovable.

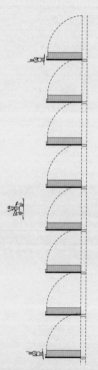

By company right wheel, &c. (No. 70).

PART SECOND.

Different modes of passing from the order in battle to the order in column.

ARTICLE FIRST.

To break to the right or the left into column.

68. Lines of battle will habitually break into column by company; they may also break by division or by platoon.

69 It is here supposed that the colonel wishes to break by company to the right; he will command:

1. *By company, right wheel.* 2. MARCH (or *double quick*—MARCH).

70. At the first command, each captain will place himself rapidly before the centre of his company, and caution it that it has to wheel to the right; each covering sergeant will replace his captain in the front rank.

71. At the command *march*, each company will break to the right, according to the principles prescribed in the school of the company, No. 173; each captain will conform himself to what is prescribed for the chiefs of platoon; the left guide, as soon as he can pass, will place himself on the left of the front rank to conduct the marching flank, and when he shall have approached near to the perpendicular, the captain will command: 1. *Such company.* 2. HALT.

72. At the second command, which will be given at the instant the left guide shall be at the distance of three paces from the perpendicular, the company will halt; the guide will advance and place his left arm lightly against the breast of the captain, who will establish him on the alignment of the man who has faced to the right; the covering sergeant will place himself correctly on the

alignment on the right of that man; which being
executed, the captain will align his company by the left,
command FRONT, and place himself two paces before its
centre.

73. The captains having commanded FRONT, the
guides, although some of them may not be in the direction
of the preceding guides, will stand fast, in order that
the error of a company that has wheeled too much or too
little may not be propagated; the guides not in the direction will readily come into it when the column is put
in march.

74. A battalion in line of battle will break into column
by company to the left, according to the same principles,
and by inverse means; the covering sergeant of each company will conduct the marching flank, and the left guide
will place himself on the left of the front rank at the
moment the company halts.

75. When the battalion breaks by division, the indication *division* will be substituted in the commands for that
of *company*; the chief of each division (the senior captain) will conform himself to what is prescribed for the
chief of company, and will place himself two paces before
the centre of his division; the junior captain, if not already
there, will place himself in the interval between the two
companies in the front rank, and be covered by the covering sergeant of the left company in the rear rank. The
right guide of the right company will be the right guide,
and the left guide of the left company the left guide, of the
division.

76. When the battalion shall break by platoon
to the right or to the left, each first lieutenant will
pass around the left of his company to place himself in
front of the second platoon, and, for this purpose, each
covering sergeant, except the one of the right company,
will step, for the moment, in rear of the right file of his
company.

77. When the battalion breaks by division to the right, and there is an odd company, the captain of this company (the left), after wheeling into column, will cause it to oblique to the left, halt it at company distance from the preceding division, place his left guide on the direction of the column, and then align his company by the left. When the line breaks by division to the left, the odd company will be in front; its captain, having wheeled it into column, will cause it to oblique to the right, halt it at division distance from the division next in the rear, place his right guide on the direction of the other guides, and align the company by the right.

78. The battalion being in column, the lieutenant colonel and major will place themselves on the directing flank, the first abreast with the leading subdivision, and the other abreast with the last, and both six paces from the flank. The adjutant will be near the lieutenant colonel, and the sergeant major near the major.

79. The colonel will have no fixed place as the *instructor* of his battalion; but in columns composed of many battalions, he will place himself habitually on the directing flack fifteen or twenty paces from the guides, and abreast with the centre of his battalion.

80. When the colonel shall wish to move the column forward without halting, he will caution the battalion to that effect, and command:

1. *By company, right wheel.*   2. MARCH (or *double quick*—MARCH).

81. At the first command; the captains of companies will execute what is prescribed for breaking into column from a halt.

82. At the second command, they will remain in front of their companies to superintend the movement; the companies will wheel to the right on fixed pivots as indicated in the school of the company No. 185; the left guides

will conform to what is prescribed above; when they shall arrive near the perpendicular the colonel will command:

3. *Forward.*   4. MARCH.   5. *Guide left.*

83. At the third command, each covering sergeant will place himself by the right side of the man on the right of the front rank of his company. At the fourth command, which will be given at the instant the wheel is completed, the companies will cease to wheel, and march straightforward. At the fifth, the men will take the touch of elbows to the left. The leading guide will march in the direction indicated to him by the lieutenant colonel. The guides will immediately conform themselves to the principles of the march in column, school of the company No. 200 and following.

84. If the battalion be marching in line of battle, the colonel will cause it to wheel to the right or left, by the same commands and the same means: but he should previously caution the battalion that it is to continue the march.

85. A battalion in line of battle will break into column by company to the left, according to the same principles and by inverse means; the covering sergeant of each company will conduct the marching flank, and the left guides will place themselves on the left of their respective companies at the command *forward.*

86. When a battalion has to prolong itself in column towards the right or left, or has to direct its march in column perpendicularly or diagonally in front, or in rear of either flank, the colonel will cause it to break by company to the right or left, as has just been prescribed; but when the line breaks to the right, in order to march towards the left, or the reverse, the colonel will command: *Break to the right to march to the left,* or *break to the left to march to the right,* before giving the command, *by company,*

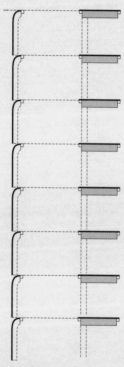

By the right of companies to the rear into column, &c.
(No. 88).

right (or *left*) *wheel*. As soon as the battalion is broken, the lieutenant colonel will place a marker abreast with the right guide of the leading company. The instant the column is put in motion, this company will wheel to the left (or right), march ten paces to the front without changing the guide, and wheel again to the left (or right). The second wheel being completed, the captain will immediately command *guide left* (or *right*). The guide of this company will march in a direction parallel to the guides of the column. The lieutenant colonel will be careful to place a second marker at the point where the first company is to change direction the second time.

Article Second.

To break to the rear, by the right or left, into column, and to advance or retire by the right or left of companies.

87. When the colonel shall wish to cause the battalion to break to the rear, by the right, into column by company, he will command:

1. *By the right of companies to the rear into column.*
2. *Battalion right*—Face. 3. March (or *double quick*—March).

88. At the first command, each captain will place himself before the centre of his company, and caution it to face to the right; the covering sergeants will step into the front rank.

89. At the second command, the battalion will face to the right; each captain will hasten to the right of his company, and break two files to the rear; the first file will break the whole depth of the two ranks; the second file less; which being executed, the captain will place himself so that his breast may touch lightly the left arm of the front rank man of the last file in the company next on the

right of his own. The captain of the right company will
place himself as if there were a company on his right, and
will align himself on the other captains. The covering sergeant of each company will break to the rear with the
right files, and place himself before the front rank of the
first file, to conduct him.

90. At the command *march*, the first file of each company will wheel to the right; the covering sergeant, placed
before this file, will conduct it perpendicularly to the rear.
The other files will come successively to wheel on the
same spot. The captains will stand fast, see their companies file past, and at the instant the last file shall have
wheeled, each captain will command:

1. *Such company.*   2. HALT.   3. FRONT.
4. *Left*—DRESS.

91. At the instant the company faces to the front, its
left guide will place himself so that his left arm may touch
lightly the breast of his captain.

92. At the fourth command, the company will
align itself on its left guide, the captain so directing it
that the new alignment may be perpendicular to that
which the company had occupied in line of battle; and,
the better to judge this, he will step back two paces from
the flank.

93. The company being aligned, the captain will command: FRONT, and take his place before its centre.

94. The battalion marching in line of battle, when the
colonel shall wish to break into column by company, to
the rear, by the right, he will command:

1. *By the right of companies to the rear into column.*
2. *Battalion, by the right flank.*   3. MARCH (or
double quick—MARCH).

95. At the first command, each captain will step

briskly in front of the centre of his company, and caution it to face *by the right flank.*

96. At the command *march*, the battalion will face to the right; each captain will move rapidly to the right of his company and cause it to break to the right; the first file of each company will wheel to the right, and the covering sergeant placed in front of this file will conduct it perpendicularly to the rear; the other files will wheel successively at the same place as the first. The captains will see their companies file past them; when the last files have wheeled, the colonel will command:

3. *Battalion, by the left flank*—MARCH.   4. *Guide left.*

97. At the command *march*, the companies will face to the left, and march in column in the new direction. The captains will place themselves in front of the centres of their respective companies. At the fourth command, the guides will conform to the principles of the march in column; the leading one will move in the direction indicated to him by the lieutenant colonel. The men will take the touch of elbows to the left.

98. To break to the rear by the left, the colonel will give the same commands as in the case of breaking to the rear by the right, substituting the indication *left*, for that of *right*.

99. The movement will be executed according to the same principles. Each captain will hasten to the left of his company, cause the first two files to break to the rear, and then place his breast against the right file of the company next on the left of his own, in the manner prescribed above.

100. As soon as the two files break to the rear, the left guide of each company will place himself before the front rank man of the headmost file, to conduct him.

101. The instant the companies face to the front, the

right guide of each will place himself so that his right arm
may lightly touch the breast of his captain.

102. The battalion may be broken by division to the
rear, by the right or left, in like manner; in this case, the
indication *divisions* will be substituted, in the first command, for that of *companies*; the chiefs of division will
conform themselves to what is prescribed for the chiefs of
company. The junior captain in each division will place
himself, when the division faces to a flank, by the side of
the covering sergeant of the left company, who steps into
the front rank.

103. If there be an odd number of companies, and the
battalion breaks by division to the rear, whether by the
right or left, the captain of the left company will conform
to what is prescribed No. 77.

104. This manner of breaking into column, being at
once the most prompt and regular, will be preferred on
actual service, unless there be some particular reason for
breaking to the front.

105. If the battalion be in line and at a halt, and the
colonel should wish to advance or retire by the right of
companies, he will command:

1. *By the right of companies to the front* (or *rear*).
2. *Battalion, right*—FACE. 3. MARCH (or *double
quick*—MARCH). 4. *Guide right* (*left*) or (*centre*).

106. At the first command, each captain will move rapidly two paces in front of the centre of his company, and
caution it to face to the right; the covering sergeants will
replace the captains in the front rank.

107. At the second command, the battalion will face to
the right, and each captain moving quickly to the right of
his company will cause files to break to the front, according to the principles indicated No. 89.

108. At the command *march*, each captain placing

himself on the left of his leading guide will conduct his company perpendicularly to the original line. At the fourth command, the guide of each company will dress to the right, left, or centre, according to the indication given, taking care to preserve accurately his distance.

109. If the colonel should wish to move to the front, or rear, by the left of companies, the movement will be executed by the same means and the same commands, substituting *left* for *right*.

110. If the battalion be in march, and the colonel should wish to advance or retire by the right of companies, he will command:

1. *By the right of companies to the front* (or *rear*).
   2. *Battalion, by the right flank.*   3. MARCH (or *double quick*—MARCH).   4. *Guide right* (*left*) or (*centre*).

111. Which will be executed according to the principles and means prescribed Nos. 95 and following, and 106 and following. At the first command, the color and general guides will take their places as in column.

112. If the colonel should wish to advance or retire by the left of companies, the movement will be executed by the same means and the same commands, substituting *left* for *right*.

113. If the battalion be advancing by the right or left of companies, and the colonel should wish to form line to the front, he will command:

1. *By companies into line.*   2. MARCH (or *double quick*—MARCH).   3. *Guide centre.*

114. At the command *march*, briskly repeated by the captains, each company will be formed into line, as prescribed in the school of the company, No. 154.

115. At the third command, the color and general

guides will move rapidly to their places in line, as will be hereinafter prescribed No. 405.

116. If the battalion be retiring by the right or left of companies, and the colonel should wish to form line facing the enemy, he will first cause the companies to face about while marching, and immediately form in line by the commands and means prescribed Nos. 113 and following.

ARTICLE THIRD.

To ploy the battalion into close column.

117. This movement may be executed by company or by division, on the right or left subdivision, or on any other subdivision, right or left in front.

118. The examples in this school will suppose the presence of four divisions, with directions for an odd company; but what will be prescribed for four will serve equally for two, three or five divisions.

119. To ploy the battalion into close column by division in rear of the first, the colonel will command:

1. *Close column, by division.*   2. *On the first division, right in front.*   3. *Battalion, right*—FACE.   4. MARCH (or *double quick*—MARCH).

120. At the second command, all the chiefs of division will place themselves before the centres of their divisions; the chief of the first will caution it to stand fast; the chiefs of the three others will remind them that they will have to face to the right, and the covering sergeant of the right company of each division will replace his captain in the front rank, as soon as the latter steps out.

121. At the third command, the last three divisions will face to the right; the chief of each division will hasten to its right, and cause files to be broken to the rear, as indicated No. 89; the right guide will break at the same time, and place himself before the front rank man of the

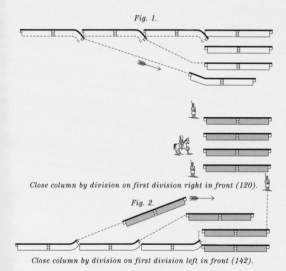

Fig. 1.

Close column by division on first division right in front (120).

Fig. 2.

Close column by division on first division left in front (142).

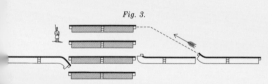

Fig. 3.

...e column by division on third (any other than 1st or 4th) division (144).

first file, to conduct him, and each chief of division will place himself by the side of this guide.

122. The moment these divisions face to the right, the junior captain in each will place himself on the left of the covering sergeant of the left company, who will place himself in the front rank. *This rule is general for all the ployments by division.*

123. At the command *march*, the chief of the first division will add, *guide left*; at this, its left guide will place himself on its left, as soon as the movement of the second division may permit, and the file closers will advance one pace upon the rear rank.

124. All the other divisions, each conducted by its chief, will step off together, to take their places in the column; the second will gain, in wheeling by file to the rear, the space of six paces, which ought to separate its guide from the guide of the first division, and so direct its march as to enter the column on a line parallel to this division; the third and fourth divisions will direct themselves diagonally towards, but a little in rear of, the points at which they ought, respectively, to enter the column; at six paces from the left flank of the column, the head of each of these divisions will incline a little to the left, in order to enter the column as has just been prescribed for the second, taking care also to leave the distance of six paces between its guide and the guide of the preceding division. At the moment the divisions put themselves in march to enter the column, the file closers of each will incline to the left, so as to bring themselves to the distance of a pace from the rear rank.

125. Each chief of these three divisions will conduct his division till he shall be up with the guide of the directing one; the chief will then himself halt, see his division file past, and halt it the instant the last file shall have passed, commanding: 1. *Such division*; 2. HALT; 3. FRONT; 4. *Left*—DRESS.

126. At the second command, the division will halt; the left guide will place himself promptly on the direction, six paces from the guide which precedes him, in order that, the column being formed, the divisions may be separated the distance of four paces.

127. At the third command, the division will face to the front; at the fourth, it will be aligned by its chief, who will place himself two paces outside of his guide, and direct the alignment so that his division may be parallel to that which precedes—which being done, he will command, FRONT, and place himself before the centre of his division.

128. If any division, after the command *front*, be not at its proper distance, and this can only happen through the negligence of its chief, such division will remain in its place, in order that the fault may not be propagated.

129. The colonel will superintend the execution of the movement, and cause the prescribed principles to be observed.

130. The lieutenant colonel, placing himself in succession in rear of the left guides, will assure them on the direction as they arrive, and then move to his place outside of the left flank of the column, six paces from, and abreast with, the first division. In assuring the guides on the direction, he will be a mere observer, unless one or more should fail to cover exactly the guide or guides already established. *This rule is general.*

131. The major will follow the movement abreast with the left of the fourth division, and afterwards take his position outside of the left flank of the column, six paces from, and abreast with, this division.

132. To ploy the battalion in front of the first division, the colonel will give the same commands, substituting the indication *left* for that of *right* in front.

133. At the second and third commands, the chiefs of

division and the junior captains will conform themselves to what is prescribed Nos. 120, 121, 122; but the chiefs of the last three divisions, instead of causing the first two files to break to the rear, will cause them to break to the front.

134. At the fourth command, the chief of the first division will add: *Guide right.*

135. The three other divisions will step off together to take their places in the column in front of the directing division; each will direct itself as prescribed, No. 124, and will enter in such manner that, when halted, its guide may find himself six paces from the guide of the division next previously established in the column.

136. Each chief of these divisions will conduct his division, till his right guide shall be nearly up with the guide of the directing one; he will then halt his division, and cause it to face to the front; at the instant it halts, its right guide will face to the rear, place himself six paces from the preceding guide, and cover him exactly—which being done, the chief will align his division by the right.

137. The lieutenant colonel, placed in front of the right guide of the first division, will assure the guides on the direction as they successively arrive, and then move outside of the right flank of the column, to a point six paces from, and abreast with, the fourth division, now in front.

138. The major will conform himself to what is prescribed No. 131, and then move outside of the right flank of the column, six paces from, and abreast with, the first division, now in the rear.

139. The movement being ended, the colonel will command:

Guides, about—FACE.

140. At this, the guides, who are faced to the rear, will face to the front.

141. To ploy the battalion in rear, or in front of the fourth division, the colonel will command:

1. *Close column by division.*   2. *On the fourth division, left* (or *right*) *in front.*   3. *Battalion, left*—FACE. 4. MARCH (*or double quick*—MARCH).

142. These movements will be executed according to the principles of those which precede, but by inverse means: the fourth division on which the battalion ploys will stand fast; the instant the movement commences, its chief will command, *guide right* (or *left*).

143. The foregoing examples embrace all the principles: thus, when the colonel shall wish to ploy the battalion on an interior division, he will command:

1. *Close column by division.*   2. *On such division, right* (or *left*) *in front.*   3. *Battalion inwards*—FACE.   4. MARCH (*or double quick* MARCH).

144. The instant the movement commences, the chief of the directing division will command, *guide left* (or *right*).

145. The divisions which, in the order in battle, are to the right of the directing division, will face to the left; those which are to the left, will face to the right:

146. If the right is to be in front, the right divisions will ploy in front of the directing division, and the left in its rear; the reverse, if the left is to be in front. And in all the foregoing suppositions, the division or divisions contiguous to the directing one, in wheeling by file to the front or rear, will gain the space of six paces, which ought to separate their guides from the guide of the directing division.

147. In all the ployments on an interior division, the lieutenant colonel will assure the positions of the guides in front, and the major those in rear of the directing division.

148. If the battalion be in march, instead of at a halt, the movement will be executed by combining the two gaits of quick and double quick time, and always in rear of one of the flank divisions.

149. The battalion being in march, to play it in rear of the first division, the colonel will command:

1. *Close column by division.* 2. *On the first division.* 3. *Battalion—by the right flank.* 4. *Double quick—* MARCH.

150. At the second command, each chief of division will move rapidly before the centre of his division and caution it to face to the right.

151. The chief of the first division will caution it to continue to march to the front, and he will command: *Quick march.*

152. At the command *march*, the chief of the first division will command: *Guide left.* At this, the left guide will move to the left flank of the division and direct himself on the point indicated.

153. The three other divisions will face to the right and move off in double quick time, breaking to the right to take their places in column; each chief of division will move rapidly to the right of his division in order to conduct it. The files will be careful to preserve their distances, and to march with a uniform and decided step. The color-bearer and general guides will retake their places in the ranks.

154. The second division will immediately enter the column, marching parallel to the first division; its chief will allow it to file past him, and, when the last file is abreast of him, will command: 1. *Second division, by the left flank—*MARCH. 2. *Guide left*, and place himself in front of the centre of his division.

155. At the command *march*, the division will face to the left; at the second command, the left guide will march in the trace of the left guide of the first division; the men will take the touch of elbow, to the left. When the second

division has closed to its proper distance, its chief will command: *Quick time*—MARCH. This division will then change its step to quick time.

156. The chiefs of the third and fourth divisions will execute their movements according to the same principles, taking care to gain as much ground as possible towards the head of the column.

157. If the battalion had been previously marching in line at double quick time, when the fourth division shall have gained its distance, the colonel will command: *Double quick*—MARCH.

158. In this movement, the lieutenant colonel will move rapidly to the side of the leading guide, give him a point of direction, and then follow the movements of the first division. The major will follow the movement abreast with the left of the fourth division.

Remarks on ploying the battalion into column.

159. The battalion may be ployed into column at full, or half distance, on the same principles, and by the same commands, substituting for the first command: *Column at full* (or *half*) *distance by division*.

160. In the ployments and movements in column, when the subdivisions execute the movements successively, such as—to take or close distances; to change direction by the flank of subdivisions, each chief of subdivision will cause his men to support arms after having aligned it and commanded, FRONT.

PART THIRD.

ARTICLE FIRST.

To march in column at full distance.

161. When the colonel shall wish to put the column in march, he will indicate to the leading guide two distinct

objects in front, on the line which the guide ought to follow. This guide will immediately put his shoulders in a square with that line, take the more distant object as the point of direction, and the nearer one as the intermediate point.

162. If only a single prominent object present itself in the direction the guide has to follow, he will face to it as before, and immediately endeavor to catch on the ground some intermediate point, by which to give steadiness to his march on the point of direction.

163. There being no prominent object to serve as the point of direction, the colonel will despatch the lieutenant colonel or adjutant to place himself forty paces in advance, facing the column, and by a sign of the sword establish him on the direction he may wish to give to the leading guide; that officer being thus placed, this guide will take him as the point of direction, conforming himself to what is prescribed in the school of the company No. 87.

164. These dispositions being made, the colonel will command:

> 1. *Column forward.*   2. *Guide left* (or *right*).
> 3. March (or *double quick*—March).

165. At the command *march*, briskly repeated by the chiefs of subdivision, the column will put itself in march, conforming to what is prescribed in the school of the company No. 200 and following.

166. The leading guide may always maintain himself correctly on the direction by keeping steadily in view the two points indicated to him, or chosen by himself; if these points have a certain elevation, he may be assured he is on the true direction, when the nearer masks the more distant point.

167. The following guides will preserve with exactness both step and distance; each will march in the trace of the guide who immediately precedes him, without occupying himself with the general direction.

168. The lieutenant colonel will hold himself, habitually, abreast with the leading guide, to see that he does not deviate from the direction, and will observe, also, that the next guide marches exactly in the trace of the first.

169. The major will generally be abreast with the last subdivision; he will see that each guide marches exactly in the trace of the one immediately preceding: if either deviate from the direction, the major will promptly rectify the error, and prevent its being propagated; but he need not interfere, in this way, unless the deviation has become sensible, or material.

170. The column being in march, the colonel will frequently cause the *about* to be executed while marching; to this effect, he will command:

1. *Battalion, right about.*   2. MARCH.   3. *Guide right.*

171. At the second command, the companies will face to the right about, and the column will then march forward in an opposite direction; the chiefs of subdivision will remain behind the front rank, the file closers in front of the rear rank, and the guides will place themselves in the same rank. The lieutenant colonel will remain abreast of the first division, now in rear; the major will give a point of direction to the leading guide, and march abreast of him.

172. The colonel will hold himself habitually on the directing flank; he will look to the step and to the distances, and see that all the principles prescribed for the march in column, school of the company, are observed.

173. These means, which the practice in that school ought to have rendered familiar, will give sufficient exactness to the direction of the column, and also enable it to form *forward* or *faced the rear*, *on the right*, or *on the left*, into line of battle, and *to close in mass*.

174. But when a column, arriving in front, or in rear of the line of battle, or, rather, on one of the extremities of that line, has to prolong itself on it, in order to form *to the*

Pl. 44.

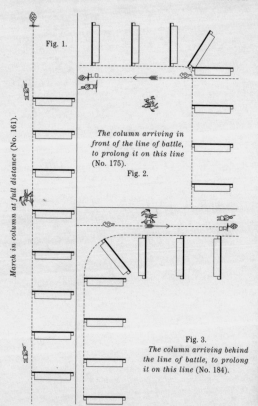

Fig. 1.

March in column at full distance (No. 161).

The column arriving in front of the line of battle, to prolong it on this line (No. 175).

Fig. 2.

Fig. 3.

The column arriving behind the line of battle, to prolong it on this line (No. 184).

left or *to the right* into line of battle, then, as it is essential, to prevent the column from cutting the line, or sensibly deviating from it, other means, as follows, will be employed.

The column arriving in front of the line of battle, to prolong it on this line.

175. If the column right in front arrive in front of the line of battle, as it should cross it and find itself four paces beyond it after having changed direction, the colonel will cause to be placed, in advance, a marker on the line to indicate the point at which the column ought to cross it, and another marker to indicate the point where the first subdivision should commence to wheel; he will be so placed that when the wheel is executed, the left guide will find himself four paces within the line of battle. The chief of the leading subdivision, when the head of the column shall have arrived near the line, will take the guide to the right, and this guide will immediately direct himself on the second marker. On arriving abreast of him, this subdivision will be wheeled to the left, and when the wheel is completed, the guide will be changed again to the left; this guide will then march parallel to the line of battle by the means to be hereinafter indicated.

176. The instant the first subdivision wheels, the right general guide, who, by a caution from the lieutenant colonel, will before have placed himself on the line of battle at the point where the column crosses, and who will have faced to the two points of direction in his front, indicated by the colonel, will march forward correctly on the prolongation of those points.

177. The color-bearer will place himself in like manner on the line of battle; and, at the instant the color subdivision wheels, he will prolong his march on that line, abreast with this subdivision, taking care to carry the color-lance before the centre of his person, and to maintain himself exactly in the direction of the general guide

who precedes him, and the point of direction in front which will have been indicated to him.

178. Finally, the left general guide will place himself in the same manner on the line of battle; and, at the instant the last subdivision of the battalion wheels, he will march correctly in the direction of the color-bearer, and the other general guide.

179. The guide of the first subdivision will march steadily abreast with the right general guide, and about four paces to his right; each of the guides of the following subdivisions will march in the trace of the guide who immediately precedes him, as prescribed No. 167.

180. The colonel, placed outside of the general guides, will see that the column marches nearly parallel to, and about four paces within, these guides.

181. The lieutenant colonel and major will look to the direction of the general guides, and, to this end, place themselves sometimes in rear of the color-bearer, or the left general guide.

182. If the column be composed of several battalions, the general guides of each will successively place themselves on the line of battle to prolong their march on this line, as the leading subdivision, that of the color, and the one in the rear of their battalion, shall wheel into the new direction; these guides will conform themselves respectively, as will also the colonel, lieutenant colonel, and major, to what is prescribed above for those of the leading battalion.

183. In the case of several battalions, the lieutenant colonel of each will maintain steadily the guide of his leading subdivision about four paces within the line of general guides, even should the last subdivisions of the battalion immediately preceding deviate from the parallelism, in order that the false direction of one battalion may not influence that of the battalions which follow.

The column arriving behind the line of battle, to prolong it on this line.

184. If the column, right in front, arrive behind the line of battle, as it ought to find itself four paces within this line, after having changed direction, the colonel will cause a marker to be placed at the point where, according to that condition, the first subdivision ought to commence wheeling. Another marker will be established on the line of battle, to indicate the point at which the general guides ought, in succession, to begin to prolong themselves on that line; he will be so placed that each subdivision, having finished its wheel, may find itself nearly in a line with this marker.

185. At the instant the first subdivision, after having wheeled to the right, begins to prolong itself, parallelly to the line of battle, the leading general guide, placed in advance on that line, will direct himself on the two points taken in his front; the color-bearer and the other general guide will successively place themselves on the same line the instant that their respective subdivisions shall have finished their wheel.

186. If the column be composed of several battalions, the general guides of the following battalions will successively execute what has been just prescribed for those of the leading battalion, and the whole will conform themselves, as well as the guides of subdivisions, and the field officers of the several battalions, to what is indicated, above, for a column arriving in front of the line of battle.

187. In a column, left in front, arriving in front or in rear of the line of battle, these movements will be executed on the same principles, and by inverse means.

The column arriving on the right or the left of the line of battle, to prolong it on this line.

188. If the column, instead of arriving in front or in rear of the line of battle, arrive on its right or left, and if it have to prolong itself on that line, in order afterwards to form to the left or right into line of battle, the colonel will bring the color and general guides on the flank of the column by the command *color and general guides on the line:* and these guides will prolong themselves on the line of battle, conforming to what is prescribed above.

Manner of prolonging a line of battle by markers.

189. When a column prolongs itself on the line of battle, it being all-important that the general guides march correctly on that line, it becomes necessary that colonels, lieutenant colonels, and majors, whose duty it is to maintain the true direction, should be able to see, as far as practicable, the two objects, on which the march of the general guides ought to be directed; consequently, when no prominent objects present themselves in the desired direction, the chief of the column will supply the want of them in advance by aids-de-camp, or other mounted officers, and in such number as may be necessary.

190. Three such officers may prolong a line as far as may be desired in the following manner: they will place themselves in advance on the line of battle, the first at the point where the head of the column ought to enter; the second, three or four hundred paces behind the first, and the third, a like distance behind the second. The first of these officers will remain in position till the leading general guide shall have entered on the line of battle, and then, at a gallop, place himself at a convenient distance behind the third. The second will do the like in respect to the first, when the lead of the column shall be near him,

and so on in continuation. These officers, without dismounting, will face to the column, and cover each other accurately in file. It will be on them that the general guides will steadily direct their march, and it will be so much the more easy for the latter to maintain themselves on the direction, as they will always be able to see the mounted officers over the heads of the preceding guides: thus the deviation from the direction, by one or more general guides, need not mislead those who follow.

191. A single mounted officer may suffice to assure the direction of a column, when the point of direction towards which it marches is very distinct. In this case, that officer will place himself on the line of battle within that point, and beyond the one at which the head of the column will halt, and remain in position till the column halts; serving thus as the intermediate point for giving steadiness to the march of the general guides.

192. For a column of one or two battalions, markers on foot will suffice to indicate the line to be followed by the general guides.

Remarks on the march in column.

193. Although the uncadenced step be that of columns in route marches, and also that which ought to be habitually employed in the *Evolutions of the Line*, because it leaves the men more at ease, and, consequently, is better adapted to movements on a large scale and to difficult grounds, nevertheless, as it is of paramount importance to confirm soldiers in the measure and the movement of the cadenced pace, the route step will be but little practised in the exercises by battalion, except in going to, and returning from, the ground of instruction, and for teaching the mechanism and movements of columns in route.

194. It is highly essential to the regularity of the march in column that each guide follow exactly in the trace of

the one immediately preceding, without occupying his
attention with the general direction of the guides.
If this principle be steadily observed, the guides will find
themselves aligned, provided that the leading one
march exactly in the direction indicated to him; and even
should obstacles in his way force him into a momentary
deviation, the direction of the column would not necessarily be changed; whereas, if the following guides
endeavor to conform themselves at once to all the movements of the leading one, in order to cover him in file,
such endeavors would necessarily cause corresponding
fluctuations in the column, from right to left, and from left
to right, and render the preservation of distances
extremely difficult.

195. As a consequence of the principle, that *each
guide shall exactly follow in the trace of the one who
immediately precedes*, if, pending the march of the column, the colonel shall give a new point of direction, too
near to the first to require a formal change of direction,
the leading guide, advancing the one or other
shoulder, will immediately direct himself on this point; the
other guides will only conform themselves to this
movement as each arrives at the point at which the
first had executed it. Each subdivision will conform
itself to the movement of its guide, the men insensibly
lengthening or shortening the step, and advancing or
refusing (throwing back) the shoulder opposite to the
guide, but without losing the touch of the elbow towards
his side.

196. The column, by company, being in march, the
colonel will cause it to diminish front by platoon, from
front to rear, at once, and to increase front by platoon in
like manner, which movements will be commanded and
executed as prescribed in the school of the company Nos.
282 and 273 and following, changing the command *form
company* to *form companies*. So may he increase and
diminish, or diminish and increase, front, according to the

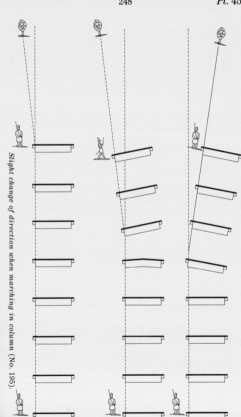

Slight change of direction when marching in column (No. 195).

same principles and at once, by company, changing the command *form companies* to *form divisions*, and the command *break into platoons* to *break into companies*. In this case, the companies and divisions will execute what is prescribed for platoons and companies respectively.

197. The column being at a halt, if the colonel should wish to march it to the rear, and the distance to be gained be so inconsiderable as to render a countermarch a disproportionate loss of time, he will cause the column to face about, and then put it in march by the commands prescribed No. 164; the chiefs of the subdivisions will remain behind the front rank, the file closers before the rear rank, and the guides will step into the rear rank, now in front. In a column, by division, the junior captains, in the intervals between companies, will replace their covering sergeants in the rear rank, and these sergeants will step into the line of file closers in front of their intervals.

ARTICLE SECOND.
Column in route.

198. A column in route, like a column in manœuvre, ought never to have a depth greater than about the front it had occupied in the line of battle, less the front of a subdivision.

199. The observance of this principle requires no particular rule for a column in manœuvre; but, as a column in route may have hourly to pass narrow ways, bridges, or other defiles, rendering it necessary to diminish the front of subdivisions, it becomes important to give rules and means by which the column may, for any length of march, preserve the ease of the route step without elongation from front to rear.

200. A column in route will be habitually formed by company.

201. When a column in route shall arrive at a pass too narrow to receive the front of a company, the column will diminish front by platoon before entering. This movement will be executed successively, or by all the companies at once.

202. If, however, the defile be very short, and it may be passed by the diminution of a few files, it will be preferable to break to the rear the limited number of files.

203. The column being by platoon, and the want of space rendering a further diminution of front necessary, it will be diminished by section, if the platoons be of twelve or more files.

204. The column being by section, will continue to march by that front as long as the defile may permit.

205. If the platoons have less than twelve files, one or two files will be broken to the rear, according to the narrowing of the defile, and the route step continued as long as six files can march abreast.

206. What has just been explained for breaking files to the rear in a column by platoon, is equally applicable to a column by section.

207. If the defile be too narrow to permit six men to march abreast, the subdivisions will be marched successively by the flank, conforming to what is prescribed Nos. 314 and 315, school of the company.

208. The battalion marching by the flank, will be formed into column, by section, by platoon, or by company, as soon as the breadth of the way may permit; the several movements which these formations include will be executed by the commands of the captains, as their companies successively clear the defile, observing the following rules.

209. As soon as the way is sufficiently broad to contain six men abreast, the captain will command:

1. *By section* (or *by platoon*) *into line.*   2. MARCH.

210. At the command *march*, the subdivisions indicated will form themselves into line; the files which have not been able to enter will follow (by the flank) the last four files of their subdivision which have entered into line.

211. The column marching in this order, the files in rear will be caused to enter into line as the increased breadth of the way may permit.

212. The column marching by section or by platoon, platoons or companies will be formed as soon as the breadth of the way may permit.

213. The leading subdivision will follow the windings of the pass or defile; the following subdivisions will not occupy themselves with the direction, but all, in succession, pass over the trace of the subdivisions which precede them respectively. The men will not seek to avoid the bad parts of the way, but pass, as far as practicable, each in the direction of his file.

214. Changes of direction will always be made without command; if the change be important, a caution merely from the respective chiefs to their subdivisions will suffice, and the rear rank, as well as the files broken to the rear, will execute successively the movement where the front rank had executed it.

215. The colonel will hold himself at the head of the battalion; he will regulate the step of the leading subdivision, and indicate to its chief the instant for executing the various movements which the nature of the route may render necessary.

216. If the column be composed of several battalions, each will conform itself, in its turn, to what shall have been commanded for the leading battalion, observing to execute each movement at the same pace, and in the same manner.

217. Finally, to render the mechanism of all those movements familiar to the troops, and to habituate them to march in the route step without elongating the column, commanders will generally cause their battalions to march in this step, going to, and returning from, fields of exercise. Each will occasionally conduct his battalion through narrow passes, in order to make it perceive the utility of the principles prescribed above; and he will several times, in every course of instruction, march it in the route step, and cause to be executed, sometimes at once, and sometimes successively, the divers movements which have just been indicated.

General remarks on the column in route.

218. The lesson relative to the column in route is, by its frequent application, one of the most important that can be given to troops. If it be not well taught and established on right principles, it will happen that the rear of the column in route will be obliged to run, to regain distances, or that the front will be forced to halt till the rear shall have accomplished that object; thus rendering the march greatly slower, or greatly more fatiguing, generally both, than if it were executed according to rule.

219. The ordinary progress of a column in route ought to be, on good roads or good grounds, at the rate of one hundred and ten paces in a minute. This rate may be easily maintained by columns of almost any depth; but over bad roads, ploughed fields, loose sands, or mountainous districts, the progress cannot be so great, and must therefore be regulated according to circumstances.

220. The most certain means of marching well in route, is to preserve always a regular and equal movement, and, if obstacles oblige one or more subdivisions to slacken or to shorten the step, to cause

the primitive rate of march to be resumed the moment the difficulties are passed.

221. A subdivision ought never to take *more* than the prescribed distance from the subdivision immediately preceding; but it is sometimes necessary to *lessen* that distance.

222. Thus: the head of the column encounters an obstacle which obliges it to relax its march; all the following subdivisions will preserve the habitual step, and close up in mass, if necessary, on the subdivision nearest to the obstacle. Distances will afterwards naturally be recovered as each subdivision shall successively have passed the obstacle. Nevertheless, if the difficulty be too great to be overcome by one subdivision, while the next is closing up, so that distances cannot afterwards be recovered without running, the chief of the column will halt the leading subdivision beyond the obstacle, at a distance sufficient to contain the whole column in mass. He will then put the column in march, the subdivisions taking distances by the head, observing to commence the movement in time, so that the last subdivision may not be obliged to halt, after having cleared the obstacle.

223. When the chief of a column shall wish to change the rate of march, he will cause the leading battalion to quicken or to relax the step insensibly, and send orders to the other battalions each to regulate itself by that which precedes it.

224. The column being composed of several battalions, the general-in-chief will always leave an aid-de-camp with its rear to bring him prompt information if it find a difficulty in following.

225. Subdivisions ought always to step out well in obliquing, both in breaking and forming companies or platoons. When either is done in succession, it is highly important that no subdivision slacken or shorten the step whilst that which precedes it is engaged in the movement.

The observance of this principle can alone prevent an elongation of the column.

226. If the battalion, marching by the flank, encounter a pass so narrow as to oblige it to defile with a front of two men, the colonel will order support arms, take the cadenced step, and undouble the files, which will be executed as prescribed in the school of the company, No. 326; the files will double again as soon as the breadth of the way will permit.

227. If the defile be only sufficient to receive a front of one map, the colonel will cause the men to pass one at a time. The men of the same file should follow each other in their order as closely as possible, and without loss of time. As soon as the defile permits a front of two or four men, the battalion will be re-formed into two or four ranks, and will march in this order until there be space to form platoons or sections, as indicated No. 209.

228. In both cases, just supposed, the head of the battalion, after having passed the defile, will march till sufficient space be left to contain the whole of the subdivisions in mass; afterwards it will be put in march by the means indicated No. 222.

229. When a command has to move rapidly over a given distance, the movements prescribed in this article will be executed in double quick time; if the distance be long, the chief of the column will not allow the march at this gait to be continued for more than fifteen minutes; at the end of this time, he will order the ordinary route step to be marched for five minutes, and then again resume the double quick. If the ground be uneven, having considerable ascents and descents, he will reserve the double quick for those parts of the ground most favorable to this march.

230. A column marching alternately in double quick time and the ordinary route step, in the manner stated,

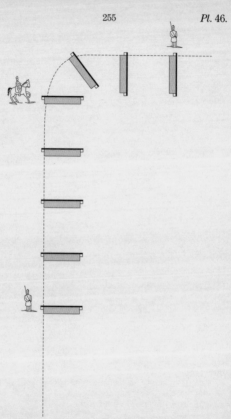

To change direction. Head of column to the right.
(No. 232).

can easily accomplish very long distances in a very short space of time; but when the distance to be passed over be not greater than two miles, it ought to be accomplished, when the ground is favorable, without changing the rate of march.

Article Third.

To change direction in column at full distance.

231. The column being in march in the cadenced step, when the colonel shall wish to cause it to change direction, he will go to the point at which the change ought to be commenced, and establish a marker there, presenting the breast to the flank of the column; this marker, no matter to which side the change of direction is to be made, will be posted on the opposite side, and he will remain in position till the last subdivision of the battalion shall have passed. The leading subdivision being within a few paces of the marker, the colonel will command:

Head of column to the left (or *right*).

232. At this, the chief of the leading subdivision will immediately take the guide on the side opposite the change of direction, if not already there. This guide will direct himself so as to graze the breast of the marker; arrived at this point, the chief will cause his subdivision to change direction by the commands and according to the principles prescribed in the school of the company. When the wheel is completed, the chief of this subdivision will retake the guide, if changed, on the side of the primitive direction.

233. The chief of each succeeding subdivision, as well as the guides, will conform to what has just been explained for the leading subdivision.

234. The colonel will carefully see that the guide of each subdivision, in wheeling, does not throw himself

without or within, but passes over all the points of the arc of the circle, which he ought to describe.

235. As often as no distinct object presents itself in the new direction, the lieutenant colonel will place himself upon it in advance, at the distance of thirty or forty paces from the marker, and be assured in this direction by the colonel; the leading guide will take, the moment he shall have changed direction, two points on the ground in the straight line which, drawn from himself, would pass between the heels of the lieutenant colonel, taking, afterwards, new points as he advances.

236. The major will see that the guides direct themselves on the marker posted at the point of change, so as to graze his breast.

237. If the column be composed of several battalions, the lieutenant colonel of the second will cause the marker of the first battalion to be replaced as soon as the last subdivision of this battalion shall have passed; this disposition will be observed by battalion after battalion, to the rear of the column.

Remarks.

238. It has been demonstrated, school of the company, how important it is, *first*, that each subdivision execute its change of direction precisely at the point where the leading one had changed, and that it arrive in a square with the direction; *second*, that the wheeling point ought, always, to be cleared in time, in order that the subdivision engaged in the wheel may not arrest the movement of the following one. The deeper the column, the more rigorously ought these principles to be observed; because, a fault that would be but slight in a column of a single battalion would cause much embarrassment in one of great depth.

Article Fourth.

To halt the column.

239. The column being in march, when the colonel shall wish to halt it, he will command:

1. *Column.*   2. Halt.

240. At the second command, briskly repeated by the captains, the column will halt; no guide will stir, though he may have lost his distance, or be out of the direction of the preceding guides

241. The column being in march, in double quick time, will be halted by the same commands. At the command *halt*, the men will halt in their places, and will themselves rectify their positions in the ranks.

242. The column being halted, when the colonel shall wish to form it into line of battle, he will move a little in front of the leading guide, and face to him; this guide and the following one will fix their eyes on the colonel, in order promptly to conform themselves to his directions.

243. If the colonel judge it not necessary to give a general direction to the guides, be will limit himself to rectifying the position of such as may be without, or within the direction, by the command, *guide of* (such) *company,* or *guides of* (such) *companies, to the right* (or *to the left*); at this command, the guides designated will place themselves on the direction; the others will stand fast.

244. If, on the contrary, the colonel judge it necessary to give a general direction to the guides of the column, he will place the first two on the direction he shall have chosen, and command:

Guides, cover.

245. At this, the following guides will promptly place themselves on the direction covering the first two in file,

and each precisely at a distance equal to the front of his
company, from the guide immediately preceding; the lieutenant colonel will assure them in the direction, and the
colonel will command:

Left (or *right*)—DRESS.

246. At this command, each company will incline to
the right or left, and dress forward or backward, so as to
bring the designated flank to rest on its guide; each captain will place himself two paces outside of his guide,
promptly align his company parallelly with that which
precedes, then command, FRONT, and return to his place
in column.

247. Finally, if the general guides march on the flank
of the column, the colonel, having halted it, will place
himself in rear of the color-bearer, to ascertain whether
the leading general guide and the color-bearer be exactly
on the direction of the two points in advance, and establish them on that direction if they be not already on it; the
major will do the like, in respect to the general guide
in the rear; which being executed, the colonel will
command:

1. *Guides*—ON THE LINE.

248. At this command, the guide of each company of
the directing flank will step promptly into the direction of
the general guides, and face to the front. The lieutenant
colonel, placed in front of, and facing to, the leading general guide, and the major, placed in rear of the rearmost
one, will promptly align the company guides.

249. The colonel, having verified the direction of the
guides, will command:

Left (or *right*)—DRESS.

250. This will be executed as prescribed No. 246.

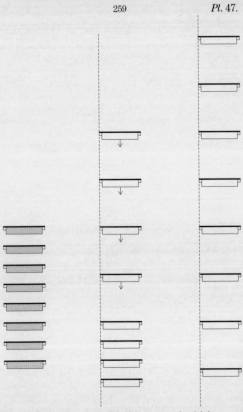

To close the column to half distance on the eighth company (No. 252).

Remarks.

251. The means indicated No. 244 and following, for giving a general direction to the guides of a column, at full distance, will apply only to a column composed of two or, at most, three battalions. If the number be more numerous, its chief will cause the colors and general guides of all the battalions to step out and place themselves on the direction which he may wish to give to the column, as is explained in the evolutions of the line.

Article Fifth.

To close the column to half distance, or in mass.

252. A column by company being at full distance right in front, and at a halt, when the colonel shall wish to cause it to close to half distance, on the leading company, he will command:

> 1. *To half distance, close column.*   2. March (or *double quick*—March).

253. At the first command, the captain of the leading company will caution it to stand fast.

254. At the command *march*, which will be repeated by all the captains, except the captain of the leading company, this company will stand fast, and its chief will align it by the left; the file closers will close one pace upon the rear rank.

255. All the other companies will continue to march, and as each in succession arrives at platoon distance from the one which precedes, its captain will halt it.

256. At the instant that each company halts, its guide will place himself on the direction of the guides who precede, and the captain will align the company by the left; the file closers will close one pace upon the rear rank.

257. No particular attention need be given to the

general direction of the guides before they respectively
halt: it will suffice if each follow in the trace of the one
who precedes him.

258. The colonel, on the side of the guides, will superintend the execution of the movement, observing that the
captains halt their companies exactly at platoon distance
the one from the other.

259. The lieutenant colonel, a few paces in front, will
face to the leading guide and assure the positions of the
following guides as they successively place themselves on
the direction.

260. The major will follow the movement abreast with
the last guide.

261. If the column be in march, the colonel will cause
it to close by the same commands.

262. If the column be marching in double quick time,
at the first command, the captain of the leading company
will command *quick time;* the chiefs of the other companies will caution them to continue their march.

263. At the command *march,* the leading company
will march in quick, and the other companies in double
quick time; and as each arrives at platoon distance from
the preceding one, its chief will cause it to march in quick
time.

264. When the rearmost company shall have gained its
distance, the colonel will command:

Double quick—MARCH.

265. When the colonel shall wish to halt the column
and to cause it to close to half distance at the same time,
he will notify the captain of the leading company of his
intention, who at the command *march* will halt his company and align it by the left.

266. If the column be marching in quick time, and the
colonel should not give the command *double quick,* the
captain of the leading company will halt his company at
the command *march,* and align it by the left. In the case,

where the colonel adds the command *double quick*, the captains of companies will conform to what is prescribed No. 262, and the movement will be executed as indicated No. 263.

To close the column on the eighth, or rearmost, company.

267. The column being at a halt, if, instead of ensuing it too close to half distance on the first company, the colonel should wish to cause it to close on the eighth, he will command:

1. *On the eighth company, to half distance close column.* 2. *Battalion about*—FACE. 3. *Column forward.* 4. *Guide right.* 5. MARCH (or *double quick*—MARCH)

268. At the second command, all the companies, except the eighth, will face about, and their guides will remain in the front rank, now the rear.

269. At the fourth command, all the captains will place themselves two paces outside of their companies on the directing flank.

270. At the command *march*, the eighth company will stand fast, and its captain will align it by the left: the other companies will put themselves in march: and, as each arrives at platoon distance from the one established before it, its captain will halt it and face it to the front. At the moment that each company halts, the left guide, remaining faced to the rear, will place himself promptly on the direction of the guides already established. Immediately after, the captain will align his company by the left, and the file closers will close one pace on the rear rank. If this movement be executed in double quick time, each captain, in turn, will halt, and command: *Such company, right about*—HALT. At this command, the company designated will face to the right about and halt.

271. All the companies being aligned, the colonel will

cause the guides, who stand faced to the rear, to face about.

272. The lieutenant colonel, placing himself behind the rearmost guide, will assure successively the positions of the other guides, as prescribed No. 259; the major will remain abreast with the rearmost company.

273. The column being in march, when the colonel shall wish to close it on the eighth company, he will command:

1. *On the eighth company, to half distance, close column.* 2. *Battalion right about.* 3. MARCH (or *double quick*—MARCH). 4. *Guide right.*

274. At the first command, the captain of the eighth company will caution his company that it will remain faced to the front; the captains of the other companies will caution their companies that they will have to face about.

275. At the command *march*, the captain of the eighth company will halt his company and align it by the left; the file closers will close one pace upon the rear rank.

276. The captains of the other companies, at the same command, will place themselves on the flank of the column; the subdivisions will face about, and, as each arrives at platoon distance from the company immediately preceding it, its chief will face it to the front and halt it as prescribed No. 270. The instant each company halts, the guide on the directing flank, remaining faced to the rear, will quickly place himself on the direction of the guides already established. After which, the captain will align the company by the left, and the file closers will close one pace upon the rear rank.

277. The lieutenant colonel will follow the movement abreast of the first company. The major will place himself a few paces in rear of the guide of the eighth company,

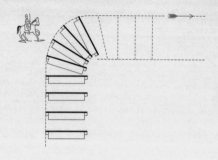

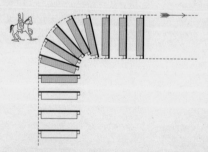

To change direction in column at half distance (No. 287).

and will assure successively the position of the other guides.

Remarks.

278. A column by division at full distance will close to half distance by the same means and the same commands.

279. A column, by company, or by division, being at full or half distance, the colonel will cause it to close in mass by the same means and commands, substituting the indication, *column, close in mass*, for that of *to half distance, close column*. Each chief of subdivision will conform himself to all that has just been prescribed, except that he will not halt his subdivision till its guide shall be at a distance of six paces from the guide of the subdivision next preceding.

280. In a column, left in front, these various movements will be executed on the same principles.

ARTICLE SIXTH.

To march in column at half distance, or closed in mass.

281. A column at half distance or in mass, being at a halt, the colonel will put it in march by the commands prescribed for a column at full distance.

282. The means of direction will also be the same for a column at half distance or in mass, as for a column at full distance, except that the general guides will not step out.

283. A column at half distance or in mass, being in march, when the colonel shall wish to halt it, he will give the commands prescribed for halting a column at full distance, and if, afterwards, he judge it necessary to give a general direction to the guides

of the column, he will employ, to this end, the commands and means indicated No. 244 and following.

284. In columns at half distance or closed in mass, chiefs of subdivision will repeat the commands *march* and *halt*, as in columns at full distance.

285. The colonel will often march the column to the rear, by the means and the commands prescribed Nos. 170 and 171.

286. A column by division or company, whether at full or half distance or closed in mass, at a halt or marching, can be faced to the right or left, and marched off in the new direction.

ARTICLE SEVENTH.

To change direction in column at half distance.

287. A column at half distance, being in march, will change direction by the same commands and according to the same principles as a column at full distance; but, as the distance between the subdivisions is less, the pivot-man in each subdivision will take steps of fourteen inches instead of nine, and of seventeen inches instead of eleven, according to the gait, in order to clear, in time, the wheeling point, and the marching flank will describe the arc of a larger circle, the better to facilitate the movement.

ARTICLE EIGHTH.

To change direction in column closed in mass.

1st. *To change direction in marching.*

288. A column by division, closed in mass, being in march, will change direction by the *front* of subdivisions.

289. Whether the change be made to the reverse, or to the pivot flank, it will always be executed on the principle of wheeling in marching; to this end, the colonel will first

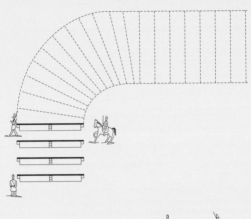

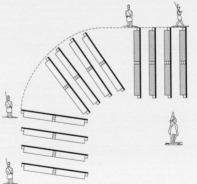

To change direction in column closed in mass while marching (No. 288).

cause the battalion to take the guide on the flank opposite to the intended change of direction, if it be not already on that flank.

290. A column by division, closed in mass, right in front, having to change direction to the right, the colonel, after having caused a marker to be placed at the point where the change ought to commence, will command:

1. *Battalion, right wheel.* 2. MARCH.

291. At the command *march*, the leading division will wheel as if it were part of a column at half distance.

292. The instant that this division commences the wheel, all the others will, at once, conform themselves to its movement; to this end the left guide of each, advancing slightly the left shoulder and lengthening a little the step, will incline to the left, and will observe, at the same time, to gain so much ground to the front that there may constantly be an interval of four paces between his division and that which precedes it; and as soon as he shall cover the preceding guide, he will cease to incline, and then march exactly in his trace.

293. Each division will conform itself to the movement of its guide; the men will feel lightly the elbow towards him and advance a little the left shoulder the instant the movement commences; each file, in inclining, will gain so much the less ground to the front, as the file shall be nearer to the pivot, and the right guide will gain only so much as may be necessary to maintain between his own and the preceding division the same distance which separates their marching flanks.

294. Each chief of division, turning to it, will regulate its march, and see that it remains constantly included between its guides, that its alignment con-

tinues nearly parallel to that of the preceding division, and that the centre bends only a little to the rear.

295. The colonel will superintend the movement, and cause the pivot of the leading division to lengthen or to shorten the step, conforming to the principle established, school of the company, No. 227—if either be necessary to facilitate the movement of the other divisions.

296. The lieutenant colonel, placed near the left guide of the leading division, will regulate his march, and take care, above all, that he does not throw himself *within* the arc he ought to describe.

297. The major, placed in the rear of the guides, will see that the last three conform themselves, each by slight degrees, to the movement of the guide immediately preceding, and that neither inclines too much in the endeavor to cover too promptly the guide in his front; he will rectify any serious fault that may be committed in either of those particulars.

298. The colonel, seeing the wheel nearly ended, will command:

1. *Forward.*   2. March.

299. At the second command, which will be given at the instant the leading division completes its wheel, it will resume the direct march; the other divisions will conform themselves to this movement; and if any guide find himself not covering his immediate leader, he will, by slight degrees, bring himself on the trace of that guide, by advancing the right shoulder.

300. If the column, right in front, has to change direction to the left, the colonel will first cause it to take the guide to the right, and then command:

1. *Battalion, left wheel.*   2. March.

301. At the command *march*, the battalion will change

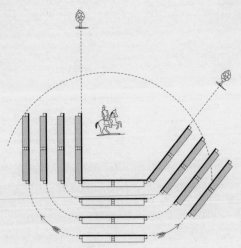

To change direction from a halt (No. 306).

direction to the left, according to the principles just prescribed, and by inverse means.

302. When the battalion shall have resumed the direct
march, the colonel will change the guide to the left, on
seeing the last three guides nearly in the direction of the
one in front.

303. The foregoing changes of direction will be executed according to the same principles in a column, left in
front.

304. A column by company, closed in mass, will
change direction in marching, by the commands and
means indicated for a column by division.

305. The guide who is the pivot of the particular
wheel ought to maintain himself at his usual distance
of six paces from the guide who precedes him; if this
distance be not exactly preserved, the divisions would
necessarily become confounded, which must be carefully
avoided.

2d. To change direction from a halt.

306. A column by company, or by division, closed in
mass, being at a halt, when the colonel shall wish to give
it a new direction, and in which it is to remain, he will
cause it to execute this movement by the flanks of subdivisions, in the following manner:

307. The battalion having the right in front, when the
colonel shall wish to cause it to change direction by the
right flank, he will indicate to the lieutenant colonel the
point of direction to the right; this officer will immediately establish, on the new direction, two markers, distant
from each other a little less than the front of the first subdivision, the first marker in front of the right file of this
subdivision; which being executed, he will command:

1. *Change direction by the right flank.* 2. *Battalion,
right*—FACE. 3. MARCH (or *double quick*—MARCH).

308. At the second command, the column will face to

the right, and each chief of subdivision will place himself by the side of his right guide.

309. At the command *march*, all the subdivisions will step off together; the right guide of the leading one will direct himself from the first step, parallelly to the markers placed in advance on the new direction; the chief of the subdivision will not follow the movement, but see it file past, and as soon as the left guide shall have passed, he will command:

> 1. *First company* (or *first division*).   2. HALT.
> 3. FRONT.   4. *Left*—DRESS.

310. At the fourth command, the subdivision will place itself against the two markers, and be promptly aligned by its chief.

311. The right guide of each of the following subdivisions will conform himself to the direction of the right guide of the subdivision preceding his own in the column, so as to enter on the new direction parallelly to that subdivision, and at the distance of four paces from its rear rank.

312. Each chief of subdivision will halt in his own person, on arriving opposite to the left guides already placed on the new direction, see his subdivision file past, and conform himself, in halting and aligning it, to what is prescribed No. 309.

313. If the change of direction be by the left flank, the colonel will cause markers to be established as before, the first in front of the left file of the leading subdivision, and then give the same commands, substituting the indication *left* for *right*.

314. At the second command, all the subdivisions will face to the left, and each chief will place himself by the side of his left guide.

315. At the command *march*, all the subdivisions will step off together, each conducted by its chief.

316. The guide of the leading subdivision will direct himself, from the first step, parallelly to the markers; the

subdivision will be conducted by its chief, and as soon as its left guide shall have passed the second marker, it will be halted and aligned as prescribed above; and so of each of the following subdivisions.

317. The colonel will hold himself on the designated flank, to see that each subdivision enters the new direction parallelly to the leading one, and at the prescribed distance from that which precedes.

318. The lieutenant colonel will place himself in front of, and facing to, the guide of the leading subdivision, and will assure the positions of the following guides, as they successively arrive on the new direction.

319. The major will follow the movement abreast with the last subdivision.

320. In order that this movement may be executed with facility and precision, it is necessary that the leading subdivision should entirely unmask the column; for example, the movement being made by the right flank, it is necessary, before halting the leading subdivision, that its left guide shall, at least, have arrived at the place previously occupied by its right guide, in order that each following subdivision which has to pass over a space at least equal to its front to put itself in the new direction, and whose left ought to pass the point at which the right had rested, may, at the command *halt*, find itself, in its whole front, parallel to the leading subdivision.

321. By this method there is no direction that may not be given to a column in mass.

ARTICLE NINTH.

Being in column at half distance, or closed in mass, to take distances.

322. A column at half distance will take full distances *by* the head of the column when it has to prolong itself on

the line of battle. If, on the contrary, it has to form itself in line of battle on the ground it occupies, it will take distances *on* the leading or *on* the rearmost subdivision, according as the one or the other may find itself at the point where the right or left of the battalion ought to rest in line of battle.

1st. To take distances by the head of the column.

323. The column being by company at half distance and at a halt, when the colonel shall wish to cause it to take full distances by the head, he will command:

By the head of column, take wheeling distance.

324. At this command, the captain of the leading company will put it in march; to this end, he will command:

1. *First company, forward.*   2. *Guide left.*   3. MARCH
        (or *double quick*—MARCH).

325. When the second shall have nearly its wheeling distance, its captain will command:

1. *Second company, forward.*   2. *Guide left.*   3. MARCH
        (or *double quick*—MARCH).

326. At the command *march*, which will be pronounced at the instant that this company shall have its wheeling distance, it will step off smartly, taking the step from the preceding company. Each of the other companies will successively execute what has just been prescribed for the second.

327. The colonel will see that each company puts itself in march at the instant it has its distance.

328. The lieutenant colonel will hold himself at the head of the column, and direct the march of the leading guide.

329. The major will hold himself abreast with the rearmost guide.

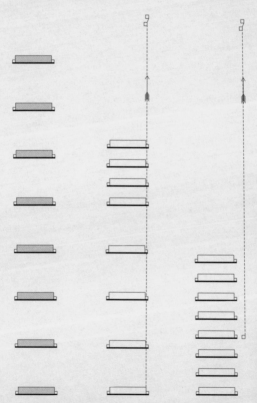

To take wheeling distance on eighth company (No. 334).

330. If the column, instead of being at a halt, be in march, the colonel will give the same commands, and add:

MARCH (or *double quick*—MARCH).

331. If the column be marching in quick time, at the command *march*, the captain of the leading company will cause *double quick time* to be taken; which will also be done by the other captains as the companies successively attain their proper wheeling distance.

332. If the column be marching in *double quick time*, the leading company will continue to march at the same gait. The captains of the other companies will cause *quick time* to be taken, and as each company gains its proper distance, its captain will cause it to retake the *double quick step*.

2d. To take distances on the rear of the column.

333. If the colonel wish to take distances on the rear-most company, he will establish two markers on the direction he shall wish to give to the line of battle, the first opposite to the rearmost company, the second marker towards the head of the column, at company distance from the first, and both facing to the rear; at the same time, the right general guide, on an intimation from the lieutenant colonel, will move rapidly a little beyond the point to which the head of the column will extend, and place himself correctly on the prolongation of the two markers. These dispositions being made, the colonel will command:

1. *On the eighth company, take wheeling distance.* 2. *Column, forward.* 3. *Guide left.* 4. MARCH (or *double quick*—MARCH).

334. At the third command, the captains will place themselves two paces outside of the directing flank; the

captain of the eighth company will caution it to stand fast.

335. At the command *march*, repeated by all the captains, except the captain of the eighth company, this latter company will stand fast; its chief will align it by the left on the first marker, who is opposite to this company, and place himself before its centre, after commanding: FRONT. At this command, the marker will retire, and the left guide will take his place.

336. All the other companies will put themselves in march, the guide of the leading one directing himself a little within the right general guide; when the seventh company has arrived opposite the second marker, its captain will halt, and align it on this marker, in the manner prescribed for the eighth company.

337. When the captain of the sixth company shall see that there is, between his company and the seventh, the necessary space for wheeling into line, he will halt his company; the guide facing to the rear will place himself promptly on the direction, and the moment he shall be assured in his position, the captain will align the company by the left, and then place himself two paces before the centre; the other companies will successively conform themselves to what has just been prescribed for the sixth company.

338. The colonel will follow the movement, and see that each company halts at the prescribed distance; he will promptly remedy any fault that may be committed, and, as soon as all the companies shall be aligned, he will cause the guides, who are faced to the rear, to face about.

339. The lieutenant colonel will successively assure the left guides on the direction, placing himself in their rear, as they arrive.

340. The major will hold himself at the head of the column, and will direct the march of the leading guide.

3d. To take distances on the head of the column.

341. The colonel, wishing to take distances on the leading company, will establish two markers in the manner just prescribed, one abreast with this company, and the other at company distance in rear of the first, but both facing to the front: the left general guide, on an intimation from the lieutenant colonel, will move rapidly to the rear and place himself correctly on the prolongation of the two markers, a little beyond the point to which the rear of the column will extend: these dispositions being made, the colonel will command:

1. *On the first company, take wheeling distance.* 2. *Battalion, about*—FACE. 3. *Column, forward.* 4. *Guide right.* 5. MARCH (or *double quick*—MARCH).

342. At the second command, all the companies, except the one designated, will face about, the guides remaining in the front rank, now become the rear.

343. At the fourth command, the captains will place themselves outside of their guides.

344. At the command *march*, the captain of the designated company will align it, as prescribed No. 335, on the marker placed by its side.

345. The remaining companies will put themselves in march: the guide of the rearmost one will direct himself a little within the left general guide; when the second company shall have arrived opposite the second marker, its captain will face it about, conforming to what is prescribed No. 270, and align it, as has just been prescribed for the first company.

346. The instant that the third company shall have its wheeling distance, its captain will halt it, facing it about, as prescribed No. 270, and align it by the left; the captains of the remaining companies will each, in succession, con-

form himself to what has just been prescribed for the captain of the third.

347. The colonel will follow the movement, as indicated No. 338; the lieutenant colonel and major will conform themselves to what is prescribed Nos. 339 and 340.

348. These various movements will be executed according to the same principles in a column with the left in front.

349. They will be executed in like manner in a column closed in mass; but, if it be the wish of the colonel to open out the column to half, instead of full distance, he will substitute, in the commands, the indication *half*, for that of *wheeling* distance.

350. In a column by division, distances will be taken according to the same principles.

ARTICLE TENTH.

Countermarch of a column at full or half distance.

351. In a column at full or half distance, the countermarch will be executed by the means indicated, school of the company; to this end, the colonel will command:

1. *Countermarch.* 2. *Battalion, right* (or *left*)—FACE. 3. *By file left* (or *right*). 4. MARCH (or *double quick*—MARCH).

To countermarch a column closed in mass.

352. If the column be closed in mass, the countermarch will be executed by the commands and means subjoined.

353. The column being supposed formed by division, right in front, the colonel will command:

1. *Countermarch.* 2. *Battalion, right and left*—FACE. 3. *By file left and right.* 4. MARCH (or *double quick*—MARCH).

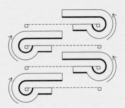

To countermarch a column closed in mass (No. 352).

354. At the first command, the chiefs of the odd numbered divisions will caution them to face to the right, and the chiefs of the others to face to the left.

355. At the second command, the odd divisions will face to the right, and the even to the left; the right and left guides of all the divisions will face about; the chiefs of odd divisions will hasten to their right and cause two files to break to the rear, and each chief place himself on the left of the leading front rank man of his division; the chiefs of even divisions will hasten to their left, and cause two files to break to the rear, and each chief place himself on the right of his leading front rank man.

356. At the command *march*, all the divisions, each conducted by its chief, will step off smartly, the guides standing fast; each odd division will wheel by file to the left around its right guide; each even division will wheel by file to the right around its left guide, each division so directing its march as to arrive behind its opposite guide, and when its head shall be up with this guide, the chief will halt the division, and cause it to face to the front.

357. Each division, on facing to the front, will be aligned by its chief by the right: to this end, the chiefs of the even divisions will move rapidly to the right of their respective divisions.

358. The divisions being aligned, each chief will command, FRONT; at this, the guides will shift to their proper flanks.

359. In a column with the left in front, the countermarch will be executed by the same commands and means; but all the divisions will be aligned by the left: to this end, the chiefs of the odd divisions will hasten to the left of their respective divisions as soon as the latter shall have been faced to the front.

360. The colonel, placed on the directing flank, will superintend the general movement.

361. The countermarch being ended, the lieutenant

colonel will always place himself abreast with the leading, and the major abreast with the rearmost division.

362. In a column by company, closed in mass, the countermarch will be executed by the same means and commands, applying to companies what is prescribed for divisions.

363. The countermarch will always take place from a halt, whether the column be closed in mass, or at full, or half distance.

Article Eleventh.

Being in column by company, closed in mass, to form divisions.

364. The column being closed in mass, right in front, and at a halt, when the colonel shall wish to form divisions, he will command:

1. *Form divisions.* 2. *Left companies, left*—Face. 3. March (or *double quick*—March).

365. At the first command, the captains of the left companies will caution them to face to the left.

366. At the second command, the left companies will face to the left, and their captains will place themselves by the side of their respective left guides.

367. The right companies, and their captains, will stand fast; but the right and left guides of each of these companies will place themselves respectively before the right and left files of the company, both guides facing to the right, and each resting his right arm gently against the breast of the front rank man of the file, in order to mark the direction.

368. At the command *march*, the left companies only will put themselves in march, their captains standing fast; as each shall see that his company, filing past, has nearly cleared the column, he will command:

Being in column by company, closed in mass, to form divisions (No. 364).

1. *Such company.*   2. HALT.   3. FRONT.

369. The first command will be given when the company shall yet have four paces to march; the second at the instant it shall have cleared its right company; and the third immediately after the second.

370. The company having faced to the front, the files, if there be intervals between them, will promptly incline to the right; the captain will place himself on the left of the right company of the division, and align himself correctly on the front rank of that company.

371. The left guide will place himself at the same time before one of the three left files of his company, face to the right, and cover correctly the guides of the right company; the moment his captain sees him established on the direction, he will command:

Right—DRESS.

372. At this, the left company will dress forward on the alignment of the right company; the front rank man, who may find himself opposite to the left guide, will, without preceding his rank, rest lightly his breast against the right arm of this guide; the captain of the left company will direct its alignment on this man, and, the alignment being assured, he will command, FRONT; but not quit his position.

373. The colonel seeing the divisions formed, will command:

Guides—POSTS.

374. At this, the guides who have marked the fronts of divisions will return to their places in column, the left guide of each right company passing through the interval of the centre of the division, and the captains will place themselves as prescribed No. 75.

375. The colonel, from the directing flank of the

column, will superintend the general execution of the movement.

376. If the column be in march, instead of at a halt, when the colonel shall wish to form divisions, he will command:

1. *Form divisions.*   2. *Left companies, by the left flank.*
3. MARCH (or *double quick*—MARCH).

377. At the first command, the captains of the right companies will command, *Mark time*, the captains of the left companies will caution their companies to *face by the left flank.*

378. At the third command, the right companies will mark time, the left companies will face to the left; the captains of the left companies will each see his company file past him, and when it has cleared the column, will command:

Such company by the right flank—MARCH.

As soon as the divisions are formed, the colonel will command:

4. *Forward.*   5. MARCH.

379. At the fifth command, the column will resume the gait at which it was marching previous to the commencement of the movement. The guides of each division will remain on the right and left of their respective companies; the left guide of the right company will pass into the line of file closers, before the two companies are united; the right guide of the left company will step into the rear rank. The captains will place themselves as prescribed No. 75.

Being in column at full or half distance, to form divisions.

380. If the column be at a halt, and, instead of being closed in mass, is at full or half distance, divisions will be

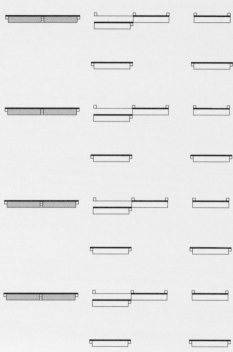

Being in column at full or half distance, to form divisions
(No. 380).

formed in the same manner; but the captains of the left companies, if the movement be made in quick time, after commanding FRONT, will each place himself before the centre of his company, and command, 1. *Such company, forward.* 2. *Guide right.* 3. MARCH. If the movement be made in double quick time, each will command, as soon as his company has cleared the column:

1. *Such company by the right flank.* 2. MARCH.

381. The right guide of each left company will so direct his march as to arrive by the side of the man on the left of the right company. The left company being nearly up with the rear rank of the right company, its captain will halt it, and the movement will be finished as prescribed No. 371 and following.

382. If the left be in front, the movement will be executed by inverse means: the right companies will conform themselves to what is prescribed above for the left companies: and the two guides, placed respectively before the right and left files of each left company, will face to the left. At the command, *Guides posts,* given by the colonel, the guides, who have marked the front of divisions, and the captains, will quickly retake their places in the column.

383. If the column be marching at full distance, the divisions will be formed as prescribed No. 196. If it be marching at half distance, the formation will take place by the commands and according to the principles indicated No. 376; if the column be marching in double quick time, the companies which should mark time will march in quick time by the command of their captains.

Remarks on the formation of divisions from a halt.

384. As this movement may be considered as the element of deployments, it ought to be executed with the utmost accuracy.

385. If companies marching by the flank do not preserve exactly their distances, there will be openings
between the files at the instant of facing to the front.

386. If captains halt their companies too early, they
will want space, and the files which have not cleared the
flanks of the standing companies will not be able to dress
into line without pushing their ranks laterally.

387. If on the contrary the companies be halted
too late, it will be necessary for them to incline to the
right or left in dressing; and in deployments, either
of these faults would lead to error in the following
companies.

388. As often as a guide shall have to step out to
place himself before his subdivision in order to mark
the direction, he will be particularly careful to place
himself so as to be opposite to one of the three outer
files of the subdivision when they shall be aligned:
if he take too much distance, and neither of those
files finds itself against him, the chiefs of the subdivision
will have no assured point on which to direct the
alignment.

PART FOURTH.

Different modes of passing from the order in column to the order in battle.

ARTICLE FIRST.

Manner of determining the line of battle.

389. The line of battle may be marked or determined
in three different manners: 1*st*, by placing two markers
eighty or a hundred paces apart, on the direction it is
wished to give to the line; 2*d*, by placing a marker at the
point at which it may be intended to rest a flank, and then
choosing a second point towards, or beyond the opposite

Manner of determining the line of battle (No. 389).

flank, and there posting a second marker distant from each other a little less than the leading subdivision; 3d, by choosing at first the points of direction for the flanks, and then determining, by intermediate points, the straight line between those selected points, both of which may sometimes be beyond reach.

ARTICLE SECOND.

Different modes of passing from column at full distance into line of battle.

1. To the left (or right)
2. On the right (or left)
3. Forward,
4. Faced to the rear,
} into line of battle.

1st. Column at full distance, right in front, to the left into line of battle.

390. A column, right in front, being at a halt, when the colonel shall wish to form it to the left into line, he will assure the positions of the guides by the means previously indicated, and then command:

1. *Left into line, wheel.*   2. MARCH (or *double quick—* MARCH).

391. At the first command, the right guide of the leading company will hasten to place himself on the direction of the left guides of the column, face to them, and place himself so as to be opposite to one of the three right files of his company, when they shall be in line: he will be assured in this position by the lieutenant colonel.

392. At the command *march*, briskly repeated by the captains, the left front rank man of each company will face to the left, and rest his breast lightly against the right arm of his guide; the companies will wheel to the left on the principle of wheeling from a halt, conforming

themselves to what is prescribed, school of the company No. 239: each captain will turn to his company, to observe the execution of the movement, and when the right of the company shall arrive at three paces from the line of battle, he will command:

1. *Such company.*   2. HALT.

393. The company being halted, the captain will place himself on the line by the side of the left front rank man of the company next on the right, align himself correctly, and command:

3. *Right*—DRESS.

394. At this command, the company will dress up between the captain and the front rank man on its left, the captain directing the alignment on that man; the front rank man on the right of the right company, who finds himself opposite to its right guide, will lightly rest his breast against the left arm of this guide.

395. Each captain, having aligned his company, will command, FRONT, and the colonel will add:

Guides—POSTS.

396. At this command, the guides will return to their places in line of battle, each passing through the nearest captain's interval; to permit him to pass, the captain will momentarily step before the first file of his company, and the covering sergeant behind the same file. *This rule is general for all the formations into line of battle.*

397. When companies form line of battle, file closers will always place themselves exactly two paces from the rear rank, which will sufficiently assure their alignment.

398. The battalion being correctly aligned, the colonel, lieutenant colonel, and major, as well as the adjutant and

sergeant major, will return to their respective places in line of battle. *This rule is general for all the formations into line of battle;* nevertheless, the battalion being in the school of elementary instruction, the colonel will go to any point he may deem necessary.

399. A column, with the left in front, will form itself *to the right into line of battle*, according to the same principles; the left guide of the left company will place himself, at the first command, on the direction of the right guides, in a manner corresponding to what is prescribed, No. 391, for the right guide of the right company.

400. At the command *guides posts*, the captains will take their places in line of battle as well as the guides. *This rule is general for all formations into line of battle in which the companies are aligned by the left.*

401. A column by division may form itself into line of battle by the same commands and means, but observing what follows: if the right be in front, at the command *halt*, given by the chiefs of division, the left guide of each right company will place himself on the alignment opposite to one of the three files on the left of his company; the left guide of the first company will be assured on the direction by the lieutenant colonel; the left guides of the other right companies will align themselves correctly on the division guides; to this end, the division guides (on the alignment) will invert, and hold their pieces up perpendicularly before the centre of their bodies, at the command *left into line, wheel.* If the column by division be with the left in front, the right guides of left companies will conform themselves to what has just been prescribed for the left guides of right companies, and place themselves on the line opposite to one of the three right files of their respective companies.

402. A column in march will be formed into line, without halting, by the same commands and means. At the

command *march*, the guides will halt in their places, and the lieutenant colonel will promptly rectify their positions.

403. If, in forming the column into line, the colonel should wish to move forward, without halting, he will command:

> 1. *By companies left wheel.*   2. MARCH (or *double quick*—MARCH).

404. At the command *march*, briskly repeated by the captains, each company will wheel to the left on a fixed pivot, as prescribed in the school of the company, No. 261; the left guides will step back into the rank of file closers before the wheel is completed; and, when the right of the companies shall arrive near the line, the colonel will command:

> 3. *Forward.*   4. MARCH.   5. *Guide centre.*

405. At the fourth command, given at the instant the wheel is completed, the companies will march directly to the front. At the fifth command, the color and the general guides will move rapidly six paces to the front. The colonel will assure the direction of the color; the captains of companies and the men will, at once, conform themselves to the principles of the march in line of battle, to be hereinafter indicated, No. 587 and following.

406. The same principles are applicable to a column left in front.

By inversion to the right (or left) into line of battle.

407. When a column, right in front, shall be under the necessity of forming itself into line faced to the reverse flank, and the colonel shall wish to execute this formation by the shortest movement, he will command:

> 1. *By inversion, right into line, wheel.*   2. *Battalion, guide right.*

408. At the first command, the lieutenant colonel will place himself in front, and facing to the right guide of the leading subdivision; at the second command, he will rectify, as promptly as possible, the direction of the right guides of the column; the captain of the odd company, if there be one, and the column be by division, will promptly bring the right of his company on the direction, and at company distance from the division neat in front; the left guide of the leading subdivision will place himself on the direction of the right guides, and will be assured in his position by the lieutenant colonel; which being executed, the colonel will command:

3. MARCH (or *double quick*—MARCH).

409. At this, the right front rank man of each subdivision will face to the right, rest his breast lightly against the left arm of his guide, and the battalion will form itself to the right into line of battle, according to the principles prescribed; which being executed, the colonel will command:

Guides—POSTS.

410. If the column be with the left in front, it will form itself, by inversion, to the left into line, according to the same principles.

411. If the colonel should wish the battalion, when formed into line of battle, to be moved forward, the movement will be executed by the commands, and according to the principles, indicated in No. 403; always preceding the command, *by companies right* (or *left*) *wheel*, by the command, *by inversion*.

Successive Formations.

412. Under the denomination of successive formations are included all those formations where the several subdivisions of a column arrive one after another on the line of battle; such are formations on the right, or left, forward

and faced to the rear into line of battle, as well as deployments of columns in mass.

413. The successive formations which may be ordered when the column is marching, and is to continue marching, will be executed by a combination of the two gaits, *quick* and *double quick* time.

2d. *Column at full distance, on the right (or on the left), into line of battle.*

414. A column by company, at full distance and right in front, having to form itself on the right into line of battle, the colonel will indicate to the lieutenant colonel, a little in advance, the point of *appui*, or rest, for the right, as well as the point of direction to the left; the lieutenant colonel will hasten with two markers, and establish them in the following manner on the direction indicated.

415. The first marker will be placed at the point of *appui* for the right front rank man of the leading company; the second will indicate the point where one of the three left files of the same company will rest when in line; they will be placed so as to present the right shoulder to the battalion when formed.

416. These dispositions being made, the colonel will command:

1. *On the right, into line.*   2. *Battalion, guide right.*

417. At the second command, the right will become the directing flank, and the touch of the elbow will be to that side; the right guide of the leading company will march straight forward until up with the turning point, and each following guide will march in the trace of the one immediately preceding.

418. The leading company being nearly up with the first marker, its captain will command: 1. *Right turn*, and when the company is precisely up with this marker, he will add: 2. MARCH.

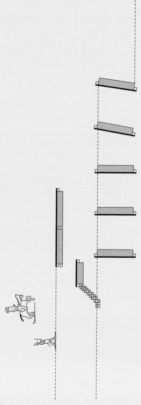

To form on the right into line (No. 417).

419. At the command *march*, the company will turn to the right; the right guide will so direct himself as to bring the man next to him opposite to the right marker, and when at three paces from him, the captain will command:

1. *First company*; 2. HALT.

420. At the second command, the company will halt; the files, not yet in line, will form promptly; the left guide will retire as a file closer; and the captain will then command:

3. *Right*—DRESS.

421. At this command, the company will align itself; the two men who find themselves opposite to the two markers will each lightly rest his breast against the right arm of his marker; the captain, passing to the right of the front rank, will direct the alignment, on these two men. *These rules are general for all successive formations.*

422. The second company will continue to march straight forward; when arrived opposite to the left flank of the preceding company, it will turn to the right, and be formed on the line of battle, as has just been prescribed; the right guide will direct himself so as to come upon that line by the side of the man on the left of the first company.

423. At the distance of three paces from the line of battle, the company will be halted by its captain, who will place himself briskly by the side of the man on the left of the preceding company, and align himself correctly on its front rank.

424. The left guide will, at the same time, place himself before one of the three left files of his company, and, facing to the right, he will place himself accurately on the direction of the two markers of the preceding company.

425. The captain will then command:

Right—DRESS.

426. At this command, the second company will dress forward on the line; the captain will direct its alignment on the front rank man who has rested his breast against the left guide of the company.

427. The following companies will thus come successively to form themselves on the line of battle, each conforming itself to what has just been prescribed for the one next to the right; and when they shall all be established, the colonel will command:

Guides—POSTS.

428. At this command, the guides will take their places in line of battle, and the markers placed before the right company will retire.

429. If the column be marching in quick time, and the colonel should wish to cause the movement to be executed in double quick time, he will add the command: *Double quick*—MARCH. At the command *march*, all the companies will take the double quick step, and the movement will be executed as prescribed No. 417 and following.

430. The colonel will follow up the formation, passing along the front, and being always opposite to the company about to turn: it is thus that he will be the better able to see and to correct the error that would result from a command given too soon or too late to the preceding company.

431. The lieutenant colonel will, with the greatest care, assure the direction of the guides; to this end, the instant that the markers are established for the leading company, he will move a little beyond the point at which the left of the next company will rest, establish himself correctly on the prolongation of the two markers, and assure the guide of the second company on this direction; this guide being assured, the lieutenant colonel will place

himself farther to the rear, in order to assure, in like manner, the guide of the third company, and so on, successively, to the left of the battalion. In assuring the guides in their positions on the line of battle, he will take care to let them first place themselves, and confine himself to rectifying their positions if they do not cover accurately, and at the proper distance, the preceding guides or markers. *This rule is general, for all successive formations.*

432. A column, left in front, will form itself on the left into line of battle according to the same principles: the captains will go to the left of their respective companies to align them, and shift afterwards to their proper flanks, as prescribed No. 400.

Remarks on the formation on the right, or left, into line of battle.

433. In order that this movement may be executed with regularity, it is necessary to establish the line of battle so that the guide of each company, after turning, may have at least ten steps to take, in order to come upon that line.

434. In the first exercises, the line of battle will be established on a direction parallel to that of the column; but, when the captains and guides shall comprehend the mechanism of the movement, the colonel will generally choose oblique directions, in order to habituate the battalion to form itself in any direction.

435. When the direction of the line of battle forms a sensible angle with that of the march of the column, the colonel, before beginning the movement, will give the head of the column a new direction parallel to that line: to this end, he will indicate to the guide of the leading company a point in advance, on which this guide will immediately direct himself, and the company will conform itself to the direction of its guide, at the command, or on a mere caution, of the captain, according as the change of

direction may require; each following company will make
the same movement, on the same ground, as it shall successively arrive. By this means the guides of all the companies in the column will have, after turning, nearly the
same number of paces to take in order to come upon the
line of battle.

436. Every captain will always observe, in placing himself on that line, not to give the command *dress*, until
after the guide of his company shall have been assured on
the direction by the lieutenant colonel. *This rule is general for all successive formations.*

437. Each captain will cause his company to support
arms, the instant that the captain, who follows him, shall
have commanded *front*. *This rule is general for all successive formations.*

438. When, in the execution of this movement, the
colonel shall wish to commence firing, he will give the
order to that effect to the captain whose company is the
first in line of battle; this captain will immediately place
himself behind the centre of his company, and as soon as
the next captain shall have commanded *front*, he will
commence the fire by file, by the commands prescribed,
school of the company. At the command *fire by file*, the
marker at the outer file of this first company will retire,
and the other will place himself against the nearest man
of the next company. The captain of the latter will
commence firing as soon as the captain of the third company, in line, shall have commanded *front*; the marker
before the nearest file of the second company, in line,
will now retire, and the guide before the opposite flank
will place himself before the nearest file of the third company, in line, and so on, in continuation, to the last
company on the left or right of the battalion, according as
the formation may have commenced with the right or left
in front.

439. In all the successive formations, the same

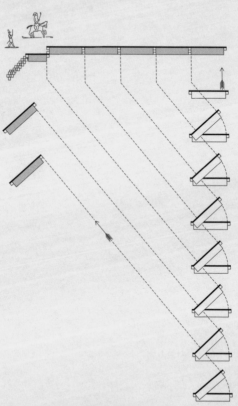

Forward into line, &c. (No. 441).

principles will be observed for the execution of the fire by file. This fire will always be executed by the command of each captain of company.

3d. Column at full distance, forward into line of battle.

440. A column being by company, at full distance, right in front, and at a halt, when the colonel shall wish to form it forward into line, he will conform to what is prescribed Nos. 414 and 415, and then command:

1. *Forward into line.*   2. *By company, left half wheel.*
3. MARCH (or *double quick*—MARCH).

441. At the first command, the captain of the leading company will add—*guide right*, put the company in march, halt it three paces from the markers, and align it against the latter by the right.

442. At the command *march*, all the other companies will wheel to the left on fixed pivots; and, at the instant the colonel shall judge, according to the direction of the line of battle, that the companies have sufficiently wheeled, he will command:

4. *Forward.*   5. MARCH.   6. *Guide right.*

443. At the fifth command, the companies, ceasing to wheel, will march straight forward; and at the sixth, the men will touch elbows towards the right. The right guide of the second company, who is nearest to the line of battle, will march straight forward; each succeeding right guide will follow the file immediately before him at the cessation of the wheel.

444. The second company having arrived opposite to the left file of the first, its captain will cause it to turn to the right, in order to approach the line of battle; and when its right guide shall be at three paces from that line, the captain will command:

1. *Second company.* 2. HALT.

445. At the second command, the company will halt; the files not yet in line with the guide will come into it promptly, the left guide will place himself on the line of battle, so as to be opposite to one of the three files on the left of the company; and, as soon as he is assured on the direction by the lieutenant colonel, the captain, having placed himself accurately on the line of battle, will command:

3. *Right*—DRESS.

446. At the instant that the guide of the second company begins to turn to the right, the guide of the third, ceasing to follow the file immediately before him, will march straight forward; and, when he shall arrive opposite to the left of the second, his captain will cause the company to turn to the right, in order to approach the line of battle, halt it at three paces from that line, and align it by the right, as prescribed for the second company.

447. Each following company will execute what has just been prescribed for the third, as the preceding company shall turn to the right, in order to approach the line of battle.

448. The formation ended, the colonel will command:

Guides—POSTS.

449. The colonel and lieutenant colonel will observe, in this formation, what is prescribed for them on the right into line.

450. A column left in front will form itself forward into line of battle according to the same principles and by inverse means.

451. When a column by company at full distance, right in front, and in march, shall arrive behind the right of the line on which it is to form into battle, the colonel and

lieutenant colonel will conform themselves to what is pre-scribed Nos. 414 and 415.

452. The head of the column having arrived at com-pany distance from the two markers established on the line, the colonel will command:

1. *Forward into line.*   2. *By company, lift half wheel.*
3. MARCH (or *double quick*—MARCH).

453. At the first command, the captain of the first company will command, *Guide right*, and caution it to march directly to the front; the captains of the other com-panies will caution them to wheel to the left.

454. At the command *march*, briskly repeated by the captains, the first company will continue to march to the front, taking the touch of elbows to the right. Its chief will halt it at three paces from the markers, and align it by the right. The other companies will wheel to the left on fixed pivots, and at the instant the colonel shall judge that they have wheeled sufficiently, he will command:

4. *Forward.*   5. MARCH.   6. *Guide right.*

455. At the fifth command, the companies will cease to wheel, and move forward. At the sixth, they will take the touch of elbows to the right. The movement will be executed as previously explained.

456. If the colonel should wish to form the column forward into line, and to continue to march in this order, he will not cause markers to be established; the move-ment will be executed in *double quick time*, by the same commands and means, but with the following modifications.

457. At the first command, the captain of the first company will add *quick time* after the command *guide right*. At the second command, the first company will con-tinue to march in quick time, and will take the touch of elbows to the right; its chief will immediately place him-self on its right, and, to assure the march, will take points

of direction to the front. The captain of the second company will cause his company to take the same gait as soon as it shall arrive on a line with the first, and will also move to the right of his company; the captains of the third and fourth companies will execute successively what has just been prescribed for the second. The companies will preserve the touch of elbows to the right until the command, *guide centre.*

458. When the color-company shall have entered the line, the colonel will command, *guide centre.* At this command, the color-bearer and the right general guide will move rapidly six paces in advance of the line. The colonel will assure the direction of the color-bearer. The lieutenant colonel and the right companies will immediately conform themselves to the principles of the march in line of battle. The left companies and the left general guide, as they arrive on the line, will also conform to the same principles. If the column be marching in double quick time, when the last company shall have arrived on the line, the colonel will cause the double quick to be resumed.

459. It is not necessary that the movement be entirely completed before halting the battalion. As soon as the part of the battalion already formed shall have arrived on the line of battle, the colonel will halt the battalion; the companies not in line will each complete the movement.

Remarks on the formation forward, into line of battle.

460. The precision of this movement depends on the direction the companies have at the moment the colonel commands, *Forward*—MARCH. The colonel will judge nicely the point of time for giving this command, observing that, if the direction of the line of battle form with that of the column a right or nearly a right angle, the companies ought to wheel about the eighth of the circle, and that

the more acute the angle formed by the two directions, so much the more the companies ought to wheel before marching straight forward.

461. It is important that each company in marching towards the line of battle should turn exactly opposite the point where its captain ought to place himself on that line; if a company turn too soon, it will find itself masked, in part, by that which preceded it on the line of battle, and be obliged to unmask itself by the oblique step, if it turn too late, it will leave an interval between itself and the preceding company to be regained in like manner. In either case, the next company will be led into error, and the fault propagated to the opposite flank of the battalion.

462. The guide of each company ought so to regulate himself in turning, as to bring his company to the halting point parallelly with the line of battle.

463. If the angle formed by the line of battle and the primitive direction of the column be so acute, that the companies, on arriving opposite to their respective places on the line of battle, find themselves nearly parallel to it, the captains will not give the command, *right* (or *left*) *turn*, but each halt his company, place himself on the line, and command:

Right (or *left*)—DRESS.

464. If, on the contrary, the angle formed by the line of battle and the primitive direction of the column be much greater than a right angle, the formation should be executed, not by the movement *forward into line of battle*, but by that of *on the right* (or *left*) *into line of battle*, and according to the principles prescribed for this formation.

465. If a company encounter an obstacle sufficient to prevent it from marching by the front, it will *right* (or *left*) *face* in marching, by the commands and means indicated

in the school of the company, Nos. 314 and 315. The guide
will continue to follow the same file behind which he was
marching, and will maintain exactly the same distance
from the company immediately preceding his own. The
obstacle being passed, the company will be formed into
line by the command of its captain.

*4th. Column at full distance, faced to the rear, into line
of battle.*

466. A column being by company, at full distance,
right in front, and at a halt, when the colonel shall wish to
form it into line faced to the rear, he and the lieutenant
colonel will conform themselves to what is prescribed
Nos. 414 and 415, and the colonel will then command:

1. *Into line, faced to the rear.* 2. *Battalion, right*—FACE.
    3. MARCH (or *double quick*—MARCH).

467. At the first command, the captain of the
leading company will cause it to face to the right, and put
it in march, causing it to wheel by file to the left, and
direct its march towards the line of battle, which it will
pass in rear of the left marker; the first file having passed
three paces beyond the line, the company will wheel again
by file to the left, in order to place itself in rear of the
two markers; being in this position, its captain will halt it,
face it to the front, and align it by the right against
the markers.

468. At the second command, all the other companies
will face to the right, each captain placing himself by the
side of his right guide.

469. At the command *march*, the companies will
put themselves in movement; the left guide of the second,
who is nearest to the line of battle, will hasten in
advance to mark that line; he will place himself on it as
prescribed above for successive formations, and thus indicate to his captain the point at which he ought to pass

Pl. 58.

Into line faced to the rear etc. (No. 467).

the line of battle, by three paces, in order to wheel by file to the left, and then to direct his company parallelly to that line.

470. As soon as the first file of this company shall have arrived near the left file of the preceding one already on the line of battle, its captain will command:

1. *Second company.* 2. HALT. 3. FRONT.
4. *Right—*DRESS.

471. The first command will be given when the company shall yet have four paces to take to reach the halting point.

472. At the second command, the company will halt.

473. At the third, the company will face to the front, and, if there be openings between the files, the latter will promptly close to the right; the captain will immediately place himself by the side of the man on the left of the preceding company, and align himself on its front rank.

474. The fourth command will be executed as prescribed No. 426.

475. The following companies will be conducted and established on the line of battle as just prescribed for the second, each regulating itself by the one that precedes it; the left guides will detach themselves in time to precede their respective companies on the line by twelve or fifteen paces, and each place himself so as to be opposite to one of the three left files of his company, when in line. If the movement be executed in double quick time, the moment it is commenced, all the left guides will detach themselves at the same time from the column, and will move at a run to establish themselves on the line of battle.

476. The formation ended, the colonel will command:

Guides—POSTS.

477. The colonel and lieutenant colonel, in this formation, will each observe what is prescribed for him in that of *on the right, into line of battle*.

478. A column, left in front, will form itself faced to the rear into line of battle according to the same principles and by inverse means.

479. If the column be in march, and should arrive in front of the right of the line on which it is to form into battle, the colonel and lieutenant colonel will conform to what is prescribed Nos. 414 and 415.

480. When the head of the column shall be nearly at company distance from the two markers established on the line, the colonel will command:

1. *Into line, faced to the rear.* 2. *Battalion, by the right flank.* 3. MARCH (or *double quick*—MARCH).

481. At the first command, the captains will caution their companies to face by the right flank.

482. At the command *march*, briskly repeated by the captains of companies, all the companies will face to the right; the first company will then wheel by file to the left, and be directed by its captain a little to the rear of the left marker; then pass three paces beyond the line, and wheel again by file to the left; having arrived on the line, the captain will halt the company, and align it by the right. The remaining part of the movement will be executed as heretofore explained.

483. The foregoing principles are applicable to a column, left in front.

484. As the companies approach the line of battle, it is necessary that their captains should so direct the march as to cross that line a little in rear of their respective guides, who are faced to the basis of the formation; hence each guide ought to detach himself in

time to find himself correctly established on the direction before his company shall come up with him.

ARTICLE THIRD.

Formation in line of battle by two movements.

485. If a column by company, right in front, and at a halt, find itself in part on the line of battle, and the colonel should think proper to form line of battle before all the companies enter the new direction, the formation will be executed in the following manner:

486. It will be supposed that the column has arrived behind the line of battle, and that five companies have entered the new direction. The colonel having assured the guides of the first five companies on the direction, will command:

1. *Left into line, wheel.*   2. *Three rear companies, forward into line.*

487. At the second command, the chief of each of the rear companies will command: *By company, left half wheel;* and the colonel will add:

3. MARCH (or *double quick*—MARCH).

488. At this command, briskly repeated, the first five companies will form themselves *to the left, into line of battle,* and the three last *forward, into line of battle,* by the means prescribed for these respective formations; each captain of the three rear companies will, when his company shall have sufficiently wheeled, command:

1. *Forward.*   2. MARCH.   3. *Guide right.*

489. If the column be in march, the colonel will command:

1. *To the left, and forward into line.*   2. MARCH (or
        double quick—MARCH).

490. At the first command, the captains of those companies which have not entered on the new direction will
command: *By company, left half wheel*. At the command
march, briskly repeated, the first five companies will form
left into line, and the last three forward into line, as prescribed for these respective formations. Those captains
who form their companies forward into line will conform
to what is prescribed No. 488.

491. If the colonel should wish, in forming the battalion into line, to march it immediately forward, he will
command:

1. *By company to the left, and forward into line.*
        2. MARCH.

492. At the first command, each captain, whose
company is not yet in the new direction, will command:
1. *By company, left half wheel*; 2. *Double quick*. At
the command *march*, briskly repeated by the captains,
the companies not in the new direction will execute
what is prescribed above for forming forward into
line while marching; each of the other companies will
wheel to the left on a fixed pivot, and when the right of
these companies shall arrive on the line, the colonel
will command:

3. *Forward.* 4. MARCH. 5. *Guide centre.*

493. The fifth command will be given when the color-
bearer arrives on the line, if not already there.

494. If the battalion be marching in double quick time,
the colonel will cause quick time to be taken before commencing the movement.

495. If, instead of arriving behind, the column
should arrive before the line of battle, the colonel will
command:

1. *Left into line, wheel.* 2. *Three rear companies into line, faced to the rear.*

496. At the second command, the captain of each of the three rear companies will command: 1. *Such company.* 2. *Right*—FACE. The colonel will then add:

3. MARCH (or *double quick*—MARCH).

497. At this command, briskly repeated, the first five companies will form themselves *to the left, into line of battle,* and the three last *faced to the rear, into line of battle,* by the means prescribed for these respective formations.

498. If the column be in march, the colonel will command:

1. *To the left, and into line faced to the rear.* 2. MARCH (or *double quick*—MARCH).

499. The movement will be executed as prescribed Nos. 391, 480, and following.

500. These several movements in a column, left in front, will be executed according to the same principles, and by inverse means.

ARTICLE FOURTH.

Different modes of passing from column at half distance, into line of battle.

1. To the left (or right)
2. On the right (or left)
3. Forward, by deployment,
4. Faced to the rear,
} into line of battle.

1st. *Column at half distance, to the left (or right) into line of battle.*

501. A column at half distance having to form itself to the left (or right) into line of battle, the colonel will cause it to take distances by one of the means prescribed Article

IX., Part Third, of this school; which being executed, he
will form the column into line of battle, as has been indicated No. 390 and following.

502. If a column by company, at half distance, be in
march, and it be necessary to form rapidly into line of battle, the colonel will command:

1. *By the rear of column left* (or *right*) *into line, wheel.*
2. MARCH (or *double quick*—MARCH).

503. At the first command, the right general guide will
move rapidly to the front, and place himself a little
beyond the point where the head of the column will rest,
and on the prolongation of the guides. The captain of the
eighth company will command: *Left into line, wheel*; the
other captains will caution their companies to continue to
march to the front.

504. At the command *march*, briskly repeated
by the captain of the eighth company, the guide of this
company will halt short, and the company will wheel to
the left, conforming to the principles prescribed for
wheeling from a halt; when its right shall arrive near
the line, the captain will halt the company, and align it by
the left. The other captains will place themselves briskly
on the flank of the column; when the captain of the
seventh sees there is sufficient distance between his
company and the eighth to form the latter into line, he
will command: *Left into line, wheel*—MARCH; the left
guide will halt short, and, facing to the rear, will
place himself on the line; the company will wheel to
the left, the man on the left of the front rank will face to
the left, and place his breast against the left arm of
the guide; the captain will halt the company when
its right shall arrive near the line, and will align it
by the left. The other companies will conform
successively to what has just been prescribed for the
seventh.

505. Each captain will direct the alignment of his

company on the left man in the front rank of the company next on his right.

506. The lieutenant colonel will be watchful that the leading guide marches accurately on the prolongation of the line of battle, and directs himself on the right general guide. The major, placed in rear of the left guide of the eighth company, will, as soon as the guide of the seventh company is established on the direction, hasten in rear of the guides of the other companies, so as to assure each of them in succession on the line.

2d. Column at half distance, on the right (or left), into line of battle.

507. A column at half distance will form itself on the right (or left) into line of battle, as prescribed for a column at full distance.

3d. Column at half distance, forward, into line of battle.

508. If it be wished to form a column at half distance, forward into line of battle, the colonel will first cause it to close in mass and then deploy it on the leading company.

4th. Column at half distance, faced to the rear, into line of battle.

509. A column at half distance will be formed into line of battle, faced to the rear, as prescribed for a column at full distance.

ARTICLE FIFTH.

Deployment of columns closed in mass.

510. A column in mass may be formed into line of battle:

    1. Faced to the front, by the deployment.
    2. Faced to the rear, by the countermarch and
           the deployment.

3. Faced to the right and faced to the left, by a
change of direction by the flank, and the
deployment.

511. When a column in mass, by division, arrives
behind the line on which it is intended to deploy it, the
colonel will indicate, in advance, to the lieutenant colonel,
the direction of the line of battle, as well as the point on
which he may wish to direct the column. The lieutenant
colonel will immediately detach himself with two markers, and establish them on that line, the first at the point
indicated, the second a little less than the front of a division from the first.

512. Deployments will always be made upon lines
parallel and lines perpendicular to the line of battle;
consequently, if the head of the column be near the
line of battle, the colonel will commence by establishing
the direction of the column perpendicularly to that line,
if it be not already so, by one of the means indicated
No. 244 and following, or No. 307 and following. If the
column be in march, he will so direct it that it may
arrive exactly behind the markers, perpendicularly to the
line of battle, and halt it at three paces from that line.

513. The column, right in front, being halted, it is supposed that the colonel wishes to deploy it on the first division; he will order the left general guide to go to a point
on the line of battle a little beyond that at which the left of
the battalion will rest when deployed, and place himself
correctly on the prolongation of the markers established
before the first division.

514. These dispositions being made, the colonel will
command:

1. *On the first division, deploy column.*   2. *Battalion,
left*—FACE.

515. At the first command, the chief of the first division will caution it to stand fast; the chiefs of the three

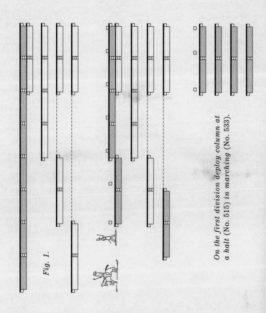

Fig. 1.

On the first division deploy column at a halt (No. 515) in marching (No. 533).

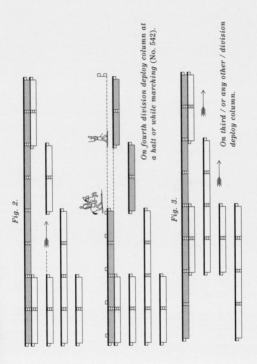

Fig. 2.

On fourth division deploy column at
a halt or while marching (No. 542).

Fig. 3.

On third / or any other / division
deploy column.

other divisions will remind them that they will have to face to the left.

516. At the second command, the three last divisions will face to the left; the chief of each division will place himself by the side of its left guide, and the junior captain by the side of the covering sergeant of the left company, who will have stepped into the front rank.

517. At the same command, the lieutenant colonel will place a third marker on the alignment of the two first, opposite to one of the three left files of the right company, first division, and then place himself on the line of battle a few paces beyond the point at which the left of the second division will rest.

518. The colonel will then command:

3. MARCH (or *double quick*—MARCH).

519. At this command, the chief of the first division will go to its right, and command:

Right—DRESS.

520. At this, the division will dress up against the markers; the chief of the division, and its junior captain, will each align the company on his left, and then command:

FRONT.

521. The three divisions, faced to the left, will put themselves in march; the left guide of the second will direct himself parallelly to the line of battle; the left guides of the third and fourth divisions will march abreast with the guide of the second; the guides of the third and fourth each preserving the prescribed distance between himself and the guide of the division which preceded his own in the column.

522. The chief of the second division will not follow its movement; he will see it file by him, and when its right guide shall be abreast with him, he will command:

1. *Second division.* 2. Halt. 3. Front.

523. The first command will be given when the division shall yet have seven or eight paces to march; the second, when the right guide shall be abreast with the chief of the division, and the third immediately after the second.

524. At the second command, the division will halt; at the third, it will face to the front, and if there be openings between the files, the chief of the division will cause them to be promptly closed to the right; the left guides of both companies will step upon the line of battle, face to the right, and place themselves on the direction of the markers established before the first division, each guide opposite to one of the three left files of his company.

525. The division having faced to the front, its chief will place himself accurately on the line of battle, on the left of the first division; and when he shall see the guides assured on the direction, he will command, *Right—* Dress. At this, the division will be aligned by the right in the manner indicated for the first.

526. The third and fourth divisions will continue to march; at the command *halt*, given to the second, the chief of the third will halt in his own person, place himself exactly opposite to the guide of the second, after this division shall have faced to the front and closed its files; he will see his division file past, and when his right guide shall be abreast with him, he will command:

1. *Third division.* 2. Halt. 3. Front.

527. As soon as the division faces to the front, its chief will place himself two paces before its centre, and command:

1. *Third division, forward.* 2. *Guide right.* 3. March.

528. At the third command, the division will march towards the line of battle; the right guide will so direct himself as to arrive by the side of the man on the left of the second division, and when the division is at three paces from the line of battle, its chief will halt it and align it by the right.

529. The chief of the fourth division will conform himself (and the chief of the fifth, if there be a fifth) to what has just been prescribed for the third.

530. The deployment ended, the colonel will command:

Guides—Posts.

531. At this command, the guides will resume their places in line of battle, and the markers will retire.

532. If the column be in march, and the colonel shall wish to deploy it on the first division without halting the column, he will make the dispositions indicated Nos. 512 and 513, and when the first division shall have arrived at three paces from the line, he will command:

1. *On the first division, deploy column.* 2. *Battalion by the left flank.* 3. March (or *double quick*—March).

533. At the first command, the chief of the first division will caution it to halt, and will command, *First division*; the other chiefs will caution their divisions to face by the left flank.

534. At the command *march*, briskly repeated by the chiefs of the rear divisions, the chief of the first division will command, Halt, and will align his division by the right against the markers; the other divisions will face to the left, their chiefs hastening to the left of their divisions. The second division will conform its movements to what is prescribed Nos. 522 and following. The third and fourth divisions will execute what is prescribed Nos. 526 and follow-

ing; but the chief of each division will halt in his own person at the command *march* given by the chief of the division which precedes him, and when the right of his division arrives abreast of him, he will command:

Such division, by the right flank—MARCH.

535. The lieutenant colonel will assure the position of the guides, conforming to what is prescribed No. 431. The major will follow the movement abreast with the fourth division.

536. If the colonel shall wish to deploy the column without halting it, and to continue the march, the markers will not be posted; the movement will be executed by the same commands and the same means as the foregoing, but with the following modifications:

537. At the first command, the chief of the first division will command, 1. *Guide right.* 2. *Quick time.* At the command, *Double quick*—MARCH, given by the colonel, the first division will march in quick time and will take the touch of elbows to the right; the captains will place themselves on the right of their respective companies; the captain on the right of the battalion will take points on the ground to assure the direction of the march. The chief of the second division will allow his division to file past him, and when he sees its right abreast of him, he will command: 1. *Second division by the right flank.* 2. MARCH. 3. *Guide right*; and when this division shall arrive an alignment of the first, he will cause it to march in quick time. The third and fourth divisions will deploy according to the same principles as the second.

538. The colonel, lieutenant colonel, major, and color-bearer will conform themselves to what is prescribed No. 458.

539. The colonel will see, pending the movement, that the principles just prescribed are duly observed, and particularly that the divisions, in deploying, be

not halted too soon nor too late. He will correct promptly and quickly the faults that may be committed, and prevent their propagation. *This rule is general for all deployments.*

540. The column being at a halt, if, instead of deploying it on the first, the colonel shall wish to deploy it on the rearmost division, he will cause the dispositions to be made indicated No. 511 and following; but it will be the right general guide whom he will send to place himself beyond the point at which the right of the battalion will rest when deployed.

541. The colonel will then command:

> 1. *On the fourth* (or such) *division, deploy column.*
> 2. *Battalion, right*—FACE.

542. At the first command, the chief of the fourth division will caution it to stand fast; the chiefs of the other divisions will caution them that they will have to face to the right.

543. At the second command, the first three divisions will face to the right; and the chief of each will place himself by the side of its right guide.

544. At the same command, the lieutenant colonel will place a third marker between the first two, so that this marker may be opposite to one of the three right files of the left company of the division; the lieutenant colonel will then place himself on the line of battle a few paces beyond the point at which the right of the third division will rest when deployed.

545. The colonel will then command:

> 3. MARCH (or *double quick*—MARCH).

546. At this command, the three right divisions will put themselves in march, the guide of the first so directing himself as to pass three paces within the line marked by the right general guide. The chief of the third division will not follow its movement: he will see it file past, halt it when its left guide shall

be abreast with him, and cause it to face to the front; and, if there be openings between the files, he will cause them to be promptly closed to the left.

547. The chief of the fourth division, when he sees it nearly unmasked by the three others, will command:

1. *Fourth division, forward.* 2. *Guide left.* 3. MARCH.

548. At the command *march*, which will be given the instant the fourth is unmasked, this division will approach the line of battle, and when at three paces from the markers on that line, its chief will halt it, and command:

Left—DRESS.

549. At this command, the division will dress forward against the markers; the chief of the division and the junior captain will each align the company on his right, and then command:

FRONT.

550. The instant that the third division is unmasked, its chief will cause it to approach the line of battle, and halt it in the manner just prescribed for the fourth.

551. The moment the division halts, its right guide and the covering sergeant of its left company will step on the line of battle, placing themselves on the prolongation of the markers established in front of the fourth division; as soon as they shall be assured in their positions, the division will be aligned as has just been prescribed for the fourth.

552. The second and first divisions which will have continued to march, will, in succession, be halted and aligned by the left, in the same manner as the third; the chiefs of these divisions will conform themselves to what is prescribed No. 526. The second being near the line of battle, the command

will not be given for it to move on this line, but it will be dressed up to it.

553. The deployment ended, the colonel will command:

*Guides—*POSTS.

554. At this command, the chiefs of division and the guides will resume their places in line of battle, and the markers will retire.

555. The lieutenant colonel will assure the positions of the guides by the means indicated No. 431, and the major will follow the movement abreast with the fourth division.

556. If the column be in march, and the colonel shall wish to deploy it on the fourth division, he will make the dispositions indicated No. 511 and following; and when the head of the column shall arrive within three paces of the line, he will command:

1. *On the fourth division, deploy column.* 2. *Battalion, by the right flank.* 3. MARCH (or *double quick—* MARCH).

557. At the first command, the chief of the fourth division will caution it to halt, and will command, *Fourth division*; the chiefs of the other divisions will caution their divisions to face to the right.

558. At the command *march*, briskly repeated by the chiefs of the first three divisions, the chief of the fourth will command: HALT. The first three divisions will face to the right, and be directed parallelly to the line of battle. The chief of each of these divisions will place himself by the side of its right guide. The chief of the third division will see his division file past him, and when his left guide is abreast of him, he will halt it, and face it to the front. The chief of the fourth division, when he shall see it nearly unmasked, will command: 1.

Fourth division, forward; 2. *Guide left*; 3. MARCH (or *double quick*—MARCH). This division will move towards the line of battle, and when at three paces from this line, it will be halted by its chief, and aligned by the left.

559. The chief of the third division will move his division forward, conforming to what has just been prescribed for the fourth.

560. The chiefs of the second and first divisions, after halting their divisions, will conform to what is prescribed No. 552.

561. If the colonel should wish to deploy on the fourth division without halting the column, and to continue to march forward, he will not have markers posted, and the movement will be executed by the same commands and the same means, with the following modifications: the fourth division, when unmasked, will be moved forward in quick time, and will continue to march, instead of being halted, and will take the touch of elbows to the left. The third division, on being unmasked, will be moved to the front in double quick time, but when it arrives on the alignment of the fourth it will take the quick step, and dress to the left until the command *Guide centre*, is given by the colonel. The chiefs of the second and first divisions will conform to what has been prescribed for the third. When the first division shall arrive on the line, the colonel may cause the battalion to take the double quick step.

562. The colonel and lieutenant colonel will conform to what has been prescribed Nos. 458 and 459.

563. To deploy the column on an interior division, the colonel will cause the line to be traced by the means above indicated, and the general guides will move briskly on the line, as prescribed Nos. 513 and 540. This being executed, the colonel will command:

1. *On such division, deploy column.* 2. *Battalion out-*
wards—FACE. 3. MARCH (or *double quick*—
MARCH).

564. Whether the column be with the right or left
in front, the divisions which, in the order in battle, belong
to the right of the directing one, will face to the right;
the others, excepting the directing division, will face
to the left; the divisions in front of the latter will
deploy by the means indicated No. 542 and following;
those in its rear will deploy as is prescribed No. 513
and following.

565. The directing division, the instant it finds itself
unmasked, will approach the line of battle, taking the
guide left or right, according as the right or left of the column may be in front. The chief of this division will align it
by the directing flank, and then step back into the rear, in
order momentarily to give place to the chief of the next
for aligning the next division.

566. The lieutenant colonel will assure the positions of
the guides of divisions, which, in the line of battle, take
the right of the directing division, and the major will
assure the positions of the other guides.

567. If the column be in march, the colonel will command:

1. *On such division, deploy column.* 2. *Battalion, by the*
right and left flanks. 3. MARCH (or *double quick*—
MARCH).

568. The divisions which are in front of the directing one will deploy by the means indicated Nos. 557
and following; those in rear, as prescribed No. 533 and
following.

569. The directing division, when unmasked, will
conform to what is prescribed for the fourth division,
No. 558.

570. The colonel, lieutenant colonel and major will conform to what has been prescribed Nos. 458 and 459.

571. In a column, left in front, deployments will be executed according to the same principles, and by inverse means.

Remarks on the deployment of columns, closed in mass.

572. All the divisions ought to deploy rectangularly, to march off abreast, and to preserve their distances towards the line of battle.

573. Each division, the instant that it is unmasked, ought to be marched towards the line of battle, and to be aligned upon it by the flank next to the directing division; the latter, whether the right or left be in front, will always be aligned by the flank next to the point of *appui*, when the deployment is made on the first or last division; but if the column be deployed on an interior division, this division will be aligned by the flank which *was* that of direction.

574. The chiefs of division will see that, in deploying, the principles prescribed for marching by the flank are well observed, and if openings between the files occur, which ought not to happen except on broken or difficult grounds, the openings ought to be promptly closed towards the directing flank as soon as the divisions face to the front.

575. If a chief of division give the command *halt*, or the command *by the right or left flank*, too soon or too late, his division will be obliged to oblique to the right or left in approaching the line of battle, and his fault may lead the following subdivision into error.

576. In the divisions which deploy by the left flank, it is always the left guide of each company who ought to place himself on the line of battle to mark the direction; in divisions which deploy by the right flank, it is the right guide.

577. A column by company, closed in mass, may be formed to the left or to the right into line, in the same manner as the column at half distance, and by the means indicated No. 502 and following.

578. A column by company, closed in mass, may be formed on the right or on the left into line of battle, as a column at half distance; but in order to execute this movement, without arresting the march of the column, it is necessary that the guides avoid, with the greatest care, shortening the step in turning, and that the men near them, respectively, conform themselves rapidly to the movements of their guides.

Remarks on inversions.

579. Inversions giving frequently the means of forming line of battle, in the promptest manner, are of great utility in the movements of an army.

580. The application that may be made of inversions in the formations to the right and to the left in line of battle, has been indicated No. 407 and following. They may also be advantageously employed in the successive formations, except in that of *faced to the rear, into line of battle.*

581. Formations, by inversion, will be executed according to the same principles as formations in the direct order; but the colonel's first command will always begin *by inversion.*

582. The battalion being in line of battle by inversion, when the colonel shall wish, by forming it into column, to bring it back to the direct order, he will cause it either to *break* or to *ploy* by company, or by division, accordingly as the column may have been by company or by division before it had been formed into line of battle by inversion.

583. When a battalion in line of battle, formed by

inversion, has to be ployed into column, the movement will be executed according to the same principles as if the line were in the direct order, but observing what follows.

584. If it be intended that the column shall be by division, with the first in front, or by company, with the first company in front, the colonel will announce in the second command—*left in front*, because the battalion being in line of battle by inversion, that subdivision is on the left.

585. Each chief whose subdivision takes position in the column in front of the directing one, will conduct his subdivision till it halts; and each chief whose subdivision takes position in rear of the directing one, will halt in his own person when up with the preceding right guide, and see his subdivision file past; and each chief will align his subdivision by the right. When the column is to be put in march, the second command will be, *guide left*, because the proper right is in front.

586. For the same reason, if it be intended that the last subdivision shall be in front, *right in front*, will be announced in the second command; the subdivisions will be aligned by the left, and to put the column in march, the second command will be, *guide right*, because the proper left is in front.

PART FIFTH.

Article First.

To advance in line of battle.

587. The battalion being correctly aligned, and supposed to be the directing one, when the colonel shall wish to march in line of battle, he will give the lieutenant colonel an intimation of his purpose, place himself about forty paces in rear of the color-file, and face to the front.

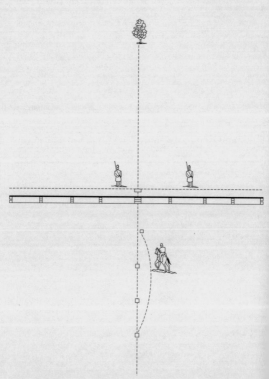

To advance in line of battle, Battalion forward (No. 592).

588. The lieutenant colonel will place himself a like distance in front of the same file, and face to the colonel, who will establish him as correctly as possible, by signal of the sword, perpendicularly to the line of battle opposite to the color-bearer. The colonel will next, above the heads of the lieutenant colonel and color-bearer, take a point of direction in the field beyond, if a distinct one present itself, exactly in the prolongation of those first two points.

589. The colonel will then move twenty paces farther to the rear, and establish two markers on the prolongation of the straight line passing through the color-bearer and the lieutenant colonel; these markers will face to the rear, the first placed about twenty-five paces behind the rear rank of the battalion, and the second at the same distance from the first.

590. The color-bearer will be instructed to take, the moment the lieutenant colonel shall be established on the perpendicular, two points on the ground in the straight line which, drawn from himself, would pass between the heels of that officer; the first of these points will be taken at fifteen or twenty paces from the color-bearer.

591. These dispositions being made, the colonel will command:

1. *Battalion, forward.*

592. At this, the front rank of the color-guard will advance six paces to the front; the corporals in the rear rank will place themselves in the front rank, and these will be replaced by those in the rank of file closers; at the same time the two general guides will move in advance, abreast with the color-bearer, the one on the right, opposite to the captain of the right company, the other opposite to the sergeant who closes the left of the battalion.

593. The captain of the left wing will shift, passing before the front rank, to the left of their respective

companies; the sergeant on the left of the battalion will
step back into the rear rank. The covering sergeant of the
company next on the left of the color-company will step
into the front rank.

594. The lieutenant colonel having assured the color-
bearer on the line between himself and the corporal of the
color-file, now in the front rank, will go to the position
which will be hereinafter indicated, No. 602.

595. The major will place himself six or eight paces on
either flank of the color-rank.

596. The colonel will then command:

2. MARCH (or *double quick—*MARCH).

597. At this command, the battalion will step off with
life; the color-bearer, charged with the step and direction,
will scrupulously observe the length and cadence of the
pace, marching on the prolongation of the two points previously taken, and successively taking others in advance
by the means indicated in the school of the company; the
corporal on his right, and the one on his left, will march in
the same step, taking care not to turn the head or shoulders, the color-bearer supporting the color-lance against
the hip.

598. The two general guides will march in the same
step with the color-rank, each maintaining himself
abreast, or nearly so, with that rank, and neither occupying himself with the movement of the other.

599. The three corporals of the color-guard, now in the
front rank of the battalion, will march well aligned, elbow
to elbow, heads direct to the front, and without deranging
the line of their shoulders; the centre one will follow
exactly in the trace of the color-bearer, and maintain the
same step, without lengthening or shortening it, except on
an intimation from the colonel or lieutenant colonel,

although he should find himself more or less than six paces from the color-rank.

600. The covering sergeant in the front rank between the color-company and the next on the left will march elbow to elbow, and on the same line, with the three corporals in the centre, his head well to the front.

601. The captains of the color-company, and the company next to the left, will constitute, with the three corporals in the centre of the front rank, the basis of alignment for both wings of the battalion; they will march in the same step with the color-bearer, and exert themselves to maintain their shoulders exactly in the square with the direction. To this end, they will keep their heads direct to the front, only occasionally casting an eye on the three centre corporals, with the slightest possible turn of the neck, and, if they perceive themselves in advance or in rear of these corporals, the captain, or two captains, will almost insensibly shorten or lengthen the step, so as, at the end of several paces, to regain the true alignment, without giving sudden checks or impulsions to the wings beyond them respectively.

602. The lieutenant colonel, placed twelve or fifteen paces on the right of the captain of the color-company, will maintain this captain and the next one beyond, abreast with the three centre corporals; to this end, he will caution either to lengthen or to shorten the step, as may be necessary, which the captain, or two captains, will execute as has just been explained.

603. All the other captains will maintain themselves on the prolongation of this basis; and, to this end, they will cast their eyes towards the centre, taking care to turn the neck but slightly, and not to derange the direction of their shoulders.

604. The captains will observe the march of their companies, and prevent the men from getting in advance of

the line of captains; they will not lengthen or shorten step
except when evidently necessary; because, to correct,
with too scrupulous attention, small faults, is apt to cause
the production of greater—loss of calmness, silence,
and equality of step, each of which it is so important to
maintain.

605. The men will constantly keep their heads well
directed to the front, feel lightly the elbow towards the
centre, resist pressure coming from the flank, give the
greatest attention to the squareness of shoulders, and
hold themselves always very slightly behind the line of the
captains, in order never to shut out from the view of the
latter the basis of alignment; they will, from time to time,
cast an eye on the color-rank, or on the general guide of
the wing, in order to march constantly in the same step
with those advanced persons.

606. Pending the march, the line determined
by the two markers (h and d) will be prolonged by
placing, in proportion as the battalion advances, a third
marker (i) in the rear of the first (h), then the marker
(d) will quit his place and go a like distance in rear
of (i); the marker (h) will, in his turn, do the like in
respect to (d), and so on, in succession, as long as the battalion continues to advance; each marker, on shifting position, taking care to face to the rear, and to cover
accurately the two markers already established on the
direction. A staff officer, or the quartermaster sergeant,
designated for the purpose, and who will hold himself
constantly fifteen or twenty paces facing the marker farthest from the battalion, will caution each marker when
to shift place, and assure him on the direction behind
the other two.

607. The colonel will habitually hold himself about
thirty paces in rear of the centre of his battalion, taking
care not to put himself on the line of markers; if, for
example, by the slanting of the battalion, or the indica-

tions which will be given Nos. 617 and following, he find that the march of the color-bearer is not perpendicular, he will promptly command:

Point of direction to the right (or *left*).

608. At this command, the major will hasten thirty or forty paces in advance of the color-rank, halt, face to the colonel, and place himself on the direction which the latter will indicate by signal of the sword; the corporal in the centre of the battalion will then direct himself upon the major, on a caution from the colonel, advancing, to that end, the opposite shoulder; the corporals on his right and left will conform themselves to his direction.

609. The color-bearer will also direct himself upon the major, advancing the opposite shoulder, the major causing him, at the same time, to incline to the right or left, until be shall exactly cover the corporal of his file; the color-bearer will then take points on the ground in this new direction.

610. The two general guides will conform themselves to the new direction of the color-rank.

611. The officer charged with observing the successive replacing of the markers in the rear of the centre, will establish them promptly on the new direction, taking for basis the color-bearer and the corporal of his file in the centre of the battalion; the colonel will verify the new direction of the markers.

612. The lieutenant colonel, from the position given No. 602, will see that the two centre companies, and successively all the others, conform themselves to the new direction of the centre, but without precipitancy or disorder; he will then endeavor to maintain that basis of alignment for the battalion, perpendicularly to the direction pursued by the color-bearer.

613. He will often observe the march of the two wings;

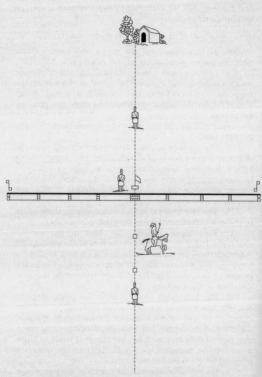

Point of direction to the right or left (No. 608).

and, if he discover that the captains neglect to conform themselves to the basis of alignment, he will recall their attention by the command—*captain of* (such) *company,* or *captains of* (such) *companies, on the line*—without, however, endeavoring too scrupulously to correct small faults.

614. The major on the flank of the color-rank will, during the march, place himself, from time to time, twenty paces in front of that rank, face to the rear, and place himself correctly on the prolongation of the markers established behind the centre, in order to verify the exact march of the color-bearer on that line; he will rectify, if necessary, the direction of the color-bearer, who will immediately take two new points on the ground between himself and the major.

615. All the principles applicable to the advance in line are the same for a *subordinate* as for the *directing* battalion; but when the battalion under instruction is supposed to be *subordinate*, no markers will be placed behind its centre.

Remarks on the advance in line of battle.

616. If, in the exercises of detail, or courses of elementary instruction, the officers, sergeants, corporals, and men, have not been well confirmed in the principles of the position under arms, as well as in the length and cadence of the step, the march of the battalion in line will be floating, unsteady, and disunited.

617. If the color-bearer, instead of marching perpendicularly forward, pursue an oblique direction, the battalion will slant; crowdings in one wing, and openings in the other, will follow; and these defects in the march, becoming more and more embarrassing in proportion to the deviation from the perpendicular, will commence near the centre.

618. It is then of the greatest importance that the color-bearer should direct himself perpendicularly

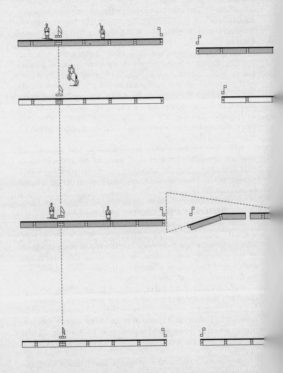

Cautions when advancing in line of battle (Nos. 616 to 622).

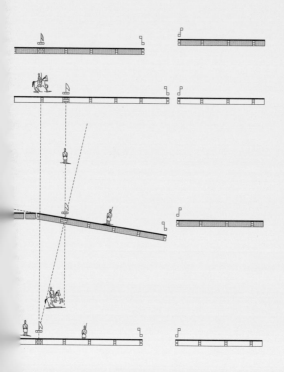

Cautions when advancing in line of battle (Nos. 616 to 622).

forward, and that the basis of alignment should always be perpendicular to the line pursued by him.

619. If openings be formed, if the files crowd each other, if, in short, disorder ensue, the remedy ought to be applied as promptly as possible, but calmly, with few words, and as little noise as practicable.

620. The object of the general guides, in the march in line of battle, is to indicate to the companies near the flanks the step of the centre of the battalion, and to afford more facility in establishing the wings on the direction of the centre if they should be too much in the rear; hence the necessity that these guides should maintain the same step, and march abreast, or very nearly so, with the color-rank, which it will be easy for them to do by casting from time to time an eye on that rank.

621. If the battalion happen to lose the step, the colonel will recall its attention by the command, *to the*—STEP; captains and their companies will immediately cast an eye on the color-rank, or one of the general guides, and promptly conform themselves to the step.

622. Finally, it is of the utmost importance to the attainment of regularity in the march in line of battle, to habituate the battalion to execute with as much order as promptness the movements prescribed No. 607 and following, for rectifying the direction; it is not less essential that commanders of battalions should exercise themselves, with the greatest care, in forming their own *coup d'œil*, in order to be able to judge with precision the direction to be given to their battalions.

ARTICLE SECOND.

Oblique march in line of battle.

623. The battalion marching in line of battle, when

the colonel shall wish to cause it to oblique, he will command:

> 1. *Right* (or *left*) *oblique.*   2. MARCH (or *double quick*—MARCH).

624. At the first command, the major will place himself in front of, and faced to, the color-bearer.

625. At the command *march*, the whole battalion will take the oblique step. The companies and captains will strictly observe the principles established in the school of the company.

626. The major in front of the color-bearer ought to maintain the latter in a line with the centre corporal, so that the color-bearer may oblique neither more nor less than that corporal. He will carefully observe also that they follow parallel directions and preserve the same length of step.

627. The lieutenant colonel will take care that the captains and the three corporals in the centre keep exactly on a line and follow parallel directions.

628. The colonel will see that the battalion preserves its parallelism; he will exert himself to prevent the files from opening or crowding. If he perceive the latter fault, he will cause the files on the flank, to which the battalion obliques, to open out.

629. The colonel, wishing the direct march to be resumed, will command:

> 1. *Forward.*   2. MARCH.

630. At the command *march*, the battalion will resume the direct march. The major will place himself thirty paces in front of the color-bearer, and face to the colonel, who will establish him, by a signal of the sword, on the direction which the color-bearer ought to pursue. The latter will immediately take two points on the ground between himself and the major.

631. In resuming the direct march, care will be taken

that the men do not close the intervals which may exist between the files at once; it should be done almost insensibly.

Remarks on the oblique march.

632. The object of the oblique step is to gain ground to the right or left, preserving all the while the primitive direction of the line of battle; as thus, for example: the battalion, departing from the line (*sz*), arrives on the line (*xx*) parallel to (*sz*).

633. It is then essential that the corporals in the centre of the battalion, and the captains of companies, should follow parallel directions, and maintain themselves at the same height; without which they will give a false direction to the battalion.

634. The colonel and lieutenant colonel will exert themselves to prevent the files from crowding; for, without such precaution, the oblique march cannot be executed with facility.

ARTICLE THIRD.

To halt the battalion, marching in line of battle, and to align it.

635. The battalion marching in the line of battle, when the colonel shall wish to halt it, he will command:

1. *Battalion.* 2. HALT.

636. At the second command, the battalion will halt; the color-rank and the general guides will remain in front; but if the colonel should not wish immediately to resume the advance in line, nor to give a general alignment, he will command:

Color and general guides—POSTS.

637. At this command, the color-rank and general guides will retake their places in line of battle, the

captains in the left wing will shift to the right of their companies.

638. If the colonel should then judge it necessary to rectify the alignment, he will command:

Captains, rectify the alignment.

639. The captains will immediately cast an eye towards the centre, align themselves accurately, on the basis of the alignment, which the lieutenant colonel will see well directed, and then promptly dress their respective companies. The lieutenant colonel will admonish such captains as may not be accurately on the alignment by the command: *Captain of* (such) *company*, or *captains of* (such) *companies, move up* or *fall back*.

640. But when the colonel shall wish to give the battalion a general alignment, either parallel or oblique, instead of rectifying it as above, he will move some paces outside of one of the general guides (the right will here be supposed), and caution the right general guide and the color-bearer to face him, and then establish them, by signal of the sword, on the direction which he may wish to give to the battalion. As soon as they shall be correctly established, the left general guide will place himself on their direction, and be assured in his position by the major. The color-bearer will carry the color-lance perpendicularly between his eyes, and the two corporals of his rank will return to their places in the front rank the moment he shall face to the colonel.

641. This disposition being made, the colonel will command:

1. *Guides*—ON THE LINE.

642. At this command, the right guide of each company in the right wing, and the left guide of each company in the left, will each place himself on the direction of the color-bearer and the two general guides, face to the

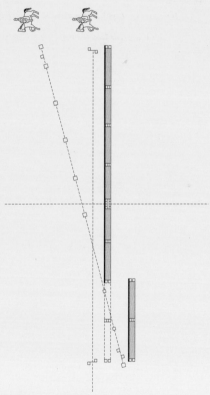

To rectify, or slightly alter, the alignment (Guides on the line) (No. 642).

color-bearer, place himself in rear of the guide who is next before him at a distance equal to the front of his company, and align himself upon the color-bearer and the general guide beyond.

643. The captains in the right wing will shift to the left of their companies, except the captain of the color-company, who will remain on its right, but step into the rear rank; the captains in the left wing will shift to the right of their companies.

644. The lieutenant colonel will promptly rectify, if necessary, the positions of the guides of the right wing, and the major those of the other; which being executed, the colonel will command:

2. *On the centre*—DRESS.

645. At this command, the companies will move up in quick time against the guides, where, having arrived, each captain will align his company according to prescribed principles, the lieutenant colonel aligning the color-company.

646. If the alignment be oblique, the captains will take care to conform their companies to it in conducting them towards the line.

647. The battalion being aligned, the colonel will command:

3. *Color and guides*—POSTS.

648. At this command, the color-bearer, the general and company guides, and the captains in the right wing, will take their places in the line of battle, and the color-bearer will replace the heel of the color-lance against the right hip.

649. If the new direction of the line of battle be such that one or more companies find themselves in advance of that line, the colonel, before establishing the general guides on the line, will cause such companies to be moved to the rear, either by the back step, or by first facing

about, according as there may be less or more ground to
be repassed to bring the companies in rear of the new
direction.

650. When the colonel shall wish to give a general
alignment, and the color and general guides are not on the
line, he will cause them to move out by the command:

1. *Color and general guides*—ON THE LINE.

651. At this command, the color-bearer and the general guides will place themselves on the line, conforming
to what is prescribed No. 640.

ARTICLE FOURTH.

Change of direction in marching in line of battle.

652. The battalion marching in line of battle, when the
colonel shall wish it to change direction to the right, he
will command:

1. *Change direction to the right.*   2. MARCH (or *double
quick*—MARCH).

653. At the command *march*, the movement will commence; the color-rank will shorten the step to fourteen or
seventeen inches, and direct itself circularly to the right,
taking care to advance the left shoulder, but only insensibly; the major will place himself before the color-bearer,
facing him, and so direct his march that he may describe
an arc of a circle neither too large nor too small; he will
also see that the color-bearer takes steps of fourteen or
seventeen inches, according to the gait.

654. The right general guide will wheel on the
right captain of the battalion as his pivot; the left general
guide will circularly march in the step of twenty-eight
inches or thirty-three inches, according to the gait,
and will align himself upon the color-bearer and the right
general guide.

To change direction while marching in line of battle (No. 652).

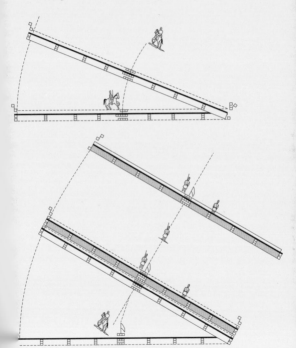

655. The corporal placed in the centre of the battalion, will take steps of fourteen or seventeen inches, and will wheel to the right by advancing insensibly the left shoulder; the battalion will conform itself to the movement of the centre; to this end, the captain of the color-company, and the captain of the next to the left, will attentively regulate their march, as well as the direction of their shoulders, on the three centre corporals. All the other captains will regulate the direction of their shoulders and the length of their step on this basis.

656. The men will redouble their attention in order not to pass the line of captains.

657. In the left wing, the pace will be lengthened in proportion as the file is distant from the centre; the captain of the eighth company who closes the left flank of the battalion will take steps of twenty-eight or thirty-three inches, according to the gait.

658. In the right wing the pace will be shortened in proportion as the file is distant from the centre; the captain who closes the right flank will only slowly turn in his person, observing to yield ground a little if pushed.

659. The colonel will take great care to prevent the centre of the battalion from describing an arc of a circle either too great or too small, in order that the wings may conform themselves to its movement. He will see also that the captains keep their companies constantly aligned upon the centre, so that there may be no opening and no crowding of files. He will endeavor to prevent faults, and, should they occur, correct them without noise.

660. The lieutenant colonel, placed before the battalion, will give his attention to the same objects.

661. When the colonel shall wish the direct march to be resumed, he will command:

1. *Forward.* 2. MARCH.

662. At the command *march*, the color-rank, the general guides, and the battalion will resume the direct march; the major will immediately place himself thirty or forty paces in front, face to the colonel, placed in rear of the centre, who will establish him by signal of the sword on the perpendicular direction which the corporal in the centre of the battalion ought to pursue; the major will immediately cause the color-bearer, if necessary, to incline to the right or left, so as to be exactly opposite to his file; the color-bearer will then take two points on the ground between himself and the major.

663. The lieutenant colonel will endeavor to give to the color-company and the next on the left a direction perpendicular to that pursued by the centre corporal; and all the other companies, without precipitancy, will conform themselves to that basis.

ARTICLE FIFTH.

To march in retreat, in line of battle.

664. The battalion being halted, if it be the wish of the colonel to cause it to march in retreat, he will command:

1. *Face to the rear.* 2. *Battalion, about*—FACE.

665. At the second command, the battalion will face about; the color-rank, and the general guides, if in advance, will take their places in line; the color-bearer will pass into the rear rank, now leading; the corporal of his file will step behind the corporal next on his own right, to let the color-bearer pass, and then step into the front rank, now rear, to re-form the color-file; the colonel will place himself behind the front rank, become the rear; the lieutenant colonel and major will place themselves before the rear rank, now leading.

666. The colonel will take post forty paces behind the

color-file, in order to assure the lieutenant colonel on the perpendicular, who will place himself at a like distance in front, as prescribed for the advance line of battle.

667. If the battalion be the one charged with the direction, the colonel will establish markers in the manner indicated No. 589, except that they will face to the battalion, and that the first will be placed twenty-five paces from the lieutenant colonel. If the markers be already established, the officer charged with replacing them in succession will cause them to face about, the moment that the battalion executes this movement, and then the marker nearest to the battalion will hasten to the rear of the two others.

668. These dispositions being made, the colonel will command:

3. *Battalion, forward.*

669. At this command, the color-bearer will advance six paces beyond the rank of file closers, accompanied by the two corporals of his guard of that rank, the centre corporal stepping back to let the color-bearer pass; the two file closers nearest this centre corporal will unite on him behind the color-guard to serve as a basis of alignment for the line of file closers; the two general guides will place themselves abreast with the color-rank, the covering sergeants will place themselves in the line of file closers, and the captains in the rear rank, now leading; the captains in the left wing, now right, will, if not already there, shift to the left of their companies, now become the right.

670. The colonel will then command:

4. MARCH (or *double quick*—MARCH).

671. The battalion will march in retreat on the same principles which govern the advance in line:

the centre corporal behind the color-bearer will march exactly in his trace.

672. If it be the directing battalion, the color-bearer will direct himself on the markers, who will, of their own accord, each place himself in succession behind the marker most distant, on being approached by the battalion; the officer charged with the superintendence of the markers will carefully assure them on the direction.

673. In the case of a subordinate battalion, the color-bearer will maintain himself on the perpendicular by means of points taken on the ground.

674. The colonel, lieutenant-colonel, and major will each discharge the same functions as in the advance in line.

675. The lieutenant colonel, placed on the outside of the file closers of the color-company, will also maintain the three file closers of the basis of alignment in a square with the line of direction: the other file closers will keep themselves aligned on this basis.

ARTICLE SIXTH.

To halt the battalion marching in retreat, and to face it to the front.

676. The colonel having halted the battalion, and wishing to face it to the front, will command:

1. *Face to the front.* 2. *Battalion, about*—FACE.

677. At the second command, the color-rank, general guides, captains, and covering sergeants, will all retake their habitual places in line of battle, and the color-bearer will repass into the front rank.

678. The battalion marching in line of battle by the front rank, when the colonel shall wish to march it in retreat, he will command:

1. *Battalion, right about.* 2. MARCH.

Third & Eighth Companies obstacle (No. 683).

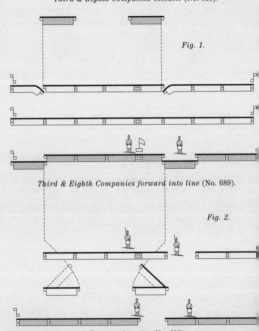

Fig. 1.

Third & Eighth Companies forward into line (No. 689).

Fig. 2.

To pass obstacles (No. 682).

679. At the command *march*, the battalion will face to the rear and move off at the same gait by the rear rank. The principles prescribed Nos. 669 and following will be carefully observed.

680. If the colonel should wish the battalion to march again by the front, he will give the same commands.

ARTICLE SEVENTH.

Change of direction, in marching in retreat.

681. A battalion retiring in line will change direction by the commands and means indicated No. 652 and following; the three file closers, united behind the color-rank, will conform themselves to the movement of this rank, and wheel like it; the centre file closer of the three will take steps of fourteen or seventeen inches, according to the gait, and keep himself steadily at the same distance from the color-bearer; the line of file closers will conform themselves to the movement of its centre, and the lieutenant colonel will maintain it on that basis.

ARTICLE EIGHTH.

Passage of obstacles, advancing and retreating.

682. The battalion advancing in line will be supposed to encounter an obstacle which covers one or more companies; the colonel will cause them to ploy into column at full distance, in rear of the next company towards the color, which will be executed in the following manner. It will be supposed that the obstacle only covers the third company, the colonel will command:

Third company, obstacle.

683. At this command, the captain of the third company will place himself in its front, turn to it, and command, 1. *Third company, by the left flank, to the rear*

into column. 2. *Double quick.* 3. MARCH. He will then hasten to the left of his company.

684. At the command *march*, the company will face to the left in marching; the two left files will promptly disengage to the rear in double quick time; the left guide, placing himself at the head of the front rank, will conduct it behind the fourth company, directing himself parallelly with this company; the captain of the third will himself halt opposite to the captain of the fourth, and see his company file past; when its right file shall be nearly up with him, he will command, 1. *Third company.* 2. *By the right flank.* 3. MARCH. 4. *Guide right*, and place himself before the centre of his company.

685. At the command *march*, the company will face to the right, preserving the same gait, but the moment it shall be at the prescribed distance, its captain will command:

1. *Quick time.* 2. MARCH.

686. This company will thus follow in column that behind which it finds itself, and at wheeling distance, its right guide marching exactly in the trace of the captain of that company.

687. As soon as the third company shall have faced to the left, the left guide of the second will place himself on the left of the front rank of his company, and maintain between himself and the right of the fourth the space necessary for the return into line of the third.

688. The obstacle being passed, the colonel will command:

Third company, forward, into line.

689. At this command, the captain, turning to his company, will add:

1. *By company, right half wheel.* 2. *Double quick.*
3. MARCH.

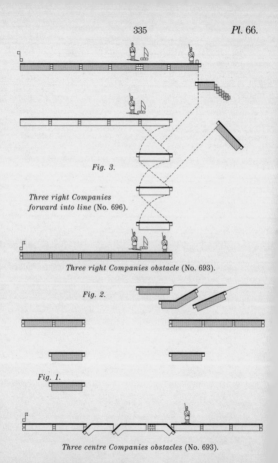

Fig. 3.

Three right Companies
forward into line (No. 696).

Three right Companies obstacle (No. 693).

Fig. 2.

Fig. 1.

Three centre Companies obstacles (No. 693).

690. At the command *march*, the company will take the double quick step, and execute a half wheel; its captain will then command, 1. *Forward.* 2. MARCH. 3. *Guide left.* The second command will be given when the company shall have sufficiently wheeled.

691. At. the command *march*, the company will direct itself straight forward towards the line of battle, and retake its position in it according to the principles prescribed for the formation forward into line of battle.

692. It will be supposed that the obstacle covers several contiguous companies (the three companies on the right, for example), the colonel will command:

1. *Three right companies, obstacle.* 2. *By the left flank, to the rear, into column.* 3. *Double quick*—MARCH.

693. At the first command, the captains of the designated companies will each place himself before the centre of his company, and caution it as to the movement about to be executed.

694. At the command *march*, the designated companies will face to the left in marching, and immediately take the double quick step; each captain will cause the head of his company to disengage itself to the rear, and the left guide will place himself at the head of the front rank; the captain of the third company will conform himself to what is prescribed No. 684 and following; the captains of the other companies will conduct them by the flank in rear of the third, inclining towards the head of the column; and, as the head of each company arrives opposite to the right of the one next before it in column, its captain will himself halt, see his company file past, and conform himself for facing it to the front, in marching, to what is prescribed No. 684 and following.

695. When the last company in column shall have passed the obstacle the colonel will command:

1. *Three right companies, forward, into line.*

696. At this command, the captain of each of these three companies will command, *By company, right half wheel.* The colonel will then add:

1. *Double quick.* 2. MARCH.

697. At this, briskly repeated by the captains of the three companies, each company will conform itself to what is prescribed No. 690 and following.

698. It is supposed, in the foregoing examples, that the companies belonged to the right wing; if they make part of the other, they will execute the passage of an obstacle according to the same principles and by inverse means.

699. When flank companies are broken off to pass an obstacle, the general guide on that flank will place himself six paces in front of the outer file of the nearest company to him remaining in line.

700. In the preceding movements, it has been supposed that the battalion was marching in quick time; but if it be marching in double quick time, and the colonel shall wish to cause several contiguous companies to break to the rear, he will first order the battalion to march in quick time; the companies will break as indicated No. 692.

701. When the movement is completed, the colonel will order the double quick step to be resumed. He will also cause the battalion to march in quick time when he shall wish to bring into line the several companies which are to the rear in column; the movement will be executed as previously indicated; and when the last company shall have nearly completed its movement, the colonel will cause the double quick step to be resumed.

702. In the movement of a single company, or of several companies not contiguous to each other, the battalion will continue to march in double quick

time; but in these cases the companies which are to ploy into column, or re-enter the line, will increase the gait.

703. In the march in retreat, these several movements will be executed on the same principles as if the battalion marched by the front rank.

704. When a battalion, advancing in line of battle, shall be obliged to execute the right about in order to retreat, if there be companies in column, behind the rear rank, these companies will also execute the right about, put themselves in march, at the same time with the battalion, and will thus precede it in the retreat; they will afterwards successively put themselves into line by the oblique step, as the ground may permit.

705. If the battalion be marching in retreat in double quick time, and many contiguous companies be marching before the rear rank of the battalion, the colonel will not change the gait of the battalion in causing them to re-enter into line.

706. When the color-company shall be obliged to execute the movement of passing an obstacle, the color-rank will return into line at the moment the company shall face to the left or right; the major will place himself six paces before the extremity of the company behind which the color-company marches in column, in order to give the step and the direction; he, himself, first taking the step from the battalion.

707. As soon as the color-company shall have returned into line, the front rank of the color-guard will again move out six paces in front of the battalion, and take the step from the major; the latter will immediately place himself twenty or thirty paces in front of the color-bearer, and face to the colonel placed behind the centre of the battalion, who will establish him on the perpendicular; and, as soon as he shall be assured on it, the color-bearer will in-

stantly take two points on the ground between himself and the major.

708. It is prescribed, as a general rule, that the companies of the right wing ought to execute the movement of passing obstacles by the left flank, and the reverse for the companies of the other wing; but if the obstacle cover at once several companies of the centre, each will file into column behind that, still in line, and of the same wing, which may be the nearest to it.

Article Ninth.

To pass a defile, in retreat, by the right or left flank.

709. When a battalion, retiring in line, shall encounter a defile which it must pass, the colonel will halt the battalion, and face it to the front.

710. It will be supposed that the defile is in rear of the left flank, and that its width is sufficient to give passage to a column by platoon; the colonel will place a marker fifteen or twenty paces in rear of the file closers at the point around which the subdivisions will have to change direction in order to enter the defile; he will then command:

To the rear, by the right flank, pass the defile.

711. The captain of the first company will immediately command:

1. *First company, right*—FACE. 2. MARCH (or *double quick*—MARCH).

712. At the command *march*, the first company will commence the movement; the first file will wheel to the right, march to the rear till it shall have passed four paces beyond the file closers, when it will wheel again to the right, and then direct itself straight forward towards the left flank. All the other files of this company will come to

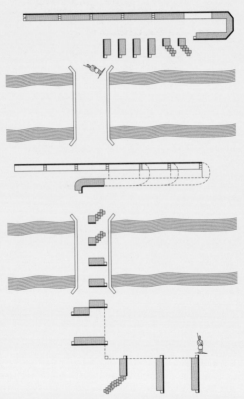

To the rear, by the right flank, pass the defile (No. 711).

wheel in succession at the same place where the first had wheeled.

713. The second company will execute, in its turn, the same movement, by the commands of its captain, who will give the command MARCH, so that the first file of his company may immediately follow the last of the first, without constraint, however, as to taking the step of the first; the first file of the second company will wheel to the right, on its ground; all the other files of this company will come in succession to wheel at the same place. The following companies will execute, each in its turn, what has just been prescribed for the second.

714. When the whole of the second company shall be on the same direction with the first, the captain of the first will cause it to form, by platoon, into line, and the moment that it is in column, the guide of the first platoon will direct himself on the marker around whom he has to change direction in order to enter the defile.

715. The second company will continue to march by the flank, directing itself parallelly with the line of battle; and it, in its turn, will form by platoon into line, when the third company shall be wholly on the same direction with itself.

716. The following companies will successively execute what has just been prescribed for the second, and each will form by platoon into line, when the next company shall be on the same direction with itself.

717. The first platoon of the leading company having arrived opposite to the marker placed at the entrance of the defile, will turn to the left, and the following platoons will all execute this movement at the same point. As the last companies will not be able to form platoons before reaching the defile, they will so direct themselves, in entering it, as to leave room to the left for this movement.

718. The battalion will thus pass the defile by platoon; and, as the two platoons of each company shall clear it, companies will be successively formed by the means indicated, school of the company, No. 273 and following.

719. The head of the column having cleared the defile, and having reached the distance at which the colonel wishes to re-form line faced to the defile, he may cause the leading company to turn to the left, to prolong the column in that direction, and then form it to the left into line of battle; or he may halt the column, and form it into line of battle faced to the rear.

720. If the defile be in the rear of the right flank, it will be passed by the left; the movement will be executed according to the same principles, and by inverse means.

721. If the defile be too narrow to receive the front of a platoon, it will be passed by the flank. Captains and file closers will be watchful that the files do not lose their distances in marching. Companies or platoons will be formed into line as the width of the defile may permit, or as the companies shall successively clear it.

Article Tenth.

To march by the flank.

722. The colonel, wishing the battalion to march by the flank, will command:

1. *Battalion.* 2. *Right* (or *left*)—Face. 3. *Forward.*
    4. March (or *double quick*—March).

723. At the second command, the captains and covering sergeants will place themselves as prescribed Nos. 136 and 141, school of the company.

724. The sergeant on the left of the battalion will place himself to the left and by the side of the last file of his company, covering the captains in file.

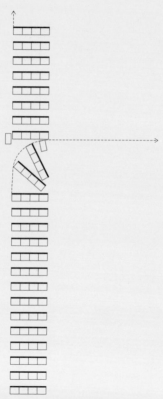

To march by the flank forming fours (No. 722).

725. The battalion having to face by the left flank, the captains, at the second command, will shift rapidly to the left of their companies, and each place himself by the side of the covering sergeant of the company preceding his own, except the captain of the left company, who will place himself by the side of the sergeant on the left of the battalion. The covering sergeant of the right company will place himself by the right side of the front rank man of the rearmost file of his company, covering the captains in file.

726. At the command *march*, the battalion will step off with life; the sergeant placed before the leading file (right or left in front) will be careful to preserve exactly the length and cadence of the step, and to direct himself straight forward; to this end, he will take points on the ground.

727. Whether the battalion march by the right or left flank, the lieutenant colonel will place himself abreast with the leading file, and the major abreast with the color-file, both on the side of the front rank, and about six paces from it.

728. The adjutant, placed between the lieutenant colonel and the front rank, will march in the same step with the head of the battalion, and the sergeant major, placed between the major and the color-bearer, will march in the same step with the adjutant.

729. The captains and file closers will carefully see that the files neither open out, nor close too much, and that they regain insensibly their distances, if lost.

730. The colonel wishing the battalion to wheel by file, will command:

1. *By file right* (or *left*).   2. MARCH.

731. The files will wheel in succession, and halt at the place where the first had wheeled, in conforming

to the principles prescribed in the school of the company.

732. The battalion marching by the flank, when the colonel shall wish it to halt, he will command:

> 1. *Battalion.* 2. HALT. 3. FRONT.

733. These commands will be executed as prescribed in the school of the company, No. 146.

734. If the battalion be marching by the flank, and the colonel should wish to cause it to march in line, either to the front or to the rear, the movements will be executed by the commands and means prescribed in the school of the company.

ARTICLE ELEVENTH.

To form the battalion on the right or left, by file, into line of battle.

735. The battalion marching by the right flank, when the colonel shall wish to form it on the right by file, he will determine the line of battle, and the lieutenant colonel will place two markers on that line, in conformity with what is prescribed No. 415.

736. The head of the battalion being nearly up with the first marker, the colonel will command:

> 1. *On the right, by file, into line.* 2. MARCH (or *double quick*—MARCH).

737. At the command *march*, the leading company will form itself on the right, by file, into line of battle, as indicated in the school of the company, No. 149; the front rank man of the first file will rest his breast lightly against the right arm of the first marker; the other companies will follow the movement of the leading company; each captain will place himself on the line at the same time with the front rank man of his first file, and on the right of this man.

738. The left guide of each company, except the leading one, will place himself on the direction of the markers, and opposite to the left file of his company, at the instant that the front rank man of this file arrives on the line.

739. The formation being ended, the colonel will command:

Guides—POSTS.

740. The colonel will superintend the successive formation of the battalion, moving along the front of the line of battle.

741. The lieutenant colonel will, in succession, assure the direction of the guides, and see that the men of the front rank, in placing themselves on the line, do not pass it.

742. If the battalion march by the left flank, the movement will be executed according to the same principles, and by inverse means.

ARTICLE TWELFTH.

Changes of front.

Change of front perpendicularly forward.

743. The battalion being in line of battle, it is supposed to be the wish of the colonel to cause a change of front forward on the right company, and that the angle formed by the old and new positions be a right angle, or a few degrees more or less than one; he will cause two markers to be placed on the new direction, before the position to be occupied by that company, and order its captain to establish it against the markers.

744. The captain of the right company will immediately direct it upon the markers by a wheel to the right on the fixed pivot; and, after having halted it, he will align it by the right.

745. These dispositions being made, the colonel will command:

1. *Change front forward on first company.* 2. *By company, right half wheel.* 3. MARCH (or *double quick*—MARCH).

746. At the second command, each captain will place himself before the centre of his company.

747. At the third, each company will wheel to the right on the fixed pivot; the left guide of each will place himself on its left as soon as he shall be able to pass; and when the colonel shall judge that the companies have sufficiently wheeled, he will command:

4. *Forward.* 5. MARCH. 6. *Guide right.*

748. At the fifth command, the companies ceasing to wheel will march straight forward; at the sixth, the men will touch elbows towards the right.

749. The right guide of the second company will march straight forward until this company shall arrive at the point where it should turn to the right; each succeeding right guide will follow the file immediately before him at the cessation of the wheel, and will march in the trace of this file until this company shall turn to the right to move upon the line; this guide will then march straight forward.

750. The second company having arrived opposite to the left file of the first, its captain will cause it to turn to the right; the right guide will direct himself so as to arrive squarely upon the line of battle, and, when he shall be at three paces from that line, the captain will command:

1. *Second company.* 2. HALT.

751. At the second command, the company will halt; the files not yet in line with the guide will come into it

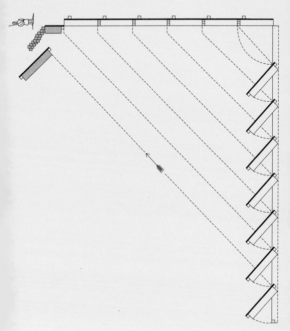

To change front forward on first company (No. 746).

promptly, the left guide will place himself on the line of battle, and as soon as he is assured in the direction by the lieutenant colonel, the captain will align the company by the right.

752. Each following company will conform to what has just been prescribed for the second.

753. The formation ended, the colonel will command:

Guides—POSTS.

754. If the battalion be in march, and the colonel shall wish to change front forward on the first company, and that the angle formed by the old and new positions be a right angle, he will cause two markers to be placed on the new direction, before the position to be occupied by that company, and will command:

1. *Change front forward on first company.* 2. *By company, right half wheel.* 3. MARCH (or *double quick*—MARCH).

755. At the first command, the captains will move rapidly before the centre of their respective companies; the captain of the first company will command: 1. *Right turn*; 2. *Quick time*; the captains of the other companies will caution them to wheel to the right.

756. At the command *march*, the first company will turn to the right, according to the principles prescribed in the school of the soldier, No. 402; its captain will halt it at three paces from the markers, and the files in rear will promptly come into line. The captain will align the company by the right.

757. Each of the other companies will wheel to the right on a fixed pivot; the left guides will place themselves on the left of their respective companies, and when the colonel shall judge they have wheeled sufficiently, he will command:

4. *Forward.* 5. MARCH. 6. *Guide right.*

758. These commands will be executed as indicated No. 746 and following.

759. The colonel will cause the battalion to change front forward on the eighth company according to the same principles and by inverse means.

Change of front perpendicularly to the rear.

760. The colonel, wishing to change front to the rear on the right company, will impart his purpose to the captain of this company. The latter will immediately face his company about, wheel it to the left on the fixed pivot, and halt it when it shall be in the direction indicated to him by the colonel; the captain will then face his company to the front, and align it by the right against the two markers, whom the colonel will cause to be established before the right and left files.

761. These dispositions being made, the colonel will command:

1. *Change front to the rear, on first company.* 2. *Battalion, about*—FACE. 3. *By company, left half wheel.* 4. MARCH (or *double quick*—MARCH).

762. At the second command, all the companies, except the right, will face about.

763. At the third, the captains, whose companies have faced about, will each place himself behind the centre of his company, two paces from the front rank, now the rear.

764. At the fourth, these companies will wheel to the left on the fixed pivot by the rear rank; the left guide of each will, as soon as he is able to pass, place himself on the left of the rear rank of his company, now become the right; and when the colonel shall judge that the companies have sufficiently wheeled, he will command:

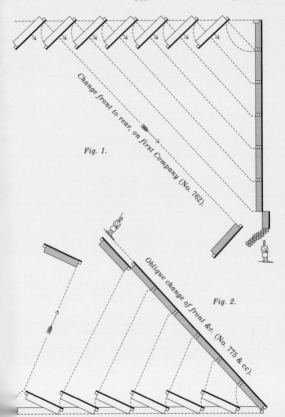

Fig. 1.

Change front to rear on first Company (No. 762).

Fig. 2.

Oblique change of front &c. (No. 775 & cc).

5. *Forward.* 6. March. 7. *Guide left.*

765. At the sixth command, the companies will cease to wheel, march straight forward towards the new line of battle, and, at the seventh, take the touch of the elbow towards the left.

766. The guide of each company on its right flank, become left, will conform himself to the principles prescribed No. 748.

767. The second company, from the right, having arrived opposite to the left of the first, will turn to the left; the guide will so direct himself as to arrive parallelly with the line of battle, cross that line, and when the front rank, now in the rear, shall be three paces beyond it, the captain will command: 1. *Second company;* 2. Halt.

768. At the second command, the company will halt; the files which may not yet be in line with the guide will promptly come into it; the captain will cause the company to face about, and then align it by the right.

769. All the other companies will execute what has just been prescribed for the second, each as it successively arrives opposite to the left of the company that precedes it on the new line of battle.

770. The formation being ended, the colonel will command:

Guides—Posts.

771. The colonel will cause a change of front on the left company of the battalion to the rear, according to the same principles and by inverse means.

772. In changes of front, the colonel will give a general superintendence to the movement.

773. The lieutenant colonel will assure the direction of the guides as they successively move out on the line of battle, conforming himself to what has been prescribed in the successive formations.

Remarks on changes of front.

774. When the new direction is perpendicular, or nearly so, to that of the battalion, the companies ought to make about a *half wheel* (the eighth of the circle) before marching straight forward; but when these two lines are oblique to each other, the smaller the angle which they form, the less ought the companies to wheel. It is for the colonel to judge, according to the angle, the precise time when he ought to give the command *march* after the caution *forward*, and if he cannot catch the exact moment, the word of execution should rather be given a little too soon, than an instant too late.

775. When the old and the new lines form an angle of forty-five or fewer degrees, the colonel will find it necessary to arrest the wheel of the companies when the marching flanks shall have taken but a few paces, or, it may be, have but disengaged, respectively, from the fixed pivots of the next companies; and in all such cases the companies will arrive so nearly parallel to the new line as to be able to align themselves upon it without the intermediate turn to the right or left: to execute the movement under either circumstance supposed, the colonel will command:

Oblique change of front, forward (or *to the rear*) *on* (*such company*).

Article Thirteenth.

To ploy the battalion into column doubled on the centre.

776. This movement consists in ploying the corresponding companies of the right and left wings into column at company distances or closed in mass, in rear of the two centre companies, according to the principles prescribed Article Third, Part Second, of this School.

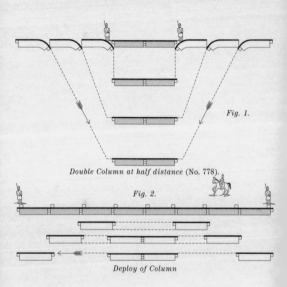

Fig. 1.

Double Column at half distance (No. 778).

Fig. 2.

Deploy of Column

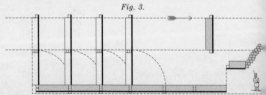

Fig. 3.

Right into line wheel left companies on the right into line (No. 804).

777. The colonel, wishing to form the double column at company distance (the battalion being in line of battle), will command:

1. *Double column, at half distance.* 2. *Battalion, inwards*—FACE. 3. MARCH (or *double quick*—MARCH).

778. At the first command, the captains will place themselves two paces in front of their respective companies; the captains of the two centre companies will caution them to stand fast, and the other captains will caution their companies to face to the left and right, respectively. The covering sergeants will step into the front rank.

779. At the second command, the fourth and fifth companies will stand fast; the others of the right wing will face to the left, and the others of the left wing will face to the right; each captain whose company has faced will hasten to break to the rear the two files at the head of his company; the left guide of each right company, and the right guide of each left company, will each place himself at the head of its front rank, and the captain by the side of his guide.

780. At the command *march*, the fourth and fifth companies, which are to form the first division, will stand fast; the senior captain of the two will place himself before the centre of the division, and command: *Guide right*; the junior captain will place himself in the interval between the two companies, and the left guide of the left company will place himself in the front rank on the left of the division, as soon as he shall be able to pass.

781. All the other companies, conducted by their captains, will step off with life to arrange themselves in column at company distance, each company behind the preceding one in the column of the same wing, so that, in the right wing, the third may be next behind the fourth, the second next to the third, and so on to the right

company; and, in the left wing, the sixth may be next
behind the fifth, the seventh next to the sixth, and so on
to the left company of the battalion.

782. The corresponding companies of the two wings
will unite into divisions in arranging themselves in column; an instant before the union, at the centre of the column, the left guides of right companies will pass into the
line of file closers, and each captain will command: 1.
Such company; 2. *Halt*; 3. FRONT.

783. At the second command, which will be given at
the instant of union, each company will halt; at the third,
it will face to the front. The senior captain in each division will place himself on its right, and command, *Right*—
DRESS, and the junior captain will place himself in the
interval between the two companies. The division being
aligned, its chief will command FRONT, and take his position two paces before its centre.

784. The column being thus formed, the divisions will
take the respective denominations of *first, second, third,*
&c., according to position in the column, beginning at the
front.

785. The lieutenant colonel, who at the second command given by the colonel will have placed himself at a little
more than company distance in rear of the right guide of the
first division, will assure the right guides on the direction as
they successively arrive, by placing himself in their rear.

786. The music will pass to the rear of the column.

787. The battalion being in march, to form the double
column at company distance without halting the battalion,
the colonel will command:

1. *Double column, at half distance.* 2. *Battalion by the
   right and left flanks.* 3. MARCH (or *double quick*—
   MARCH).

788. At the first command, each captain will move

briskly in front of the centre of his company; the captains of the fourth and fifth will caution their companies to march straight forward; the other captains will caution their companies to face to the right and left.

789. At the command *march*, the fourth and fifth companies will continue to march straight forward; the senior captain will place himself before the centre of his division, and command, *Guide right*; the junior captain will place himself in the interval between the two companies. The left guide of the fifth company will place himself on the left of the front rank of the division. The men will take the touch of elbows to the right. The color and general guides will retake their places. The three right companies will face to the left, and the three left companies will face to the right. Each captain will break to the rear two files at the head of his company; the left guides of the right companies, and the right guides of the left companies, will each place himself at the head of the front rank of his company, and the captain by the side of his guide.

790. The third and sixth companies will enter the column and direct themselves parallelly to the first division. Each of the other companies will, in like manner, place itself behind the company of the wing to which it belongs, and will be careful to gain as much ground as possible towards the head of the column.

791. The corresponding companies of each wing will unite into divisions on taking their positions in column, and each captain, the instant the head of his company arrives at the centre of the column, will command: 1. *Such company by the right* (or *left*) *flank*. 2. MARCH. The senior captain of the two companies will place himself in front of the centre of his division, and command, *Guide right*; the junior captain will place himself in the interval between the two companies. The two companies thus formed into

division will take the touch of elbows to the right, and when each division has gained its proper distance, its chief will cause it to march in quick time.

792. When the battalion presents an odd number of companies, the formation will be made in like manner, and the company on either flank which shall find itself without a corresponding one, will place itself at company distance behind the wing to which it belongs.

793. The double column, closed in mass, will be formed according to the same principles and by the same commands, substituting the indication, *closed in mass*, for that of *at half distance*.

794. The double column never being formed when two or more battalions are to be in one general column, it will habitually take the guide to the right, sometimes to the left, or in the centre of the column; in the last case, the command will be, *Guide centre*. The column will march and change direction according to the principles prescribed for a simple column by division.

795. The double column at company distance will be closed in mass, or, if in mass, will take half distance, by the commands and means indicated for a simple column by division.

Deployment of the double column, faced to the front.

796. The colonel, wishing to deploy the double column, will place a marker respectively before the right and left files of the first division, and a third before the left file of the right company, same division; which being done, he will cause the two general guides to spring out on the alignment of the markers a little beyond the points at which the respective flanks of the battalion ought to rest; he will then command:

1. *Deploy column.*   2. *Battalion outwards*—FACE.
    3. MARCH (or *double quick*—MARCH).

797. The column will deploy itself on the two companies at its head, according to the principles prescribed for the deployment of columns to mass. The captains of these companies will each, at the command *march*, place himself on the right of his own company, and align it by the right; the captain of the fourth will then place himself in the rear rank, and the covering sergeant in the rank of file closers, at the moment the captain of the third shall come to its left to align it.

798. The deployment being ended, the colonel will command:

Guides—POSTS.

799. If it be the wish of the colonel to cause the fire to commence pending the deployment, he will give an order to that effect to the captains of the fourth and fifth companies, and the fire will be executed according to the principles prescribed No. 438.

800. The battalion being in double column and in march, if the colonel shall wish to deploy it without halting the column, he will cause three markers to be posted on the line of battle, and when the head of the column shall arrive near the markers, he will command:

1. *Deploy column.* 2. *Battalion, by the right and left flanks.* 3. MARCH (or *double quick*—MARCH).

801. The column will deploy on the two leading companies, according to the principles prescribed for the deployment of a close column, No. 533 and following; at the command *march*, the chief of the first division will halt it, and the captains of the fourth and fifth companies will align their companies by the right.

802. If the column be in march, and it be the wish of the colonel to deploy the column and to continue to march in the order of battle, he will not cause markers to be established at the head of the column. The movement

will be executed by the commands and means indicated No. 800, observing what follows. At the first command, the chief of the first division will command, *Quick time*. At the command *march*, the first division will continue to march in quick time; the colonel will command, *Guide centre*. The captains of the fourth and fifth companies, the color, and the men, will immediately conform to the principles of the march in line of battle. The companies will take the quick step by the command of their captains, as they successively arrive in line. The movement completed, the colonel may cause the battalion to march in double quick time.

To form the double column into line of battle, faced to the right or left.

803. The double column, being at company distance and at a halt, may be formed into line of battle faced to the right or left; when the colonel shall wish to form it faced to the right, he will command:

1. *Right into line wheel, left companies on the right into line.* 2. *Battalion, guide right.* 3. MARCH (or *double quick*—MARCH).

804. At the first command, each captain will place himself before the centre of his company; the right companies will be cautioned that they will have to wheel to the right into line, the left companies that they will have to march straight forward.

805. At the second command, the left guide of the fourth company will place himself briskly on the direction of the right guides of the column, face to them, and opposite to one of the three last files of his company when in line of battle; the lieutenant colonel will assure him in that position.

806. At the command *march*, briskly repeated by all the captains, the right companies will form *to* the right into line of battle, the left companies will put themselves

in march in order to form *on* the right into line of battle; these formations will be executed by the means indicated No. 391 and following, No. 416 and following; the lieutenant colonel will assure the guides of the left wing on the line of battle as they successively come upon it.

807. If the column be in march, the colonel will command:

1. *Right into line wheel.* 2. *Left companies, on the right into line.* 3. *Battalion, guide right.* 4. MARCH (or *double quick*—MARCH).

808. At the first command, each captain will place himself promptly before the centre of his company; the right companies will be cautioned that they will have to wheel to the right, and the left companies that they will have to form on the right into line.

809. At the command *march*, briskly repeated, the right companies will form to the right into line, and the left companies on the right into line. These formations will be executed as prescribed Nos. 402, 417, and following.

810. If the colonel should wish to move the battalion forward, at the moment the right companies have completed the wheel, he will command:

5. *Forward.* 6. MARCH (or *double quick*—MARCH).

811. At the command *forward*, the captains of the right companies will command, *Quick time*. At the command *march*, the right companies will cease to wheel, and march straight forward. The colonel will then add:

7. *Guide centre.*

812. The movement of the left companies will be executed in double quick time as prescribed above, and as they arrive on the line each captain will cause his company to march in quick time.

813. The column may be formed faced to the left into line of battle according to the same principles.

814. If the column be closed in mass instead of at company distance, these movements will be executed according to the principles prescribed Nos. 417, 502, and 510.

Remark on the deployment of the double column.

815. The depth of the double column, at company distance, being inconsiderable, closing it in mass, if at a halt, in order to deploy it, may be dispensed with; but if it be in march, it will be preferable to cause it so to close, in halting, before deploying.

816. The double column will be deployed habitually on the centre companies, but the colonel may sometimes deploy it on any interior company, or on the first or eighth company.

Article Fourteenth.

Dispositions against Cavalry.

817. A battalion being in column by company, at full distance, right in front, and at a halt, when the colonel shall wish to form it into square, he will first cause divisions to be formed; which being done, he will command:

1. *To form square.* 2. *To half distance, close column.*
3. March (or *double quick*—March).

818. At the command *march*, the column will close to company distance, the second division taking its distance from the rear rank of the first division.

819. At the moment of halting the fourth division, the file closers of each company of which it is composed, passing by the outer flank of their companies, will place themselves two paces before the front rank opposite to their respective places in line of battle, and face towards the head of the column.

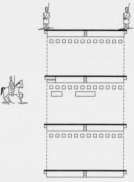

To form square, to half distance, close column (No. 818).

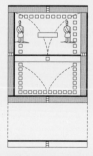

Form square, right and left into line, wheel (No. 822).

820. At the commencement of the movement, the major will place himself on the right of the column abreast with the first division; the buglers formed in two ranks will place themselves, at platoon distance, behind the inner platoons of the second division.

821. These dispositions being made, the colonel may, according to circumstances, put the column in march or cause it to form square; if he wish to do the latter, he will command:

1. *Form square.* 2. *Right and left into line, wheel.*

822. At the first command, the lieutenant colonel, facing to the left guides, and the major, facing to those of the right, will align them, from the front, on the respective guides of the fourth division, who will stand fast, holding up their pieces, inverted, perpendicularly; the right guides, in placing themselves on the direction, will take their exact distances.

823. At the second command, the chief of the first division will caution it to stand fast; all the captains of the second and third divisions will place themselves before the centres of their respective companies, and caution them that they will have to wheel, the right companies to the right, and the left companies to the left into line of battle.

824. The color-bearer will step back into the line of file closers, opposite to his place in line of battle, and will be replaced by the corporal of his file who is in the rear rank; the corporal of the same file who is in the rank of file closers will step into the rear rank.

825. The chief of the fourth division will command: 1. *Fourth division, forward*; 2. *Guide left*, and place himself at the same time two paces outside of its left flank.

826. These dispositions ended, the colonel will command:

MARCH (or *double quick*—MARCH).

827. At this command, briskly repeated, the first division will stand fast; but its right file will face to the right, and its left file to the left.

828. The companies of the second and third divisions will wheel to the right and left into line, and the buglers will advance a space equal to the front of a company.

829. The fourth division will close up to form the square, and when it shall have closed, its chief will halt it, face it about, and align it by the rear rank upon the guides of the division, who will, for this purpose, remain faced to the front. The junior captain will pass into the rear rank, now become the front, and the covering sergeant of the left company will place himself in the front rank, become rear. The file closers will, at the same time, close up a pace on the front rank, and the outer file on each flank of the division will face outwards.

830. The square being formed, the colonel will command:

Guides—POSTS.

831. At this command, the chiefs of the first and fourth divisions, as well as the guides, will enter the square.

832. The captains whose companies have formed to the right into line will remain on the left of their companies; the left guide of each of those companies will, in the rear rank, cover his captain, and the covering sergeant of each will place himself as a file closer behind the right file of his company.

833. The field and staff will enter the square, the lieutenant colonel placing himself behind the left, and the major behind the right, of the first division.

834. If the battalion present ten instead of eight companies, the fourth division will make the same movements prescribed above for the second and third divisions, and

the fifth the movements prescribed for the fourth division.

835. A battalion ought never to present, near the enemy's cavalry, an odd company. The odd company, under that circumstance, ought, when the battalion is under arms, to be consolidated, for the time, with the other companies.

836. The fronts of the square will be designated as follows: the first division will always be the *first front*; the last division, the *fourth front*; the right companies of the other divisions will form the *second front*; and the left companies of the same divisions the *third front*.

837. A battalion being in column by company, at full distance, right in front, and in march, when the colonel shall wish to form square, he will cause this movement to be executed by the commands and means indicated No. 817.

838. At the command *march*, the column will close to company distance, as is prescribed No. 278. When the chief of the fourth division shall command, *Quick, march*, the file closers of this division will place themselves before the front rank.

839. The major and the buglers will conform to what is prescribed No. 820.

840. If the colonel shall wish to form square, he will command:

1. *Form square.*   2. *Right and left into line, wheel.*
3. MARCH.

841. At the first command, the chief of the first division will caution it to halt; all the captains of the second and third divisions will rapidly place themselves before the centres of their respective companies, and caution them that they will have to wheel, the right companies to the right, and the left companies to the left into line. The chief of the fourth division will caution it to continue its

march, and will hasten to its left flank. At the third
command, briskly repeated, the chief of the first division
will halt his division and align it to the left, the outer
files will face to the right and left, the rest of the movement will be executed as prescribed No. 828 and
following.

842. The lieutenant colonel and the major, at the
command *march*, will conform to what is prescribed No.
822.

843. If the battalion, before the square is formed, be in
double column, the two leading companies will form the
first front, the two rear companies the fourth: the other
companies of the right half battalion will form the second,
and those of the left half battalion the third front.

844. The first and fourth fronts will be commanded by
the chiefs of the first and fourth divisions; each of the
other two by its senior captain.

845. The commander of each front will place himself
four paces behind its present rear rank, and will be
replaced momentarily in the command of his company by
the next in rank therein.

846. If the column be at full distance, instead
of at company distance, as has been supposed, the
square will be formed in the manner prescribed No. 817
or 838, and following; and the dispositions indicated Nos.
819 and 820 will be executed at the command *form
square*.

847. If the column by division, whether double or simple, be in mass, and the colonel shall wish to form it into
square, he will first cause it to take company distance; to
this effect, he will command:

1. *To form square.*   2. *By the head of column, take half
distance.*

848. The divisions will take half distance by the means
indicated No. 324 and following. What is prescribed No.

820 will be executed as the first and second divisions are put in motion.

849. The colonel will halt the column the moment the third division shall have its distance. As soon as the column is halted, the dispositions indicated No. 819 will be executed, and when these are completed, the colonel may proceed to form square.

850. If the column be in march, he will also, in the first place, cause company distance to be taken, and, for this purpose, will command:

1. *To form square.* 2. *By the head of column, take half distance.* 3. MARCH (or *double quick*—MARCH).

851. This movement will be executed as prescribed No. 330 and following. What is prescribed No. 820 will be executed as the first and second divisions are put in motion.

852. The colonel will proceed to form square the moment the third division shall have its distance; at the command *form square*, the dispositions indicated No. 819 will be executed. If it be intended merely to *dispose the column for square*, the colonel will not halt the column until the last division has its distance.

853. In a simple column, left in front, these several movements will be executed according to the same principles and by inverse means; but the fronts of the square will have the same designations as if the right of the column were in front, that is, the first division will constitute the first front, and thus of the other subdivisions.

854. The battalion being formed into square, when the colonel shall wish to cause it to advance a distance less than thirty paces, he will command:

1. *By* (such) *front, forward.* 2. MARCH.

855. If it be supposed that the advance be made

by the first front, the chief of this front will command:

1. *First division, forward.*   2. *Guide centre.*

856. The chief of the second front will face his front to
the left. The captains of the companies composing this
front will place themselves outside, and on the right of
their left guides, who will replace them in the front rank;
the chief of the third front will face his front to the right,
and the captains in this front will place themselves outside, and on the left of their covering sergeants; the chief
of the fourth front will face his front about, and command: 1. *Fourth division, forward*; 2. *Guide centre.* The
captain who is in the centre of the first front will be
charged with the direction of the march, and will regulate
himself by the means indicated in the school of the company, No. 89.

857. At the command *march*, the square will put
itself in motion; the companies marching by the flank
will be careful not to lose their distances. The chief
of the fourth division will cause his division to keep
constantly closed on the flanks of the second and third
fronts.

858. This movement will only be executed in quick
time.

859. The lieutenant colonel will place himself
in rear of the file of direction in order to regulate his
march.

860. If the colonel should wish to halt the square, he
will command:

1. *Battalion.*   2. HALT.

861. At the second command, the square will halt; the
fourth front will face about immediately, and without further command; the second and third fronts will face outwards; the captains of companies will resume their places
as in square.

862. In moving the square forward by the second, third, or fourth fronts, the same rules will be observed.

863. The battalion being formed into square, when the colonel shall wish to cause it to advance a greater distance than thirty paces, he will command:

1. *Form column.*

864. The chief of the first front will command:

1. *First division forward.*   2. *Guide left.*

865. The commander of the fourth front will caution it to stand fast; the commander of the second front will cause it to face to the left, and then command, *By company, by file left.* The commander of the third front will cause it to face to the right, and then command, *By company, by file right.* At the moment the second and third fronts face to the left and right, each captain will cause to break to the rear the two leading files of his company.

866. These dispositions being made, the colonel will command:

3. MARCH (or *double quick*—MARCH).

867. At this command, the first front will march forward; its chief will halt it when it shall have advanced a space equal to half its front, and align it by the left.

868. The corresponding companies of the second and third fronts will wheel by file to the left and right, and march to meet each other behind the centre of the first division, and the moment they unite, the captain of each company will halt his company and face it to the front. The division being re-formed, its chief will align it by the left.

869. The commander of the fourth front will cause it to face about: its file closers will remain before the front rank.

870. The column being thus re-formed, the colonel

may put it in march by the commands and means prescribed No. 164 and following; the right guides will preserve company distance exactly as the directing guides.

871. When the colonel shall wish to re-form square, he
will give the commands indicated No. 840.

872. To cause the square to march in retreat a distance
greater than thirty paces, the colonel will first cause column to be formed as indicated No. 863; and when formed,
he will cause it to face by the rear rank; to this end, he
will command:

> 1. *To march in retreat.*   2. *Face by the rear rank.*
> 3. *Battalion about*—FACE.

873. At the second command, the file closers of the
interior divisions will place themselves, passing by the
outer flanks of their respective companies, behind the
front rank opposite to their places in line of battle; the file
closers of the other divisions will stand fast.

874. At the third command, the battalion will face
about; each chief of division will place himself before its
rear rank, become front, passing through the interval
between its two companies; the guides will step into the
rear rank, now front.

875. The column being thus disposed, the colonel may
put it in march, or cause it to form square as if it were
faced by the front rank. The square being formed, its
fronts will preserve the same designations they had when
faced by the front rank.

876. The battalion being in square by the rear
rank, when the colonel shall wish to march it in retreat or
in advance, a distance less than thirty paces, he will
conform to what is prescribed No. 854 and following; otherwise, he will re-form the column according to the principles prescribed No. 863, by marching forward the fourth
front.

877. If the square is to be marched to the front a

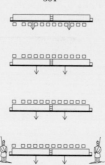

Column faced by the rear rank, to march in retreat
(No. 873).

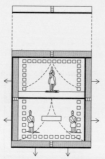

To form square, marching in retreat (No. 875).

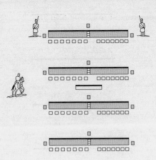

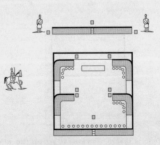

To reduce the square (No. 883).

distance greater than thirty paces, the colonel will face the column by the front rank; to this end, he will command:

1. *To march in advance.* 2. *Face by the front rank.*
    3. *Battalion about*—FACE.

878. Which will be executed as prescribed No. 873 and following.

879. If the column be marching in advance, and the colonel shall wish to march it in retreat, he will command:

1. *To march in retreat.* 2. *Battalion right about.*
    3. MARCH (or *double quick*—MARCH).

880. At the second command, the file closers of the second and third divisions will place themselves rapidly before the front rank of their respective divisions. At the command *march*, the column will face about and move off to the rear; the chiefs of divisions and the guides will conform to what is prescribed No. 874.

881. If the column be marching in retreat, and the colonel shall wish to march it in advance, he will command:

1. *To march in advance.* 2. *Battalion right about.*
    3. MARCH (or *double quick*—MARCH).

882. At the second command, the file closers of the second and third divisions will place themselves before the rear rank of their respective divisions; at the third, the column will face by the front rank.

To reduce the square.

883. The colonel, wishing to break the square, will command:

1. *Reduce square.* 2. MARCH (or *double quick*—
    MARCH).

884. This movement will be executed in the manner indicated No. 863 and following; but the file closers of the fourth front will place themselves behind the rear rank the moment it faces about; the field and staff, the color-bearer and buglers, will, at the same time, return to their places in column.

To form square from line of battle.

885. A battalion deployed may be formed into square in a direction either parallel or perpendicular to the line of battle.

886. In the first case, the colonel will cause the battalion to break by division to the rear, by the right or left, and then close the column to half distance, as indicated No. 817 and following.

887. In the second case, he will ploy the battalion into simple column by division at half distance in rear of the right or left division, or into column doubled on the centre.

888. To ploy the battalion into column upon one of the flank divisions, the colonel will command:

1. *To form square.* 2. *Column at half distance by division.* 3. *On the first* (or *fourth*) *division.* 4. *Battalion right* (or *left*)—FACE 5. MARCH. (or *double quick*—MARCH).

889. This movement will be executed according to the principles prescribed No. 119 and following.

890. If the battalion be marching in line of battle, and the colonel shall wish to form square in a direction perpendicular to the line of battle, he will command;

1. *To form square.* 2. *On the first* (or *fourth*) *division, form column.* 3. *Battalion by the right* (or *left*) *flank.* 4. MARCH (or *double quick*—MARCH).

891. This movement will be executed according to the principles prescribed for ploying a column by division at half distance, No. 150. The chief of the first division will halt his division at the command *march*.

892. To ploy the battalion into double column, the colonel will command:

1. *To form square.* 2. *Double column at half distance.* 3. *Battalion inwards*—FACE. 4. MARCH (or *double quick*—MARCH).

893. This movement will be executed as prescribed No. 778 and following.

894. The battalion being in march, to ploy it into double column to form square, the colonel will command:

1. *To form square.* 2. *Form double column.* 3. *Battalion by the right and left flanks.* 4. MARCH (or *double quick*—MARCH).

895. This movement will be executed as prescribed No. 788. The chief of the leading division will halt his division at the command *march*.

Observations relative to the formation of squares in two ranks.

896. When the colonel shall judge it proper to have a reserve, this reserve, in a column of three divisions, will be formed of the inner platoons of the second division. The second division will, in this case, close to platoon distance on the first division. When the square is formed, the reserve platoons will move forward a distance nearly equal to a platoon front.

897. In re-forming column, the first division will move forward platoon, instead of company distance.

898. If the column be formed of four divisions, the inner platoons of the third division will compose the reserve; then, in re-forming column, the first division will

conform to the general rule, and the chief of the third, as
soon as his division is formed, will close it to platoon distance on the second division. The colonel may, if necessary, form the reserve of the entire third division. In this
case, the movement will be executed in the following
manner.

899. If the column be at full distance, when it shall
close, at the command *to form square*, to half distance,
the chief of the third division will cause four files to break
to the rear from the right and left of his division; the
guides will close upon the outer files remaining in line,
and the left guide will march exactly in the trace of the
file immediately in front of him. This division will then
close in mass on the second division; and the chief of the
fourth division will close to half distance on the same
division.

900. At the command *form square*, the chief of the
reserve division will command, 1. *Third division forward.* 2. *Guide centre;* at this command, the guides on the
flanks will fall into the line of file closers. At the command *march*, the reserve will move forward the distance
of a company front. When halted, its chief will cause
the platoons to be doubled, and for this purpose will
command:

1. *On the centre double platoons.* 2. MARCH.

901. At the first command, the chiefs of platoon will
place themselves in front of the centre of their respective
platoons; the chief of each outer platoon will face his platoon towards the centre, and cause to break to the rear
two files from the left or right. At the command *march*,
the outer platoons will direct their march so as to double
on the centre platoon at the distance of four paces; their
chiefs will align these outer platoons on the centre, and
the files previously broken to the rear will come into line.

902. If the column be at half instead of full distance,
the colonel before forming square will order the chiefs of

the third and fourth divisions to move forward their divisions as prescribed No. 899.

903. If the column be closed in mass, at the command *to form square*, the chief of the third division will break four files to the rear from each of the flanks as prescribed No. 899.

904. The colonel will halt the column as soon as the second division shall have gained its distance.

905. If the colonel shall wish the column to continue marching, at the command, *by the head of column take half distance*, the chief of the reserve division will give his cautionary commands in sufficient time to place his division in motion simultaneously with the one which precedes it. The chief of the fourth division will give the command *march* at the instant there is company distance between his division and the second.

906. When the colonel shall wish to re-form the column, at the command *form column*, the chief of the third division will command, *Form division*; at this command, the chiefs of the outer platoons which have doubled in rear of the centre platoons, will give the commands and make the preparatory movements for deploying on the centre platoons, which will be executed at the command *march* given by the colonel and briskly repeated by the chief of this division. The division being re-formed, the chiefs of the outer platoons will retake their places in column, and the chief of this division will again cause four files from each of its flanks to break to the rear.

907. If before the formation of the square, the column had been left in front, it would be formed by the same commands and according to the same principles. The second division, in this case, would form the reserve.

908. The column being formed, if the colonel should wish to march it in retreat he will face it by the rear rank. The files of the third division broken off to the rear, will

face about with the battalion, and when the column is put in motion will march in front of the rear rank. But should the colonel wish to re-form the square, he will cause the battalion to face by the front rank.

909. If the battalion be in line, instead of in column, the chief of the reserve division will bring it into column in such manner that there may be a distance of only four paces between this division and the one which is to be immediately in front of it; and when this division is halted and aligned, its chief will cause the usual number of files to be broken to the rear. The chief of the division which should occupy in column a position immediately in rear of the reserve division will, on entering the column, take a distance of twelve paces between it and the division established immediately in front of the reserve division.

Squares in four ranks.

910. If the square formed in two ranks, according to the preceding rules, should not be deemed sufficiently strong, the colonel may cause the square to be formed in four ranks.

911. The battalion being in column by company at full distance, right in front, and at a halt, when the colonel shall wish to form square in four ranks, he will first cause divisions to be formed, which being executed, he will command:

1. *To form square in four ranks.* 2. *To half distance, close column.* 3. MARCH (or *double quick*—MARCH).

912. At the first command, the chief of the first division will caution the right company to face to the left, and the left company to face to the right. The chiefs of the other divisions will caution their divisions to move forward.

913. At the command *march*, the right company of the

first division will form into four ranks on its left file, and
the left company into four ranks on its right file. The formation ended, the chief of this division will align it by the
left.

914. The other divisions will move forward and double
their files marching; the right company of each division
will double on its left file, and the left company on its
right file. The formation completed, each chief of division
will command, *Guide left.* Each chief will halt his division
when it shall have the distance of a company front in four
ranks from the preceding one, counting from its rear rank,
and will align his division by the left. At the instant the
fourth division is halted, the file closers will move rapidly
before its front rank.

915. The colonel will form square, re-form column, and
reduce square in four ranks, by the same commands and
means as prescribed for a battalion in two ranks.

916. If the square formed in four ranks be reduced and
at a halt, and the colonel shall wish to form the battalion
into two ranks, he will command:

1. *In two ranks undouble files.*   2. *Battalion outwards—*
FACE.   3. MARCH.

917. At the first command, the captains will step
before the centres of their respective companies, and
those on the right will caution them to face to the right,
and those on the left to face to the left.

918. At the second command, the battalion will face to
the right and left.

919. At the command *march*, each company will
undouble its files and re-form into two ranks as indicated
in the school of the company No. 376 and following. Each
captain will halt his company and face it to the front. The
formation completed, each chief of division will align his
division by the left.

920. If the column be in march, with divisions formed

in four ranks, and the colonel shall wish to re-form them
into two ranks, he will command:

1. *Guide centre.*   2. *In two ranks, undouble files.*
3. MARCH.

921. The captain, placed in the centre of each division,
will continue to march straight to the front, as will also
the left file of the right company, and the right file of the
left company. Each company will then be re-formed into
two ranks, as prescribed in the school of the company.

922. The battalion being formed into two ranks, the
colonel will command, *Guide left* (or *right*).

923. To form square in four ranks on one of the flank
divisions, the colonel will command:

1. *To form square, in four ranks.*   2. *Column at half distance, by division.*   3. *On the first* (or *fourth*) *division.*   4. *Battalion, right* (or *left*)—FACE.   5. MARCH
(or *double quick*—MARCH).

924. At the second command, each chief of division
will place himself before the centre of his division, and
caution it to face to the right.

925. At the fourth command, the right guide of the
first division will remain faced to the front, the battalion
will face to the right.

926. At the command *march*, the first file of four men
of the first division will face to the front, remaining doubled. All the other files of four men will step off together,
and each in succession will close up to its proper distance
on the file preceding it, and face to the front, remaining
doubled. When the last file shall have closed, the chief of
division will command, *Left*—DRESS.

927. The other divisions will ploy into column in the
same manner as with a battalion in two ranks, observing
what follows: the chiefs of division, instead of allowing
their divisions to file past them on entering the column,

will continue to lead them, and as each division shall arrive on a line with the right guide of the first division, its chief will halt the right guide, who will immediately face to the front; the first file of four men will also halt at the same time and face to the front, remaining doubled. The second file will close on the first, and, when closed, halt, and face to the front, remaining doubled. All the other files will execute successively what has just been prescribed for the second. When the last file shall have closed, the chief of division will command, *Left*—DRESS.

928. If the battalion be in march, the colonel will command:

1. *To form square, in four ranks.* 2. *On the first division, form column.* 3. *Battalion, by the right flank.* 4. MARCH (or *double quick*—MARCH).

929. At the second command, each chief of division will step in front of the centre of his division and caution it to face by the right flank. The chief of the first division will caution his covering sergeant to halt, and remain faced to the front.

930. At the command *march*, the battalion will face to the right; the covering sergeant of the first division will halt and remain faced to the front, the first division will then form into four ranks as heretofore prescribed. The other divisions will ploy into column in the same manner as if the movement had taken place from a halt.

931. If the colonel should wish to form a perpendicular square in four ranks, by double column, he will command:

1. *To form square, in four ranks.* 2. *Double column, at half distance.* 3. *Battalion inwards*—FACE. 4. MARCH (or *double quick*—MARCH).

932. At the second command, the captains of companies will place themselves before the centres of their

respective companies, and caution those on the right to face to the left, and those on the left to face to the right. The captain of the fifth company will caution his covering sergeant to stand fast.

933. At the third command, the battalion will face to the left and right; at the command *march*, the left file of the fourth and the right file of the fifth company will face to the front, remaining doubled. The fourth company will close successively by file of fours on the left file, and the fifth company, in like manner, on the right file; the files will face to the front, remaining doubled. The formation completed, the chief of division will command, *Right dress*. The junior captain will place himself in the interval between the two companies.

934. The other companies will close as prescribed for the double column in two ranks, observing what follows: each captain will halt the leading guide of his company the moment the head of his company arrives on a line with the centre of the column. In the right companies, the left guides will step into the line of file closers, and the left file of four men will face immediately to the front, remaining doubled, and by the side of the right guide of the left company. The companies will each form into four ranks, as prescribed No. 926, the right companies on the left file, and the left companies on the right file. The formation completed, the junior captain will place himself between the two companies, and the senior will command, *Right dress*.

935. If the battalion be in march, the colonel will command:

1. *To form square, in four ranks.* 2. *Form double column.* 3. *Battalion by the right and left flanks.* 3. MARCH (or *double quick*—MARCH).

936. At the second command, the captains will place themselves before the centres of their respective

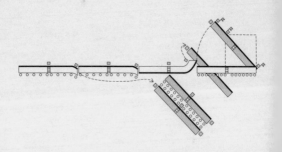

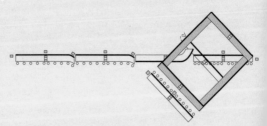

To form oblique square (No. 939).

companies, and those on the right will caution them to face by the left flank, and those on the left to face by the right flank; the captain of the fifth company will caution his covering sergeant to halt and remain faced to the front.

937. At the command *march*, the fourth and fifth companies will halt. The battalion will face to the left and right; the covering sergeant of the fifth company will halt and remain faced to the front; the movement will then be executed as if the battalion was at a halt.

Oblique squares.

938. The battalion being in line of battle, when the colonel shall wish to form the oblique square, he will command:

1. *To form oblique square.* 2. *On the first division form column.*

939. At the second command, the lieutenant colonel will trace the alignment of the first division in the following manner: he will place himself before and near the right file of this division, face to the left, march twelve paces along the front rank, halt, face to the right, march twelve paces perpendicularly to the front, halt again, face to the right, and immediately place a marker at this point. The covering sergeant of the right company will step, at the same time, before its right file, face to the left, and conform the line of his shoulders to that of the shoulders of the marker established by the lieutenant colonel. These two markers being established, the lieutenant colonel will place a third marker on the same alignment, at the point where the left of the division will halt.

940. The chiefs of division will place themselves in front of the centres of their divisions; the chief of the first division will immediately establish it by a wheel to the right on a fixed pivot, against the markers, and align it by

the left. The chiefs of the other divisions will caution
them to face to the right. The colonel will then command:

3. *Battalion, right*—FACE.   4. MARCH (or *double
quick*—MARCH).

941. The three rear divisions will direct their march so
as to place themselves at half distance from each other,
and in the rear of the first division, as previously indicated, observing what follows:

942. The chief of the second division, instead of breaking the headmost files to the rear, will break them to the
front, and, at the command *march*, will conduct his division towards the point of entrance into the column.
Arrived at this point, he will halt in his own person, cause
his division to wheel by file to the right, instructing the
right guide to direct himself parallelly to the first division;
and as soon as the left file has passed, its chief will halt
the division, and align it by the left. The other divisions
will break to the rear, but slightly; each will enter the column as prescribed for the second, and the moment the
battalion is ployed into column the colonel will cause it to
form square.

943. The formation of a battalion into oblique square
on the left division, will be executed according to the
same principles and by inverse means.

944. Should the battalion be in march, the colonel will
first cause it to halt.

945. In the preceding example, the battalion was supposed to be deployed; but if it be already formed in column, the desired obliquity will be established by causing
it to change direction by the flank; to this end, the colonel
will command:

1. *To form oblique square.*   2. *Change direction by the
right* (or *left*) *flank.*

946. At the second command, the lieutenant colonel

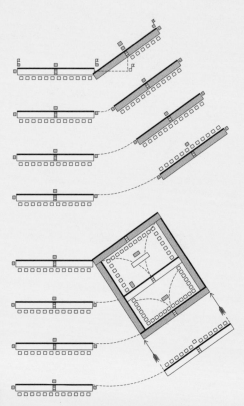

To form oblique square (No. 946).

will trace the new direction in the following manner: he will place before the right and left files of the headmost division, two markers, and a third on the prolongation of the first two, on the side of the change of direction, and at twelve paces from the flank of the column. He will then place himself before the third marker, march twelve paces perpendicularly to the front, halt, and finish tracing the new direction in the manner indicated No. 939.

947. The colonel will then command:

3. *Battalion right* (or *left*)—FACE. 4. MARCH (or *double quick—*MARCH).

948. The change of direction having been executed, the colonel will cause the square to be formed.

949. Should the column be in march, the colonel will first cause it to halt.

950. Oblique squares in four ranks will be executed by the same means, and according to the principles prescribed for the formation of squares in four ranks.

951. Whether the battalion be ployed into simple or double column, the particular dispositions for the formation of the square will be executed as prescribed No. 819 and following. The division which is to form the rear of the column will be closed in mass, and, as soon as it is aligned, the major will rectify the position of the guides on the side of the column opposite to the direction.

952. If it be the wish of the colonel merely to prepare for square, he will in all formations with that view substitute the command *prepare for square* in place of *to form square*, and in that case the last division will enter the column at company distance.

Remarks on the formation of squares.

953. It is a general principle that a column by company, which is to be formed into square, will first form

divisions, and close to half distance. Nevertheless, if it find itself suddenly threatened by cavalry without sufficient time to form divisions, the colonel will cause the column to close to platoon distance, and then form square by the commands and means which have been indicated; the leading and rearmost companies will conform themselves to what has been prescribed for divisions in those positions. The other companies will form by platoon to the right and left into line of battle, and each chief of platoon, after having halted it, will place himself on the line, as if the platoon were a company, and he will be covered by the guide in the rear rank.

954. A battalion in column at full distance, having to form square, will always close on the leading subdivision; and a column closed in mass will always, for the same purpose, take distances by the head. In either case, the second subdivision should be careful, in taking its distance, to reckon from the rear rank of the subdivision in front of it.

955. If a column by company should be required to form square in four ranks, the doubling of files will always take place on the file next the guide.

956. When a column, disposed to form square, shall be in march, it will change direction as a column at half distance; thus, having to execute this movement, the column will take the guide on the side opposite to that to which the change of direction is to be made, if *that* be not already the side of the guide.

957. A column doubled on the centre at company distance or closed in mass, may be formed into square according to the same principles as a simple column.

958. When a battalion is ployed, with a view to the square, it will always be in rear of the right or left division, in order that it may be able to commence firing, pending the execution of the movement. The double column, also, affords this advantage, and being more promptly formed than any other, it will habitually be

employed, unless particular circumstances cause a different formation to be preferred.

959. A battalion, in square, will never use any other than the fire by file and by rank; the color being in the line of file closers, its guard will not fall back as prescribed No. 41; it will fire like the men of the company of which it forms a part.

960. If the square be formed in four ranks, the first two ranks will alone execute the firings prescribed above; the other two ranks will remain either at shoulder or support arms.

961. The formation of the square being often necessary in war, and being the most complicated of the manœuvres, it will be as frequently repeated as the supposed necessity may require, in order to render its mechanism familiar to both officers and men.

962. In the execution of this manœuvre, the colonel will carefully observe that the divers movements which it involves succeed each other without loss of time, but also without confusion; for, if the rapidity of cavalry movements requires the greatest promptitude in the formation of squares, so, on the other hand, precipitancy always results in disorder; and in no circumstance is disorder more to be avoided.

963. When the colonel shall wish to cover by skirmishers the movements of a column preparing to form square, he will detach for this purpose one or two inner platoons of one of the interior divisions of the column. In this case, the exterior platoons of this division and the following subdivisions, will, according to circumstances, close on the preceding subdivision, in such manner, that there may be between them only the distance necessary for forming into line.

964. When the colonel shall be ready to form square, he will, in order to recall the skirmishers, cause *to the color* to be sounded. If, on the return of the skirmishers, there be not room for them to form into line of battle, they

will double on the outer platoons of their respective companies.

Column against Cavalry.

965. When a column closed in mass has to form square, it will begin by taking company distance; but, if so suddenly threatened by cavalry as not to allow time for this disposition, it will be formed in the following manner:

966. The colonel will command:

1. *Column against cavalry.* 2. MARCH.

967. At the first command, the chief of the leading division will caution it to stand fast and pass behind the rear rank; in the interior divisions each captain will promptly designate the number of files necessary to close the interval between his company and the one in front of it. The captains of the divisions next to the one in rear, in addition to closing the interval in front, will also close up the interval which separates this division from the last; the chief of the fourth division will caution it to face about, and its file closers will pass briskly before the front rank.

968. At the command *march*, the guides of each division will place themselves rapidly in the line of file closers. The first division will stand fast, the fourth will face about, the outer file of each of these divisions will then face outwards; in the other divisions the files designated for closing the intervals will form to the right and left into line, but in the division next to the rearmost one, the first files that come into line will close to the right or left until they join the rear division. The files of each company which remain in column will close on their outer files, formed into line, in order to create a vacant space in the middle of the column.

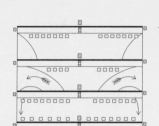

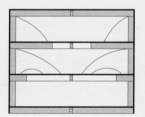

Column against cavalry (No. 967).

969. If the column be in march, the *column against cavalry* will be formed by the same commands and means. At the command *march*, the first and fourth divisions will halt and the latter division will face about; the interior divisions will conform to what has been prescribed above.

970. The battalion being no longer threatened by cavalry, the colonel will command:

1. *Form column.*   2. MARCH.

971. At the command *march*, the files in column will close to the left and right to make room for those in line, who will retake their places in column by stepping backwards, except those closing the interval between the two rear divisions, who will take their places in column by a flank movement. The fourth division will face about, the guides will resume their places.

972. If the colonel should be so pressed as not to have time to order bayonets to be fixed, the men will fix them, without command or signal, at the cautionary command, *column against cavalry.*

973. As this manœuvre is often used in war, and with decided advantage, the colonel will frequently cause it to be executed in order to render it familiar.

ARTICLE FIFTEENTH.

The Rally.

974. The battalion being in line of battle, the colonel will sometimes cause the disperse to be sounded, at which signal, the battalion will break and disperse.

975. When the colonel shall wish to rally the battalion, he will cause *to the color* to be sounded, and at the same time place two markers and the color-bearer in the direction he may wish to give to the battalion.

976. Each captain will rally his company about six paces in rear of the place it is to occupy in line of battle.

977. The colonel will cause the color-company to be promptly established against the markers, and each company by the command of its captain will be aligned on the color-company according to the principles heretofore prescribed.

978. When the colonel shall wish to rally the battalion in column, he will cause *the assembly* to be sounded, and place two markers before the position to be occupied by the first company; the captain of this company will rally his company in rear of the two markers, and each of the other captains will rally his company at platoon distance, behind the one which should precede it in the order in column.

ARTICLE SIXTEENTH.

Rules for manœuvring by the rear rank.

979. It may often be necessary to cause a battalion to manœuvre by the rear rank; when the case presents itself, the following rules will be observed.

980. The battalion being by the front rank, when the colonel shall wish to manœuvre by the rear rank, he will command:

1. *Face by the rear rank.*   2. *Battalion.*
3. *About*—FACE.

981. If the battalion be deployed, this movement will be executed as has been indicated for the fire by the rear rank.

982. If the battalion be in column by company, or by platoon, right or left in front, the chiefs of subdivision, to take their new places in column, will each pass by the left flank of his subdivision, and the file closers by the right flank; the guides will place themselves in the rear rank.

983. If the column be formed by division, the chiefs of division will each pass by the interval in the centre of his division, and the file closers by the outer flanks of their respective companies; the junior captain in each division will step into the rear rank, and be covered in the front rank by the covering sergeant of the left company.

984. The lieutenant colonel will place himself abreast with the leading subdivision, and the major abreast with the rearmost one.

985. The battalion being faced by the rear rank, companies, divisions, and wings, will preserve their prior denominations respectively.

986. The manœuvres by the rear rank will be executed by the same commands and on the same principles as if the battalion faced by the front rank; but in such manner that when the battalion shall be brought to its proper front, all the subdivisions may find themselves in their regular order from right to left.

987. According to this principle, when a column faced by the rear rank is deployed, the subdivisions which, in line of battle by the front rank, ought to find themselves on the right of the subdivision on which the deployment is made, will face to the left; and those which ought to be placed on its left, will face to the right.

988. When a battalion in line of battle, faced by the rear rank, is to be ployed into column, the colonel will announce, in the commands, *left* or *right in front*, according as it may be intended that the first or last subdivision shall be at the head of the column, because the first subdivision is on the left, and the last on the right of the battalion faced by the rear rank. The column by the rear rank will take the guide to the right, if the first subdivision be front, and to the left in the reverse case.

989. A column, faced by the rear rank, will be brought to its proper front by the means heretofore prescribed. If the column be formed by company, or by platoon, the chiefs of subdivision, in order to take their new places in column, will pass by the left subdivisions, now right, and the file closers by the right, now left.

SCHOOL OF THE BATTALION,

ARRANGED INTO LESSONS.

———

LESSON FIRST.

ARTICLE I.—Open ranks (No. 23).

ARTICLE II.—Close ranks (No. 29).

ARTICLE III.—Manual of arms (No. 30). Loading at will (No. 31).

ARTICLE IV.—Different fires by the front rank (No. 39), and by the rear rank (No. 54).

LESSON SECOND.

ARTICLE I.—Break by company to the right (No. 69), or to the left (No. 74).

ARTICLE II.—March in column, at the cadenced step, a considerable distance (No. 164). Change of direction (No. 231). Diminish and increase front in marching (No. 196.) March in retreat (No. 170).

ARTICLE III.—Halt the column (No. 239). Form it to the left or right into line of battle (No. 390). Execute this formation, the column marching (No. 402).

ARTICLE IV.—Execute the countermarch, and repeat the same movements (No. 351).

ARTICLE V.—Form column into line of battle, to the right or left, by inversion (No. 407).

LESSON THIRD.

ARTICLE I.—Break by company to the rear by the right or left, the battalion being at a halt (No. 87), or marching (No. 94).

ARTICLE II.—March in the route step (No. 198). Cause to be executed, at this gait and in double quick time, the divers movements incident to the column in route, and cause the cadenced step to be resumed.

ARTICLE III.—Form the column forward into line of battle (Nos. 440, 452), faced to the rear into line of battle (Nos. 466, 480), the battalion being at a halt, or marching. Form the column forward into line, and continue the march in this order (No. 456).

ARTICLE IV.—Form the column on the right (No. 416), or the left (No. 432), into line of battle.

ARTICLE V.—March by the flank (No. 722), and form companies into line, marching.

ARTICLE VI.—The column supposed to arrive before (No. 175) or behind the line of battle (No. 184), to prolong it on that line.

ARTICLE VII.—Change front forward (No. 743), or in rear (No. 760), on the right or left of companies, in directions perpendicular or oblique.

ARTICLE VIII.—March by the right flank (No. 722), or by the left flank (No. 725). Change direction by file (No. 730). Form the battalion into line of battle, on the right or left, by file (No. 735).

ARTICLE IX.—Pass the defile in retreat by the right (No. 709), or by the left flank (No. 720).

LESSON FOURTH.

ARTICLE I.—Break by division to the rear, by the right or left, the battalion being at a halt or marching (No. 102).

ARTICLE II.—March in column by division (No. 161). Diminish and increase front by company (No. 196).

ARTICLE III.—Close the column to half distance on the headmost or the rearmost division (No. 278).

ARTICLE IV.—March in column at half distance (No. 281), and change direction (No. 287).

ARTICLE V.—The column being at half distance, to form square at a halt (No. 817), or marching (No. 837).

ARTICLE VI.—The battalion being in square, to march to the front (No. 854). Halt the square (No. 860). Form column to march to the front (No. 863), or in retreat (No. 872). Re-form the square (No. 875).

ARTICLE VII.—Reduce the square (No. 883).

ARTICLE VIII.—Close the column in mass on the headmost or rearmost division (No. 279).

ARTICLE IX.—March in column closed in mass, and change direction by the front of subdivisions (No. 288).

ARTICLE X.—Form the column against cavalry (No. 966).

ARTICLE XI.—Take distances by the head (Nos. 323 and 330), or on rear of the column (No. 333), the column being at a halt or marching.

ARTICLE XII.—The column being by company, cause to be executed the movements indicated in Nos. 3, 4, 5, 6, 7, 8, 9, 10, and 11 of this lesson. The column being at half distance, or closed in mass, to form to the left, or right, into line, wheel, on the rear of the column (No. 502).

ARTICLE XIII.—The column being by company, form divisions from a halt (No. 364), or in march (No. 376).

ARTICLE XIV.—The column being by division, to form it to the left or right into line of battle at a halt (No. 401), or in march (No. 402).

LESSON FIFTH.

ARTICLE I.—The battalion being in line of battle, and at a halt, to ploy it by division into column closed in mass on the right division (No. 119), or on the left division (No. 141), or on an interior division (No. 143), the right or left in front. Ploy the battalion marching in line of battle on the right or left division (No. 149).

ARTICLE II.—Execute the countermarch (No. 352).

ARTICLE III.—Change direction to the right (No. 307), to the left (No. 313), by the flank of the column.

ARTICLE IV.—Deploy the column on the right division (No. 514), on the left division (No. 541), or on any interior division, the column being at a halt, or marching (No. 563).

ARTICLE V.—Ploy the battalion into column by division at half distance, marching (No. 556).

ARTICLE VI.—Ploy the battalion by company, closed in mass, and form it on the right or left into line of battle (No. 577).

ARTICLE VII.—Ploy the battalion into double column, at half distance (No. 777), or closed in mass (No. 793), the battalion being at a halt, or marching.

ARTICLE VIII.—March in this order, and change direction (No. 794).

ARTICLE IX.—Deploy the column at a halt (No. 796), or marching (No. 800), and without suspending the march (No. 802).

ARTICLE X.—The double column being at half distance, form it into line of battle faced to the right or left (No. 803), the column being in march (No. 807). Execute the same movement without suspending the march (No. 810).

ARTICLE XI.—Perpendicular or parallel squares, the battalion being deployed (Nos. 889, 895). Oblique squares, the battalion being in line of battle (No. 938), or in column (No. 945). Squares in four ranks (No. 911).

Lesson Sixth.

ARTICLE I.—March in line of battle (No. 587). Halt the battalion (No. 635), and align it (No. 640).

ARTICLE II.—Change direction in line of battle advancing (No. 652), or in retreat (No. 681). Execute passage of obstacles (No. 682).

ARTICLE III.—Oblique march in line of battle (No. 623).

ARTICLE IV.—Disperse and rally the battalion in line of battle (No. 974), and rally the battalion in column by company (No. 978).

Remarks

ON THE SCHOOL OF THE BATTALION.

In every course of instruction, the first lesson will be executed several times in the order in which it is arranged; but as soon as the battalion shall be confirmed in the principles of the lesson, the fires will be executed after the advance in line, and after the various formations into line of battle, and into square. Particular attention will be given to the fire by file, which is that principally used in war.

Every lesson of this school will be executed with the utmost precision; but the second, which comprehends the march in column and the march in line of battle, being of the most importance, will be the oftenest repeated, especially in the beginning.

Great attention ought, also, to be given to the fourth lesson, which comprehends the march in column by division, and the dispositions against cavalry.

The successive formations will sometimes be executed by inversion.

In the beginning, the march in column, the march in line of battle, and the march by the flank, will be executed only in quick time, and will be continued until the battalion shall have become well established in the cadence of this step.

The non-cadenced step will be employed in this school only in the repetition of the movements incident to a column in route, or when great celerity may be required.

When it may be desired to give the men relief, arms may be supported, if at a halt, or marching by the flank.

In marching by the front, arms may be shifted to the right shoulder; but not in the march in line of battle until the battalions shall be well instructed.

After arms have been carried for some time on the right shoulder, they may be shifted, in like manner, to the left shoulder.

When a battalion is manœuvring, its movements will be covered by skirmishers.

All the companies will be exercised, successively, in this service.

STREET FIRING.

STREET firing is the method of firing adapted to defend or clear a street, lane, or narrow pass, in the execution of which the company or platoon must be formed according to the width of the place, leaving sufficient space on the flanks for the platoons to file successively to the rear.

When the column has arrived at the place where the firing is to commence, the commanding officer will give the word, Column, halt—Prepare for street firing. At this command, all the captains will pass by the right flank to the rear of their companies, covering the centre. The colonel next commands—Commence firing. The captain of the first company will promptly command: First company—ready—aim—fire—recover arms—outward face—quick march.

The first platoon face to the right, the second to the left; the first platoon conducted by the captain, the second by the first lieutenant, will file right and left around the flanks towards the rear, halt on the flanks opposite the centre of the column, re-load, and as soon as the rear of the column has passed the platoons, the captain will command: Platoons—right and left face—march. At which command, the first platoon faces to the left, and files left, and the second to the right, and files right, and unite in rear of the column. At the instant the men of the first company recover their arms after firing, the captain of the second will order such company: Ready—and wait in that position until the front is cleared by the first company, when the captain will cause it to advance twice its front (followed by all the companies in rear), and fire, file down the ranks in the name order prescribed for the first company.

Firing in retreat is conducted on the same principle as on the advance, except that the companies fire without advancing, on the front being cleared by the former company; and, instead of halting on the flanks, the platoons will pass immediately to the rear of the column, counter-march, form, and re-load. The same principle will be observed in column of platoons as column of company.

If a column by company find itself in a narrow street or pass, or in any position without cover for either flank or rear, and is suddenly menaced at different points, the colonel will cause it to form square, notwithstanding the general principle that a column by company, with a view to the square, will first form divisions; the colonel will close the column to half or platoon distance; the file closers of the eighth company will conform themselves to what is prescribed in paragraph 823, p. 357, for the file closers of the fourth division.

These dispositions ended, he will command: Right and left, into line, wheel, quick—march! At this, briskly repeated, the leading company will stand fast, the second, third, fourth, fifth, sixth, and seventh companies will wheel by platoons, right and left, into line of battle, the right platoons to the right and the left to the left; the eighth company will close up to form the square, and when it shall have closed up, its captain will halt it, face it about, and align it by the rear rank; the right file of the first company will face to the right, and its left file to the left, and the outer files on each flank of the eighth company will face outward. The square being formed, the colonel will command: "Guides post"; at this, the field and staff, captains of the first and eighth companies, will enter the square.

In case it becomes necessary to use artillery in the suppression of riots or insurrection, the mounted howitzer can be used with much effect, and without injury to property in the vicinity; the lightness and ready manner to which they can be conveyed from place to place make this arm peculiarly adapted for this purpose.

APPENDIX.

ARTICLES OF WAR.

AN ACT FOR ESTABLISHING RULES AND ARTICLES FOR THE
GOVERNMENT OF THE ARMIES OF THE UNITED STATES.*

SECTION 1. *Be it enacted, by the Senate and House of Representatives of the United States of America, in Congress assembled,* That, from and after the passing of this act, the following shall be the rules and articles by which the armies of the United States shall be governed:

ARTICLE 1. Every officer now in the army of the United States shall, in six months from the passing of this act, and every officer who shall hereafter be appointed shall, before he enters on the duties of his office, subscribe these rules and regulations.

ART. 2. It is earnestly recommended to all officers and soldiers diligently to attend divine service; and all officers who shall behave indecently or irreverently at any place of divine worship shall, if commissioned officers, be brought before a general court-martial, there to be publicly and severely reprimanded by the president; if non-commissioned officers or soldiers, every person so offending shall, for his first offence, forfeit one-sixth of a dollar, to be deducted out of his next pay; for the second offence, he shall not only forfeit a like sum, but be confined twenty-four hours; and for every like offence, shall suffer and pay in like manner; which money, so forfeited, shall be applied, by the captain or senior officer of the troop or company, to the use of the sick soldiers of the company or troop to which the offender belongs.

ART. 3. Any non-commissioned officer or soldier who shall

---

* These rules and articles, with the exceptions indicated by the notes annexed to articles 20, 65, and 87, remain unaltered, and in force at present.

use any profane oath or execration shall incur the penalties expressed in the foregoing article; and a commissioned officer shall forfeit and pay, for each and every such offence, one dollar, to be applied as in the preceding article.

ART. 4. Every chaplain commissioned in the army or armies of the United States, who shall absent himself from the duties assigned him (excepting in cases of sickness or leave of absence), shall, on conviction thereof before a court-martial, be fined not exceeding one month's pay, besides the loss of his pay during his absence; or be discharged, as the said court-martial shall judge proper.

ART. 5. Any officer or soldier who shall use contemptuous or disrespectful words against the President of the United States, against the Vice-President thereof, against the Congress of the United States, or against the Chief Magistrate or Legislature of any of the United States in which he may be quartered, if a commissioned officer, shall be cashiered, or otherwise punished, as a court-martial shall direct; if a non-commissioned officer or soldier, he shall suffer such punishment as shall be inflicted on him by the sentence of a court-martial.

ART. 6. Any officer or soldier who shall behave himself with contempt or disrespect toward his commanding officer, shall be punished, according to the nature of his offence, by the judgment of a court-martial.

ART. 7. Any officer or soldier who shall begin, excite, cause, or join in, any mutiny or sedition, in any troop or company in the service of the United States, or in any party, post, detachment, or guard, shall suffer death, or such other punishment as by a court-martial shall be inflicted.

ART. 8. Any officer, non-commissioned officer, or soldier, who, being present at any mutiny or sedition, does not use his utmost endeavor to suppress the same, or, coming to the knowledge of any intended mutiny, does not, without delay, give information thereof to his commanding officer, shall be punished by the sentence of a court-martial with death, or otherwise, according to the nature of his offence.

ART. 9. Any officer or soldier who shall strike his superior officer, or draw or lift up any weapon, or offer any violence against him, being in the execution of his office, on any pretense whatsoever, or shall disobey any lawful command of his superior officer, shall suffer death, or such other punishment as shall, according to the nature of his offence, be inflicted upon him by the sentence of a court-martial.

ART. 10. Every non-commissioned officer or soldier, who shall enlist himself in the service of the United States, shall, at the time of his so enlisting, or within six days afterward, have the Articles for the government of the armies of the United States read to him, and shall, by the officer who enlisted him, or by the commanding officer of the troop or company into which he was enlisted, be taken before the next justice of the peace, or chief magistrate of any city or town corporate, not being an officer of the army, or, where recourse cannot be had to the civil magistrate, before the judge advocate, and in his presence shall take the following oath or affirmation : "I, A. B., do solemnly swear or affirm (as the case may be) that I will bear true allegiance to the United States of America, and that I will serve them honestly and faithfully against all their enemies or opposers whatsoever; and observe and obey the orders of the President of the United States, and the orders of the officers appointed over me, according to the Rules and Articles for the government of the armies of the United States." Which justice, magistrate, or judge advocate is to give to the officer a certificate, signifying that the man enlisted did take the said oath or affirmation.

ART. 11. After a non-commissioned officer or soldier shall have been duly enlisted and sworn, he shall not be dismissed the service without a discharge in writing; and no discharge granted to him shall be sufficient which is not signed by a field officer of the regiment to which he belongs, or commanding officer, where no field officer of the regiment is present; and no discharge shall be given to a non-commissioned officer or soldier before his term of service has expired, but by order of the President, the Secretary of War, the commanding officer of a department, or the sentence of a general court-martial; nor shall a commissioned officer be discharged the service but by order of the President of the United States, or by sentence of a general court-martial.

ART. 12. Every colonel, or other officer commanding a regiment, troop, or company and actually quartered with it, may give furloughs to non-commissioned officers or soldiers in such numbers, and for so long a time, as he shall judge to be most consistent with the good of the service; and a captain or other inferior officer, commanding a troop or company, or in any garrison, fort, or barrack of the United States (his field officer being absent), may give furloughs to non-commissioned officers or soldiers, for a time not exceeding twenty days in six months, but not to more than two persons to be absent at the same time, excepting some extraordinary occasion should require it.

ART. 13. At every muster, the commanding officer of each regiment, troop, or company, there present, shall give to the commissary of musters, or other officer who musters the said regiment troop, or company, certificates signed by himself, signifying how long such officers, as shall not appear at the said muster, have been absent, and the reason of their absence. In like manner, the commanding officer of every troop or company shall give certificates, signifying the reasons of the absence of the non-commissioned officers and private soldiers; which reasons and time of absence shall be inserted in the muster-rolls, opposite the names of the respective absent officers and soldiers. The certificates shall, together with the muster rolls, be remitted by the commissary of musters, or other officer mustering, to the Department of War, as speedily as the distance of the place will admit.

ART. 14. Every officer who shall be convicted before a general court-martial of having signed a false certificate relating to the absence of either officer or private soldier or relative to his or their pay, shall be cashiered.

ART. 15. Every officer who shall knowingly make a false muster of man or horse, and every officer or commissary of musters who shall willingly sign, direct, or allow the signing of muster-rolls wherein such false muster is contained, shall, upon proof made thereof, by two witnesses, before a general court-martial, be cashiered, and shall be thereby utterly disabled to have or hold any office or employment in the service of the United States.

ART. 16. Any commissary of musters, or other officer, who shall be convicted of having taken money, or other thing, by way of gratification, on mustering any regiment, troop, or company, or on signing muster-rolls, shall be displaced from his office, and shall be thereby utterly disabled to have or hold any office or employment in the service of the United States.

ART. 17. Any officer who shall presume to muster a person as a soldier who is not a soldier, shall be deemed guilty of having made a false muster, and shall suffer accordingly.

ART. 18. Every officer who shall knowingly make a false return to the Department of War, or to any of his superior officers, authorized to call for such returns, of the state of the regiment, troop, or company, or garrison, under his command, or of the arms, ammunition, clothing, or other stores thereunto belonging, shall, on conviction thereof before a court-martial, be cashiered.

ART. 19. The commanding officer of every regiment, troop, or independent company, or garrison, of the United States, shall, in the beginning of every month, remit, through the proper channels, to the Department of War, an exact return of the regiment, troop, independent company, or garrison, under his command, specifying the names of the officers then absent from their posts, with the reasons for and the time of their absence. And any officer who shall be convicted of having, through neglect or design, omitted sending such returns, shall be punished, according to the nature of his crime, by the judgment of a general court-martial.

ART. 20. All officers and soldiers who have received pay, or have been duly enlisted in the service of the United States, and shall be convicted of having deserted the same, shall suffer death, or such other punishment as, by sentence of a court-martial, shall be inflicted.*

ART. 21. Any non-commissioned officer or soldier who shall, without leave from his commanding officer, absent himself from his troop, company, or detachment, shall, upon being convicted thereof, be punished according to the nature of a court-martial.

ART. 22. No non-commissioned officer or soldier shall enlist himself in any other regiment, troop, or company, with-

---

*Modified by Act of 29th May, 1830.

out a regular discharge from the regiment, troop, or company in which he last served, on the penalty of being reputed a deserter and suffering accordingly. And in case any officer shall knowingly receive and entertain such non-commissioned officer or soldier, or shall not, after his being discovered to be a deserter, immediately confine him, and give notice thereof to the corps in which he last served, the said officer shall, by a court-martial, be cashiered.

Art. 23. Any officer or soldier who shall be convicted of having advised or persuaded any other officer or soldier to desert the service of the United States, shall suffer death, or such other punishment as shall be inflicted upon him by the sentence of a court-martial.

Art. 24. No officer or soldier shall use any reproachful or provoking speeches or gestures to another, upon pain, if an officer, of being put in arrest; if a soldier, confined, and of asking pardon of the party offended, in the presence of his commanding officer.

Art. 25. No officer or soldier shall send a challenge to another officer or soldier, to fight a duel, or accept a challenge if sent, upon pain, if a commissioned officer, of being cashiered; if a non-commissioned officer or soldier, of suffering corporeal punishment, at the discretion of a court-martial.

Art. 26. If any commissioned or non-commissioned officer commanding a guard shall knowingly or willingly suffer any person whatsoever to go forth to fight a duel, he shall be punished as a challenger; and all seconds, promoters, and carriers of challenges, in order to duels, shall be deemed principals, and be punished accordingly. And it shall be the duty of every officer commanding an army, regiment, company, post, or detachment, who is knowing to a challenge being given or accepted by any officer, non-commissioned officer, or soldier, under his command, or has reason to believe the same to be the case, immediately to arrest and bring to trial such offenders.

Art. 27. All officers, of what condition soever, have power to part and quell all quarrels, frays, and disorders, though the persons concerned should belong to another regiment, troop, or company; and either to order officers into arrest, or non-commissioned officers or soldiers into confinement, until their proper superior officers shall be acquainted therewith; and whosoever shall refuse to obey such officer (though of an inferior rank), or shall draw his sword upon him, shall be punished at the discretion of a general court-martial.

ART. 28. Any officer or soldier who shall upbraid another for refusing a challenge, shall himself be punished as a challenger; and all officers and soldiers are hereby discharged from any disgrace or opinion of disadvantage which might arise from their having refused to accept of challenges, as they will only have acted in obedience to the laws, and done their duty as good soldiers who subject themselves to discipline.

ART. 29. No sutler shall be permitted to sell any kind of liquors or victuals, or to keep their houses or shops open for the entertainment of soldiers, after nine at night, or before the beating of the reveille, or upon Sundays, during divine service or sermon, on the penalty of being dismissed from all future suttling.

ART. 30. All officers commanding in the field, forts, barracks, or garrisons of the United States are hereby required to see that the persons permitted to suttle shall supply the soldiers with good and wholesome provisions, or other articles, at a reasonable price, as they shall be answerable for their neglect.

ART. 31. No officer commanding in any of the garrisons, forts, or barracks of the United States, shall exact exorbitant prices for houses or stalls let out to sutlers, or connive at the like exactions in others; nor by his own authority, and for his private advantage, lay any duty or imposition upon, or be interested in, the sale of any victuals, liquors, or other necessaries of life brought into the garrison, fort, or barracks, for the use of the soldiers, on the penalty of being discharged from the service.

ART. 32. Every officer commanding in quarters, garrisons, or on the march, shall keep good order, and, to the utmost of his power, redress all abuses or disorder which may be committed by any officer or soldier under his command; if, upon complaint made to him of officers or soldiers beating or otherwise ill treating any person, or disturbing fairs or markets, or of committing any kind of riots, to the disquieting of the citizens of the United States, he, the said commander, who shall refuse or omit to see justice done to the offender or offenders, and reparation made to the party or parties injured, as far as part of the offender's pay shall enable him or them, shall, upon proof thereof, be cashiered, or otherwise punished, as a general court-martial shall direct.

ART. 33. When any commissioned officer or soldier shall be accused of a capital crime, or of having used violence or committed any offence against the person or property of any citizen of any of the United States, such as is punishable by the known laws of the land, the commanding officer and officers of every regiment, troop, or company, to which the person or persons so accused shall belong, are hereby required, upon application duly made by or in behalf of the party or parties injured, to use their utmost endeavors to deliver over such accused person or persons to the civil magistrate, and likewise to be aiding and assisting to the officers of justice in apprehending and securing the person or persons so accused, in order to bring him or them to trial. If any commanding officer or officers shall wilfully neglect, or shall refuse, upon the application aforesaid, to deliver over such accused person or persons to the civil magistrates, or to be aiding and assisting to the officers of justice in apprehending such person or persons, the officer or officers so offending shall be cashiered.

ART. 34. If any officer shall think himself wronged by his colonel, or the commanding officer of the regiment, and shall, upon due application being made to him, be refused redress, he may complain to the general commanding in the State or Territory where such regiment shall be stationed, in order to obtain justice; who is hereby required to examine into said complaint, and take proper measures for redressing the wrong complained of, and transmit, as soon as possible, to the Department of War, a true state of such complaint, with the proceedings had thereon.

ART. 35. If any inferior officer or soldier shall think himself wronged by his captain or other officer, he is to complain thereof to the commanding officer of the regiment, who is hereby required to summon a regimental court-martial, for the doing justice to the complainant; from which regimental court-martial either party may, if he thinks himself still aggrieved, appeal to a general court-martial. But if, upon a second hearing, the appeal shall appear vexatious and groundless, the person so appealing shall be punished at the discretion of the said court-martial.

ART. 36. Any commissioned officer, store-keeper, or commissary, who shall be convicted at a general court-martial of having sold, without a proper order for that purpose, embezzled, misapplied, or wilfully, or through neglect, suffered any of the provisions, forage, arms, clothing, ammunition, or other military stores belonging to the United States to be spoiled or damaged, shall, at his own expense, make good the loss or damage, and shall, moreover, forfeit all his pay, and be dismissed from the service.

ART. 37. Any non-commissioned officer or soldier who shall be convicted at a regimental court-martial of having sold, or designedly, or through neglect, wasted the ammunition delivered out to him, to be employed in the service of the United States, shall be punished at the discretion of such court.

ART. 38. Every non-commissioned officer or soldier who shall be convicted before a court-martial of having sold, lost, or spoiled, through neglect, his horse, arms, clothes, or accoutrements, shall undergo such weekly stoppages (not exceeding the half of his pay) as such court-martial shall judge sufficient for repairing the loss or damage; and shall suffer confinement, or such other corporeal punishment as his crime shall deserve.

ART. 39. Every officer who shall be convicted before a court-martial of having embezzled or misapplied any money with which he may have been intrusted, for the payment of the men under his command, or for enlisting men into the service, or for other purposes, if a commissioned officer, shall be cashiered, and compelled to refund the money; if a non-commissioned officer, shall be reduced to the ranks, be put under stoppages until the money be made good, and suffer such corporeal punishment as such court-martial shall direct.

ART. 40. Every captain of a troop or company is charged with the arms, accoutrements, ammunition, clothing, or other warlike stores belonging to the troop or company under his command, which he is to be accountable for to his colonel in case of their being lost, spoiled, or damaged, not by unavoidable accidents, or of actual service.

ART. 41. All non-commissioned officers and soldiers who shall be found one mile from the camp without leave, in writing, from their commanding officer, shall suffer such punishment as shall be inflicted upon them by the sentence of a court-martial.

ART. 42. No officer or soldier shall lie out of his quarters, garrison, or camp without leave from his superior officer, upon penalty of being punished according to the nature of his offence, by the sentence of a court-martial.

ART. 43. Every non-commissioned officer and soldier shall retire to his quarters or tent at the beating of the retreat; in default of which he shall be punished according to the nature of his offence.

ART. 44. No officer, non-commissioned officer, or soldier shall fail in repairing, at the time fixed, to the place of parade, of exercise, or other rendezvous appointed by his commanding officer, if not prevented by sickness or some other evident necessity, or shall go from the said place of rendezvous without leave from his commanding officer, before he shall be regularly dismissed or relieved, on the penalty of being punished, according to the nature of his offence, by the sentence of a court-martial.

ART. 45. Any commissioned officer who shall be found drunk on his guard, party, or other duty, shall be cashiered. Any non-commissioned officer or soldier so offending shall suffer such corporeal punishment as shall be inflicted by the sentence of a court-martial.

ART. 46. Any sentinel who shall be found sleeping upon his post, or shall leave it before he shall be regularly relieved, shall suffer death, or such other punishment as shall be inflicted by the sentence of a court-martial.

ART. 47. No soldier belonging to any regiment, troop, or company shall hire another to do his duty for him, or be excused from duty but in cases of sickness, disability, or leave of absence; and every such soldier found guilty of hiring his duty, as also the party so hired to do another's duty, shall be punished at the discretion of a regimental court-martial.

ART. 48. And every non-commissioned officer conniving at such hiring of duty aforesaid, shall be reduced; and every commissioned officer knowing and allowing such ill practices in the service, shall be punished by the judgment of a general court-martial.

ART. 49. Any officer belonging to the service of the United States, who, by discharging of firearms, drawing of swords, beating of drums, or by any other means whatsoever, shall occasion false alarms in camp, garrison, or quarters, shall suffer death, or such other punishment as shall be ordered by the sentence of a general court-martial.

ART. 50. Any officer or soldier who shall, without urgent necessity, or without the leave of his superior officer, quit his guard, platoon, or division, shall be punished, according to the nature of his offence, by the sentence of a court-martial.

ART. 51. No officer or soldier shall do violence to any person who brings provisions or other necessaries to the camp, garrison, or quarters of the forces of the United States, employed in any parts out of the said States, upon pain of death, or such other punishment as a court-martial shall direct.

ART. 52. Any officer or soldier who shall misbehave himself before the enemy, run away, or shamefully abandon any fort, post, or guard which he or they may be commanded to defend, or speak words inducing others to do the like, or shall cast away his arms and ammunition, or who shall quit his post or colors to plunder and pillage, every such offender, being duly convicted thereof, shall suffer death, or such other punishment as shall be ordered by the sentence of a general court-martial.

ART. 53. Any person belonging to the armies of the United States who shall make known the watchword to any person who is not entitled to receive it according to the rules and discipline of war, or shall presume to give a parole or watchword different from what he received, shall suffer death, or such other punishment as shall be ordered by the sentence of a general court-martial.

ART. 54. All officers and soldiers are to behave themselves orderly in quarters and on their march; and whoever shall commit any waste or spoil, either in walks of trees, parks, warrens, fish-ponds, houses, gardens, corn-fields, enclosures of meadows, or shall maliciously destroy any property whatsoever belonging to the inhabitants of the United States, unless by order of the then commander-in-chief of the armies of the said States, shall (besides such penalties as they are liable to by law) be punished according to the nature and degree of the offence, by the judgment of a regimental or general court-martial.

ART. 55. Whosoever, belonging to the armies of the United States in foreign parts, shall force a safeguard, shall suffer death.

ART. 56. Whosoever shall relieve the enemy with money, victuals, or ammunition, or shall knowingly harbor or protect an enemy, shall suffer death, or such other punishment as shall be ordered by the sentence of a court-martial.

ART. 57. Whosoever shall be convicted of holding correspondence with, or giving intelligence to, the enemy, either directly or indirectly, shall suffer death, or such other punishment as shall be ordered by the sentence of a court-martial.

ART. 58. All public stores taken in the enemy's camp, towns, forts, or magazines, whether of artillery, ammunition, clothing, forage, or provisions, shall be secured for the service of the United States; for the neglect of which the commanding officer is to be answerable.

ART. 59. If any commander of any garrison, fortress, or post shall be compelled, by the officers and soldiers under his command, to give up to the enemy, or to abandon it, the commissioned officers, non-commissioned officers, or soldiers who shall be convicted of having so offended, shall suffer death, or such other punishment as shall be inflicted upon them by the sentence of a court-martial.

ART. 60. All sutlers and retainers to the camp, and all persons whatsoever, serving with the armies of the United States in the field, though not enlisted soldiers, are to be subject to orders, according to the rules and discipline of war.

ART. 61. Officers having brevets or commissions of a prior date to those of the regiment in which they serve, may take place in courts-martial and on detachments, when composed of different corps, according to the ranks given them in their brevets or dates of their former commissions; but in the regiment, troop, or company to which such officers belong, they shall do duty and take rank, both in courts-martial and on detachments which shall be composed of their own corps, according to the commissions by which they are mustered in the said corps.

ART. 62. If upon marches, guards, or in quarters, different corps of the army shall happen to join, or do duty together, the officer highest in rank of the line of the army, marine corps, or militia, by commission, there on duty or in quarters, shall command the whole, and give orders for what is needful to the service, unless otherwise specially directed by the President of the United States, according to the nature of the case.

ART. 63. The functions of the engineers being generally confined to the most elevated branch of military science, they are not to assume, nor are they subject to be ordered on any duty beyond the line of their immediate profession, except by the special order of the President of the United States; but they are to receive every mark of respect to which their rank in the army may entitle them respectively, and are liable to be transferred, at the discretion of the President, from one corps to another, regard being paid to rank.

ART. 64. General courts-martial may consist of any number of commissioned officers, from five to thirteen, inclusively; but they shall not consist of less than thirteen where that number can be convened without manifest injury to the service.

ART. 65.* Any general officer commanding an army, or colonel commanding a separate department, may appoint general courts-martial whenever necessary. But no sentence of a court-martial shall be carried into execution until after the whole proceedings shall have been laid before the officer ordering the same, or the officer commanding the troops for the time being; neither shall any sentence of a general court-martial, in the time of peace, extending to the loss of life, or the dismission of a commissioned officer, or which shall, either in time of peace or war, respect a general officer, be carried into execution, until after the whole proceedings shall have been transmitted to the Secretary of War, to be laid before the President of the United States for his confirmation or disapproval, and orders in the case. All other sentences may be

---

*Modified by Act of 29th May, 1830.

confirmed and executed by the officer ordering the court to assemble, or the commanding officer for the time being, as the case may be.

ART. 66. Every officer commanding a regiment or corps may appoint, for his own regiment or corps, courts-martial, to consist of three commissioned officers, for the trial and punishment of offences not capital, and decide upon their sentences. For the same purpose, all officers commanding any of the garrisons, forts, barracks, or other places where the troops consist of different corps, may assemble courts-martial, to consist of three commissioned officers, and decide upon their sentences.

ART. 67. No garrison or regimental court-martial shall have the power to try capital cases or commissioned officers; neither shall they inflict a fine exceeding one month's pay, nor imprison, nor put to hard labor, any non-commissioned officer or soldier for a longer time than one month.

ART. 68. Whenever it may be found convenient and necessary to the public service, the officers of the marines shall be associated with the officers of the land forces, for the purpose of holding courts-martial, and trying offenders belonging to either; and, in such cases, the orders of the senior officer of either corps who may be present and duly authorized, shall be received and obeyed.

ART. 69. The judge advocate, or some person deputed by him, or by the general, or officer commanding the army, detachment, or garrison, shall prosecute in the name of the United States, but shall so far consider himself as counsel for the prisoner, after the said prisoner shall have made his plea, as to object to any leading question to any of the witnesses, or any question to the prisoner, the answer to which might tend to criminate himself; and administer to each member of the court, before they proceed upon any trial, the following oath, which shall also be taken by all members of the regimental and garrison courts-martial:

"You, A. B., do swear that you will well and truly try and determine, according to evidence, the matter now before you, between the United States of America and the prisoner to be tried, and that you will duly administer justice, according to the provisions of 'An act establishing Rules and Articles for the government of the armies of the United States,' without partiality, favor, or affection; and if any doubt should arise, not explained by said Articles, according to your conscience, the best of your understanding, and the custom of war in like cases; and you do further swear that you will not divulge the sentence of the court until it shall be published by the proper authority; neither will you disclose or discover the vote or opinion of any particular member of the court-martial, unless required to give evidence thereof, as a witness, by a court of justice, in a due course of law. So help you God."

And as soon as the said oath shall have been administered to the respective members, the president of the court shall administer to the judge advocate, or person officiating as such, an oath in the following words:

"You, A. B., do swear, that you will not disclose or discover the vote or opinion of any particular member of the court-martial, unless required to give evidence thereof, as a witness, by a court of justice, in due course of law; nor divulge the sentence of the court to any but the proper authority, until it shall be duly disclosed by the same. So help you God."

ART. 70. When a prisoner, arraigned before a general court-martial, shall, from obstinacy and deliberate design, stand mute, or answer foreign to the purpose, the court may proceed to trial and judgment as if the prisoner had regularly pleaded not guilty.

ART. 71. When a member shall be challenged by a prisoner, he must state his cause of challenge, of which the court shall, after due deliberation, determine the relevancy or validity, and decide accordingly; and no challenge to more than one member at a time shall be received by the court.

ART. 72. All the members of a court-martial are to behave with decency and calmness, and in giving their votes are to begin with the youngest in commission.

ART. 73. All persons who give evidence before a court-martial are to be examined on oath or affirmation, in the following form:

"You swear, or affirm (as the case may be), the evidence you shall give in the cause now in hearing shall be the truth, the whole truth, and nothing but the truth. So help you God."

ART. 74. On the trials of cases not capital, before courts-martial, the deposition of witnesses, not in the line or staff of the army, may be taken before some justice of the peace, and read in evidence; provided the prosecutor and person accused are present at the taking the same, or are duly notified thereof.

ART. 75. No officer shall be tried but by a general court-martial, nor by officers of an inferior rank, if it can be avoided. Nor shall any proceedings of trials be carried on, excepting between the hours of eight in the morning and three in the afternoon, excepting in cases which, in the opinion of the officer appointing the court-martial, require immediate example.

ART. 76. No person whatsoever shall use any menacing words, signs, or gestures, in presence of a court-martial, or shall cause any disorder or riot, or disturb their proceedings, on the penalty of being punished at the discretion of the said court-martial.

ART. 77. Whenever any officer shall be charged with a crime, he shall be arrested and confined in his barracks, quarters, or tent, and deprived of his sword by the commanding officer. And any officer who shall leave his confinement before he shall be set at liberty by his commanding officer, or by a superior officer, shall be cashiered.

ART. 78. Non-commissioned officers and soldiers, charged with crimes, shall be confined until tried by a court-martial, or released by proper authority.

ART. 79. No officer or soldier who shall be put in arrest shall continue in confinement more than eight days, or until such time as a court-martial can be assembled.

ART. 80. No officer commanding a guard, or provost marshal, shall refuse to receive or keep any prisoner committed to his charge by an officer belonging to the forces of the United States; provided the officer committing shall, at the same time, deliver an account in writing, signed by himself, of the crime with which the said prisoner is charged.

ART. 81. No officer commanding a guard, or provost marshal, shall presume to release any person committed to his charge without proper authority for so doing, nor shall he suffer any person to escape, on the penalty, of being punished for it by the sentence of a court-martial.

ART. 82. Every officer or provost marshal, to whose charge prisoners shall be committed, shall, within twenty-four hours after such commitment, or as soon as he shall be relieved from his guard, make report in writing, to the commanding officer, of their names, their crimes, and the names of the officers who committed them, on the penalty of being punished for disobedience or neglect, at the direction of a court-martial.

ART. 83. Any commissioned officer convicted before a general court-martial of conduct unbecoming an officer and a gentleman, shall be dismissed the service.

ART. 84. In cases where a court-martial may think it proper to sentence a commissioned officer to be suspended from command, they shall have power also to suspend his pay and emoluments for the same time, according to the nature and heinousness of the offence.

ART. 85. In all cases where a commissioned officer is cashiered for cowardice or fraud, it shall be added in the sentence, that the crime, name, and place of abode, and punishment of the delinquent, be published in the newspapers in and about the camp, and of the particular State from which the offender came, or where he usually resides; after which it shall be deemed scandalous for an officer to associate with him.

ART. 86. The commanding officer of any post or detachment, in which there shall not be a number of officers adequate to form a general court-martial, shall, in cases which require the cognizance of such a court, report to the commanding officer of the department, who shall order a court to be assembled at the nearest post or department, and the party accused, with necessary witnesses, to be transported to the place where the said court shall be assembled.

ART. 87.* No person shall be sentenced to suffer death but by the concurrence of two-thirds of the members of a general court-martial, nor except in the cases herein expressly mentioned; *nor shall more than fifty lashes be inflicted on any*

---

* So much of these rules and articles as authorizes the infliction of corporeal punishment by stripes or lashes, was specially repealed by act of 16th May, 1812. By act of 2d March, 1833, the repealing act was repealed, so far as it applied to the crime of desertion, which, of course, revived the punishment by lashes for that offence.

offender, at the discretion of a court-martial; and no officer, non-commissioned officer, soldier, or follower of the army shall be tried a second time for the same offence.

ART. 88. No person shall be liable to be tried and punished by a general court-martial for any offence which shall appear to have been committed more than two years before the issuing of the order for such trial, unless the person, by reason of having absented himself, or some other manifest impediment, shall not have been amenable to justice within that period.

ART. 89. Every officer authorized to order a general court-martial shall have power to pardon or mitigate any punishment ordered by such court, except the sentence of death, or of cashiering an officer; which, in the cases where he has authority (by Article 65) to carry them into execution, he may suspend, until the pleasure of the President of the United States can be known; which suspension, together with copies of the proceedings of the court-martial, the said officer shall immediately transmit to the President for his determination. And the colonel or commanding officer of the regiment or garrison where any regimental or garrison court-martial shall be held, may pardon or mitigate any punishment ordered by such court to be inflicted.

ART. 90. Every judge advocate, or person officiating as such, at any general court-martial, shall transmit, with as much expedition as the opportunity of time and distance of place can admit, the original proceedings and sentence of such court-martial to the Secretary of War; which said original proceedings and sentence shall be carefully kept and preserved in the office of said Secretary, to the end that the persons entitled thereto may be enabled, upon application to the said office, to obtain copies thereof.

The party tried by any general court-martial shall, upon demand thereof, made by himself, or by any person or persons in his behalf, be entitled to a copy of the sentence and proceedings of such court-martial.

ART. 91. In cases where the general or commanding officer may order a court of inquiry to examine into the nature of any transaction, accusation, or imputation against any officer or soldier, the said court shall consist of one or more officers, not exceeding three, and a judge advocate, or other suitable person, as a recorder, to reduce the proceedings and evidence to writing; all of whom shall be sworn to the faithful performance of their duty. This court shall have the same power to summon witnesses as a court-martial, and to examine them on oath. But they shall not give their opinion on the merits of the case, excepting they shall be thereto specially required. The parties accused shall also be permitted to cross-examine and interrogate the witnesses, so as to investigate fully the circumstances in the question.

ART. 92. The proceedings of a court of inquiry must be authenticated by the signature of the recorder and the president, and delivered to the commanding officer, and the said proceedings may be admitted as evidence by a court-martial, in cases not capital, or extending to the dismission of an officer, provided that the circumstances are such that oral testimony cannot be obtained. But as courts of inquiry may be perverted to dishonorable purposes, and may be considered as engines of destruction to military merit, in the hands of weak and envious commandants, they are hereby prohibited, unless directed by the President of the United States, or demanded by the accused.

ART. 93. The judge advocate or recorder shall administer to the members the following oath:

"You shall well and truly examine and inquire, according to your evidence, into the matter now before you, without partiality, favor, affection, prejudice, or hope of reward. So help you God."

After which the president shall administer to the judge advocate or recorder the following oath:

"You, A. B., do swear that you will, according to your best abilities, accurately and impartially record the proceedings of the court, and the evidence to be given in the case in hearing. So help you God."

The witnesses shall take the same oath as witnesses sworn before a court-martial.

ART. 94. When any commissioned officer shall die or be killed in the service of the United States, the major of the regiment, or the officer doing the major's duty in his absence, or, in any post or garrison, the second officer in command, or the assistant military agent, shall immediately secure all his effects or equipage, then in camp or quarters, and shall make an inventory thereof, and forthwith transmit the same to the office of the Department of War, to the end that his executors or administrators may receive the same.

ART. 95. When any non-commissioned officer or soldier shall die, or be killed in the service of the United States, the then commanding officer of the troop or company shall, in the presence of two other commissioned officers, take an account of what effects he died possessed of, above his arms and accoutrements, and transmit the same to the office of the Department of War, which said effects are to be accounted for, and paid to the representatives of such deceased non-commissioned officer or soldier. And in case any of the officers, so authorized to take care of the effects of deceased officers and soldiers, should, before they have accounted to their representatives for the same, have occasion to leave the regiment or post, by preferment or otherwise, they shall, before they be permitted to quit the same, deposit in the hands of the commanding officer, or of the assistant military agent, all the effects of such deceased non-commissioned officers and soldiers, in order that the same may be secured for, and paid to, their respective representatives.

ART. 96. All officers, conductors, gunners, matrosses, drivers, or other persons whatsoever, receiving pay or hire in the service of the artillery, or corps of engineers of the United States, shall be governed by the aforesaid Rules and Articles, and shall be subject to be tried by courts-martial, in like manner with the officers and soldiers of the other troops in the service of the United States.

ART. 97. The officers and soldiers of any troops, whether militia or others, being mustered and in pay of the United States, shall, at all times and in all places, when joined or acting in conjunction with the regular forces of the United States, be governed by these rules and articles of war, and shall be subject to be tried by courts-martial, in like manner with the officers and soldiers in the regular forces; save only that such courts-martial shall be composed entirely of militia officers.

ART. 98. All officers serving by commission from the authority of any particular State, shall, on all detachments, courts-martial, or other duty, wherein they may be employed in conjunction with the regular forces of the United States, take rank next after all officers of the like grade in said regular forces, notwithstanding the commissions of such militia or State officers may be elder than the commissions of the officers of the regular forces of the United States.

ART. 99. All crimes not capital, and all disorders and neglects which officers and soldiers may be guilty of, to the prejudice of good order and military discipline, though not mentioned in the foregoing articles of war, are to be taken cognizance of by a general or regimental court-martial, according to the nature and degree of the offence, and be punished at their discretion.

ART. 100. The President of the United States shall have power to prescribe the uniform of the army.

ART. 101. The foregoing articles are to be read and published, once in every six months, to every garrison, regiment, troop, or company, mustered, or to be mustered, in the service of the United States, and are to be duly observed and obeyed by all officers and soldiers who are, or shall be, in said service.

SEC. 2. *And be it further enacted,* That in time of war, all persons not citizens of, or owing allegiance to, the United States of America, who shall be found lurking as spies in or about the fortifications or encampments of the armies of the United States, or any of them, shall suffer death, according to the law and usage of nations, by sentence of a general court-martial.

SEC. 3. *And be it further enacted,* That the rules and regulations by which the armies of the United States have heretofore been governed, and the resolves of Congress thereunto annexed, and respecting the same, shall henceforth be void and of no effect, except so far as may relate to any transactions under them prior to the promulgation of this act, at the several posts and garrisons respectively, occupied by any part of the army of the United States. [APPROVED, April 10, 1806.]

A DICTIONARY

OF

MILITARY WORDS AND PHRASES.

ABANDON.—To retire from, and yield to the enemy, a position which cannot be defended or ought not to be retained.

ABATIS *(pron. Ab-bat tee,).*—Felled trees, with their sharp branches placed outward, and so interlaced as to present an irregular and thick row of pointed stakes towards the enemy.

They are easily prepared, and expose the enemy to a destructive fire while endeavoring to remove them.

ABSENCE (Leave of).—The permission obtained by officers to absent themselves from their regiments or posts.

(Without leave.)—Every absence without permission, or after the term of the leave is expired, is entered upon the daily roll as absence *without leave*, and constitutes a military offence.

ACCOUTREMENTS.—A word which comprises the belts, cartridge-box, bayonet-scabbard, &c. of a soldier. When besides these he has his *arms*, he is said to be *armed and accoutred.*

ADJUTANT (From a Latin verb meaning *to help*).—Is the regimental staff officer who assists the colonel or other commander in the details of regimental or garrison duty. When serving with a detachment of a regiment at

417

a post, he is called a *post adjutant*. The adjutant is usually selected from the rank of lieutenants, and receives extra pay and allowances. He receives and issues orders, forms the daily parade, details and mounts the guards, &c.

ADJUTANT GENERAL.—The principal staff officer of an army, to whom the communications for the head-quarters are addressed. He keeps careful and systematic account of the strength, posts, and condition of the various corps, and is the organ of the general commanding in issuing orders. In the U. S. Army there is a department called the Adjutant General's Department, composed of one colonel, one lieutenant colonel, four brevet majors, and eight brevet captains: all except the colonel are called *assistant adjutant generals*.

AFFAIR.—An engagement between hostile bodies, less in importance than a battle, and usually of short duration.

AIDE-DE-CAMP (Commonly called *aid*).—An officer on the personal staff of a general, whose orders he receives and executes. Aids are usually regimental officers temporarily detached.

ALIGNMENT (From the French *aligner, to place in line*).—The line upon which troops are formed in battle order.

AMBULANCE.—A large spring wagon for conveying the wounded. A flying hospital.

AMBUSCADE.—A body of troops concealed from the enemy's approach, designed to surprise him and cause confusion. The place where they lie is called an *ambush*.

AMMUNITION.—Powder, either loose or in cartridges, balls, shells, and other projectiles; in short, every thing designed to supply cannon and firearms.

AMNESTY.—Pardon and release from all charges connected with war,—usually stipulated for in treaties of peace, or conceded by monarchs upon coming into power.

ANGLE.—In gunnery, the inclination which the barrel of the

piece makes with a horizontal line is called the *angle of elevation*, or the angle of the piece.

APPROACHES.—The lines of entrenchment, ditches, &c. by which the besiegers approach a fortified place. The principal trenches are called the first, second, and third parallels.

APRON.—A piece of sheet-lead, used to cover the vent of a cannon, to keep it from the weather.

ARMISTICE (Latin, *armisticium*)—A temporary suspension of hostilities.

ARMORY.—A store-house in which arms are deposited. Sometimes, also, the place where arms are made and repaired. The person who makes or repairs them is called an *armorer*.

ARMSTRONG GUN.—A rifle cannon loaded at the breech. Its projectile is made of cast iron, surrounded by two cylindrical leaden rings placed at the extremity of the cylindrical part, for the purpose of fitting the grooves when it is forced through the bore.

ARMY.—A body of troops of various corps (infantry, cavalry, artillery, and engineers), organized and commanded by a general. They constitute a military unit.

ARREST.—The confinement of an officer, and his temporary suspension from duty, preparatory to his trial on military charges.

ARSENAL.—A place where arms are made, repaired, and deposited. Military stores are also placed in arsenals.

ARTICLES OF WAR.—The various sections and articles of an act of Congress "for establishing rules and articles for the government of the armies of the United States."

ARTILLERY.—In this term are included all kinds of cannon, mortars, howitzers, &c., with all the munitions and implements requisite for service.

ASSEMBLY.—An army-call beaten upon the drum, for assembling the troops by company.

ATTACK.—Any onset upon the enemy. In sieges it implies the works carried on by the besiegers. When an assault is only partly made, with the design of deceiving the enemy and diverting his attention, it is called a *false attack.*

ATTENTION.—A word of command preparatory to the drill or exercise of troops, as, *Attention, squad* (or company, or battalion).

BAGGAGE.—The utensils, tents, provision, &c. of an army or corps. The wagons in which these are carried constitute the *baggage train,* which is always defended by a guard.

BAND.—A number of trained musicians, attached to a regiment or corps, usually under the immediate direction of the adjutant.

BANQUETTE.—A small elevation of earth on the inside of a fort, upon which the soldiers stand to fire over the parapet which shelters them when loading. It is usually three or four feet wide and less than five feet high.

BARBETTE GUNS.—Are guns which fire entirely over the parapet, on raised platforms, and thus have a free range in all outer directions. They are distinguished from guns in *embrasure,* which fire through a narrow cut in the parapet, and have but a limited field of fire.

BARRACKS (From the Spanish *Barruca.*)—Government buildings for lodging troops. They are provided with kitchens, mess-rooms, soldiers' quarters, &c., and are in reality a kind of military hotel.

BARRICADE.—To obstruct the avenues of access, as roads, streets, &c. This is done by wagons, heaps of stones, abatis, &c.; ditches are also dug across the approaches, and trees felled.

BASTION.—In fortification, the advanced portion of a regular work, consisting of two faces enclosing a salient angle, and two flanks. When two such bastions are united by a retired line called a curtain, they constitute a *bastioned front*. The advantages of bastions consist in their flanking arrangements.

BATTALION.—One-half of a regiment of infantry. This word is loosely used. Two companies are sometimes a battalion, while the whole regiment at drill is also called thus. It is commonly understood, however, that a regiment is composed of two battalions.

BATTER.—To beat down with cannon-balls. To batter in *breach* is to discharge cannon for the purpose of making a break or breach in a fortification sufficiently large for attacking troops to enter.

BATTERY.—A number of cannon of any kind arranged for firing together. Sometimes the place where they are parked receives the name of *battery*.

BATTLE.—A contest between considerable bodies of hostile troops. A battle is more important than an *affair* or a *skirmish*.

BAYONET (So called because first made at *Bayonne*.)—The sharp-pointed steel instrument made to fit upon the end of a musket or rifle, as an additional weapon. The new rifles are armed with sabre-bayonets.

BERM.—A narrow space between the parapet and the ditch, left vacant in the construction, so that the mass of the parapet may be secure from falling into the ditch.

BESIEGE.—To surround and shut in a place by an armed force. The dwellers in the place are called the besieged; the force surrounding them, the besiegers.

BILLETING.—The temporary lodgment of soldiers in the houses of the inhabitants of a town or village. It is often attended with evil consequences, and is only resorted to when separate quarters cannot be had.

BIVOUAC.—When an army passes the night without shelter, except such as can be hastily made of plants, branches,

&c., it is said to bivouac. (From *bis*, *double*, and *wache*, the German for *guard*.)

BLOCKADE.—Shutting in a fortress or place so that there is neither ingress nor egress practicable. On land, this is done by troops. By sea, a competent force of vessels must be provided.

BOMB.—A word formerly used to mean a *shell*, such as is thrown from a mortar. When mortars are fired upon a place, they are said to *bombard* it.

BOYAU.—Zigzag ditches by which the besiegers approach a fortified place. The plural is *boyaux*.

BREACH.—An opening made by cannon in a wall or fort, by which infantry troops may attack it.

BREASTWORK.—Any wall of defence breast-high, which shelters infantry in loading and firing upon the enemy.

BREECH.—The extremity of a gun near the vent.

BREVET.—An honorary commission given to officers for meritorious service, but not affecting the lineal rank except under special circumstances.

BRIGADE.—A body of troops consisting of two or three regiments.

BRIGADE INSPECTOR.—The officer appointed to inspect troops in companies, before they are mustered into service.

BRIGADIER GENERAL.—An officer who commands a brigade. The second rank in our service, next below a major-general and above a colonel.

CADENCE.—Exact *time* in marching and executing the manual of arms. It is indispensable to uniformity of motion.

CAISSON.—The ammunition carriage accompanying a field-piece.

CALIBRE.—The diameter of the bore of a cannon of any kind.

CAMP.—Implies the ground upon which troops encamp, the form of the encampment, and the tents or temporary shelters of any kind which are used.

CAMPAIGN.—The strategic arrangements of troops in a war for some definite end.

CANNON.—The name given to pieces of artillery of every form.

CANTEEN.—A small flat bottle, or runlet, in which a soldier carries water. Canteens are made of wood, tin, or India-rubber.

CAPTAIN.—The commander of a company.

CARBINE.—A small musket or rifle used by cavalry.

CARTRIDGE.—A charge of powder for any kind of fire arms. Those for muskets are rolled in paper; those for cannon are put up in flannel. A ball cartridge is one which has a ball inserted at the end of the powder, so that the piece is entirely loaded at once.

CARTRIDGE-BOX.—The leather box worn on the right hip, in which cartridges are kept.

CASCABLE.—The knob of a cannon at the end of the breech.

CASEMATE.—Casemates are bomb-proof chambers in fortifications, through holes in which, called *embrasures*, heavy guns are fired.

CASHIER.—To dismiss an officer ignominiously from the army.

CAVALRY.—This term includes all kinds of mounted troops, dragoons, hussars, light and heavy cavalry, &c.

CHAMBER.—The cavity at the bottom of the bore of a mortar or howitzer into which the charge of gunpowder is put.

CHEVAU-DE-FRISE.—A square beam (or hexagonal) of timber or iron, from six to nine feet long, in each side of which pointed stakes are placed at right angles to the sides. They are designed as obstacles for stopping a breach, or for obstructing the ditch. (Plural, *chevaux-de-frise*.)

COLONEL.—The commander of a regiment.

COLORS (*Regimental*).—The two silken flags belonging to a regiment. The *regimental colors* contain the name and number of the regiment. The *national colors* are the flag of the United States. In our service the colors are borne by *color-sergeants*; in the English, by *ensigns*.

COLUMBIAD.—A gun of very large calibre, used for throwing solid shot or shells. The old columbiads had *chambers*; the modern are made without them.

COMMISSARY.—An officer who purchases and issues provisions.

COMPANY.—A body of men, from fifty to one hundred, commanded by a captain.

CORPORAL.—The lowest grade of non-commissioned officers.

COUNTERMARCH.—To change the direction of a company or battalion from front to rear, by a flank movement, retaining the same ground.

COUNTERSCARP.—The outer wall or slope of the ditch of a fort.

COUNTERSIGN.—A secret word of communication to the sentinels on post, without a knowledge of which no one is permitted to pass the lines.

COUP-DE-MAIN.—A sudden attack connected with a surprise.

COURT-MARTIAL.—A military court of justice to try and punish all offences against military law. It is composed of military officers. They are divided into *general courts*, to try important cases, *garrison courts*, for lesser delinquencies, and *drum-head courts*, for summary punishment. (Plural, *courts-martial*.)

CUIRASSIERS.—Heavy cavalry protected by breastplates. There are no cuirassiers in the United States service.

DAHLGREN GUN.—An improved cannon, bearing the name of the inventor.

DEFILE.—A narrow passage or road, in marching through which the troops can show but a small front.

DEPLOY.—To open the order of troops from column into line of battle.

DITCH.—The excavation in front of a fort, from which earth has been taken to build the parapet, and which offers an obstacle to the enemy.

DRAGOON.—A kind of cavalry, who sometimes serve also on foot.

ECHELON (A French word, meaning ladder).—A formation of troops, where battalions or brigades follow each other on separate lines like the steps of a ladder.

EMBRASURE.—An opening cut in a parapet, for cannon to fire through. When guns fire *over* a parapet, they are called *barbette guns*.

ENFILADE.—To sweep with a battery the whole length of a work or line of troops.

ENGINEERS.—Officers who build fortifications. There is a corps of engineers in the United States service. The top-ographical engineers are those who make military surveys or reconnoissances.

ENLISTMENT.—The mode of bringing soldiers into service. The *term* of enlistment varies according to circumstances.

ENTRENCH.—To throw up a parapet with a ditch in front of it, so as to render a position stronger.

EPAULETTES.—Ornaments of gold or silver worn upon the shoulders of commissioned officers, and marked so as to determine their rank.

EPROUVETTE.—A small mortar for testing the strength and equality of gunpowder.

ESCALADE.—The attack upon a fort with scaling-ladders.

EVOLUTIONS OF THE LINE.—Movements by which troops, consisting of more regiments than one, change their position with order and regularity upon the field of battle.

FASCINES.—Brushwood, or long twigs, such as osier or willow, collected together and bound into bundles of convenient size: used to revet a parapet, or to make firm footing on marshy ground, and for other purposes.

FIELD OFFICERS.—The colonel, lieutenant colonel, and major of a regiment are called field officers.

FILE.—The front and rear rank man constitute *a file*.

FILE CLOSER.—The officers and non-commissioned officers of a company, whose habitual position is two paces behind the rear rank, are called *file closers*.

FORAGE.—The hay, straw, and oats required for the horses.

FLANK.—Literally, *side*. The right or left flank is the right or left side or at right angles. The flanks of an army are the troops on the right or left.

FORLORN HOPE.—A party of officers and men selected—generally volunteers—to attack a breach in storming a work. The duty is very dangerous, and the survivors receive promotion.

FORT.—Any military work designed to strengthen a point against every attack is a fort. If it be an important and complete fort, it is called a fortress.

FORTIFICATIONS.—Are works of strong character to defend a city or some extensive front. When they are made entirely of earth, they are called *field fortifications*; when of masonry, *permanent fortifications*.

FURLOUGH.—Leave of absence granted to warrant and non-commissioned officers and soldiers.

FUSE.—A tube filled with combustible materials, which is fixed in a shell: it burns, when ignited, for a calculated time before it reaches the powder in the shell and explodes it.

GABION.—Cylindrical baskets, without top or bottom, made of pliant twigs, filled with earth, and placed to resist cannon-shot.

GARRISON.—A strong place in which troops are quartered. Often the troops themselves are called the garrison.

GENERALS.—All officers above the rank of colonel. We have in the United States service only two grades, major general and brigadier general. By special act, the brevet of *lieutenant general* was conferred on General Winfield Scott.

GLACIS.—The declivity of ground running from beyond the counterscarp of the ditch to the open country, and swept by the fire of the parapet.

GRAPE.—Large shot (usually *nine*) sewed together in cylindrical bags, which are made to fit like cartridges into cannon.

GRENADE.—A small shell with a short fuse, which may be thrown into the enemy's works.

GRENADIERS.—The infantry company on the right of the regiment is called the grenadier-company, because they formerly carried hand-grenades.

GUARD.—A portion of troops regularly detailed, whose duty is to watch against surprise and disorder. The individual soldiers of the guard are called sentinels.

GUIDON.—Small silken flags borne by cavalry and light artillery.

GUNPOWDER.—A composition of saltpetre (76 parts), charcoal (14 parts), and sulphur (10 parts). The charcoal is the combustible part; the saltpetre furnishes the oxygen, and changes the mass into gas; the sulphur gives intensity of heat.

HANDSPIKE.—A wooden lever, placed at the rear end of a gun-carriage for convenience in turning it.

HAVERSACK.—A coarse bag of linen, cotton, or India rubber, in which a soldier carries his rations for daily use.

HOLSTERS.—Cases fixed to the front of cavalry saddles to hold a pair of pistols.

HORS DE COMBAT (French: literally, *out of combat*).—Not able to take part in immediate action. The term includes all dead, wounded, missing, or those who from any cause are thus disabled.

HOWITZER.—A chambered cannon, which fires a species of shell called a *howitz*. They are of various calibres and dimensions.

INFANTRY.—The foot troops of an army. They constitute the chief element, and are usually armed with the musket or rifle. They are divided into infantry of the line and light infantry.

INSPECTOR.—A stated examination, by commanders, of the condition of their troops in every respect.

INSPECTOR GENERAL.—The officer (with the rank of colonel) who makes regular tours of inspection in the different departments of a country, and reports to headquarters on the condition of the troops.

INTERVAL.—The distances between platoons, companies, regiments, or any other divisions of troops are called *intervals*. In manœuvring it is important to preserve the interval.

INVEST.—To take measures for besieging a town or place, by shutting in the inhabitants and shutting off all approach.

JUDGE ADVOCATE.—A person (commonly an officer) who conducts the prosecution before courts-martial. He also acts as counsel to the prisoner, should there be no other counsel. He summons witnesses, and makes all the arrangements for trial.

KNAPSACK.—A square frame, to fit across the shoulder, covered with canvas or India-rubber, and containing the entire necessaries of an infantry soldier.

LADDERS (SCALING).—Are made of flat staves, fastened in ropes, which are provided at the end with hooks for grappling the enemy's ramparts that soldiers may mount them.

LIEUTENANT (*lieu-tenant*, French, *holding the place of*).—An officer below the rank of captain, who has specific company duties.

LIEUTENANT GENERAL.—A general of rank next above a major general. We have no such lineal rank in the United States service. It is conferred by brevet upon General Scott.

LIGHT INFANTRY.—Infantry whose habitual order is that of skirmishers, or dispersed as sharp-shooters.

LIMBER.—A two-wheeled carriage fastened to the trail of a cannon when it is to be removed to a considerable distance; when the piece is brought into action, it is unlimbered.

LINSTOCK.—A piece of wood shod with iron, and easily stuck in the ground, through a hole in the upper end of which a piece of prepared tow-rope is kept burning.

LOGISTICS.—That branch of the art of war which concerns *moving* and *supplying* armies.

LUNETTE.—Small triangular field forts, with the base angles cut away.

MAGAZINE.—The place where arms, ammunition, provisions, and all other army stores are collected.

MAJOR.—A field officer just below the lieutenant colonel.

MALINGERER.—A soldier who feigns ill health to avoid doing his duty. When discovered, his conduct is declared *disgraceful*, and he is tried.

MANŒUVRE.—Any concerted movement of troops at drill.

MARTIAL LAW.—A subordination of the civil law to the military, by which the *habeas corpus* act is suspended. Subjection to the articles of war.

MÉTRE.—A French measure of distances, containing three feet and a third.

MINE.—A subterraneous passage dug under a work or glacis, and stocked with gunpowder, which may be exploded by a long train fired without danger.

MINIÉ.—A kind of rifle invented by Captain Minié, of France, which carries a conical ball, hollow at the base.

MORTARS.—Short pieces of ordnance, with large calibres and chambers, from which shells are fired at an elevated angle.

MUSTER-ROLL.—A roll, prepared at intervals of two months, containing all the details of company organization. At the same time the troops are *mustered* and inspected.

MUTINY.—Seditious or refractory conduct among troops: the name is given to insubordination associated with violence.

MUZZLE.—The extremity of a cannon, or any firearm, through which the ball makes its exit.

NON-COMMISSIONED.—Officers, are sergeants of various grades and corporals: they are appointed by authorities lower than the President,—commissions issuing from him. As a punishment, non-commissioned officers may be reduced to the ranks.

ORDERLY.—A soldier of any grade, appointed to wait officially upon a general or other officer, to carry orders or messages. The orderly sergeant is the first sergeant of the company. The officer of the day is sometimes called the orderly officer.

ORDNANCE CORPS.—A corps of officers with regimental grades, having charge of the making, keeping, and issuing of arms and ammunition. They are usually quartered at arsenals and armories.

OUTPOST.—A body of troops—usually considered as guards, and relieved from time to time—posted beyond the lines, to guard against surprise of the main body.

OUTWORKS.—The detailed works constructed outside the regular fortification, but connected with it according to the principles of defence.

PAIXHAN.—A large howitzer, similar to a columbiad, and throwing very large shells and balls. It is named after the inventor.

PARADE.—The assembling of troops in a prescribed manner. When equipped with arms, it is called a dress parade; when without, undress.

PARALLELS.—The deep trenches parallel to the general direction of a fort, by means of which the besiegers approach it.

PARAPET.—The mass of earth or masonry elevated so as to screen a place from the fire of the enemy. It is made so thick that shot cannot penetrate it.

PARK.—A number of cannon arranged in close order. Also, the place where they are.

PAROLE (French).—The word of honor given by a prisoner to his captor.

PATROL.—A small party, under a non-commissioned officer, which goes through or around an encampment at night, to keep order.

PAY.—The stipend or salary allowed to officers and soldiers. Besides the pay, certain *allowances*, such as *rations*, are made to soldiers; while officers have also servants, fuel, stationery, and other allowances.

PICKET.—A small outpost guard.

PIONEERS.—Soldiers equipped with axes, saws, and other instruments for clearing the way before an advancing army, or to entrench.

PLATOON.—One-half a company. The two platoons are called, respectively, first and second platoon.

PLOY.—To close a battalion, or any other division of troops, from line of battle into column.

POINT-BLANK.—The point of distance at which when a cannon or firearm is aimed, the axis of the piece is on the line with it.

POLICE.—In military parlance, keeping the camp or barracks clean and neat.

PONTOON, or PONTON.—Boats, or India-rubber bags, made into compartments, and filled with air, which are anchored in a stream at different distances, and upon which planks are placed to form a bridge.

PORT-FIRE.—A cylindrical case of stiff paper filled with a combustible material, and used sometimes in firing cannon.

PROJECTILES.—All kinds of shot and shells. Every thing which is projected from firearms.

QUARTER-MASTER, &c.—The quarter-master is the officer charged with providing quarters and furnishing clothing. In the United States service, there is a Quarter-Master Department, containing officers of all grades from the colonel commanding to captains.

QUARTERS.—The places where troops are lodged. Headquarters are the residence of the commander.

RALLY.—To reform disordered troops; to bring skirmishers into close order; to collect retreating troops for a new attack.

RAMPART.—A broad embankment surrounding a fortified place. It includes the parapet and other raised works.

RANK.—The range or order of seniority in commission.

RANK and FILE.—The corporals and privates of an army, or those who parade in the ranks habitually. Lineal rank is the order of promotion by seniority. Brevet rank is honorary rank conferred for meritorious service.

RATIONS.—The daily allowance of meat, bread, and other provisions to a soldier.

RECONNOISSANCE.—The survey and examination of a portion of country, or any point, with a view to military movements.

RECRUIT.—Literally, a soldier enlisted to take a vacant place in a company; commonly, any new soldier.

REDAN.—A portion of fortification included in a single salient angle.

REDOUBT.—Any small isolated fort. It is usually defensible on all sides.

REGIMENT.—A body of troops comprising ten companies, and commanded by a colonel.

REGULATIONS.—A system of orders and instructions on all subjects connected with the management of the army. They are published together, and constitute "The Army Regulations." The last were issued in 1857.

RELIEF.—A division of the guard,—usually one-third. These are called first, second, and third relief. The sentinels of each relief are on post for two hours, and off for four.

RESERVE.—A select body of troops held back for a decisive moment. In light infantry, the compact nucleus upon which the skirmishers rally.

RETREAT.—The parade at sunset, when the evening gun is fired, and the flag taken down for the night.

REVEILLE (pronounced *rev-il-lee'*).—The early morning drum-beat and roll-call, usually accompanied by the morning gun.

REVETMENT.—Any wall or strengthening process of the earth-works of a fort. Sometimes a work is revetted with sand-bags or fascines. Permanent forts are revetted with masonry.

RICOCHET.—The rebounding of a shot, usually propelled by a small charge, and with the gun pointed at an elevation of less than 10°. By striking in more spots than one, it does greater damage.

RIFLE.—Any firearm which has a curved groove running down its length from the muzzle to the bottom of the bore. Cannon are rendered more effective by rifling.

ROLL-CALLS.—Stated daily parades of the company, with or without arms, for calling the roll and seeing that every man is in his place.

ROSTER.—A list of officers and men, from which details for guard and other duties are made,—on the principle that the longest off any duty shall be detailed for the next tour.

SABRETASCHE (German, *Sabel*, sabre, and *Tasche*, pocket).— A leathern case, suspended at the left side of a mounted officer, in which papers are carried.

SAFEGUARD.—A passport given by competent authority to a person passing through military lines. It is usually both for persons and property.

SALIENT.—Any advanced point or angle in fortification.

SALLY-PORT.—The chief entrance to a fort, to afford egress to bodies of troops, as in a sortie.

SALUTE.—A discharge of artillery or musketry in honor of

persons of rank. The rank is denoted by the number of guns fired.

SAND-BAGS.—Coarse bags filled with sand, for revetting earth-works and repairing breaches made in them by shot.

SAP.—A ditch constructed rapidly by the besiegers in advancing upon a besieged place. According to the dimensions, it is called a full sap, a flying sap, or a double sap. Those who make them are called sappers.

SENTINEL.—An individual of the guard who is posted to watch for the safety of the camp, and who paces on his post, always alert, and holding no communication with any persons unauthorized to approach him.

SERGEANT.—The highest grade of non-commissioned officer. Besides the sergeants who form part of the company organization, in each regiment there is a sergeant major, who assists the adjutant, a quartermaster sergeant, who assists the quarter-master, a color-sergeant, who carries the colors, and, at military posts, an ordnance sergeant, who has charge of the ammunition.

SHELLS.—Hollow balls, filled with combustible matter, which is fired by a fuse. They are shot from guns and mortars, and explode when they reach the object aimed at.

SIEGE.—The act of surrounding a fort or place with an army, with a view to reducing it by regular approaches.

SKIRMISH.—A loose, desultory kind of engagement, generally between light troops thrown forward to test the strength and position of the enemy.

SORTIE.—A secret movement, made by a strong detachment of troops in a besieged place, to destroy or retard the enemy's approaches.

SPHERICAL CASE.—A very thin shell, filled with musket balls and powder.

SPIKE.—To close the vent of a gun with a nail forcibly driven in, so as to render it temporarily useless.

SQUAD.—A small party of men assembled for drill or inspection. Squads of recruits for drill should not number more than four or five.

SQUADRON.—A body of cavalry, comprising two troops or companies.

STAFF.—The officers connected with head-quarters, who assist in the general conduct of affairs. Such are quartermasters, commissaries, adjutants, adjutant-generals, and aids.

STRATEGY.—The science by which armies are conducted in a campaign. It implies a thorough knowledge of the theatre of the war, and the power to avail one's self of the natural features. The art of throwing masses of troops upon important points.

SUBALTERN.—Any commissioned below a captain. (Pronounced sub'al-tern.)

SUBSISTENCE DEPARTMENT.—The department, regularly organized, with a colonel and officers of all grades, including captains, who have charge of supplying troops with provisions and forage.

SURGEON.—An officer of the medical staff, with a thorough medical education, who is charged with the health and comfort of the troops, hospitals, and all care of the wounded, &c.

TACTICS.—As opposed to strategy, the movements of armies upon the battle-field, within sight and reach of the enemy.

TATTOO.—The drum-beat, sometimes with roll-call, just

preceding the retirement of troops, the putting out of lights, &c. It is usually at 9 1/2 o'clock.

TENTS.—Small canvas houses, easily erected or pitched, for the shelter of troops in camp.

TIME.—The regular cadence in marching. Common time is 90 steps to the minute; quick time, 110; double quick, 165.

TRAVERSES.—Masses of earth thrown up at short distances in forts along the line of the work, to screen the troops from shot and shells fired in ricochet.

TRENCHES.—The parallels dug by the besiegers in approaching a work. The boyaux are sometimes included in this term.

TROOP.—A company of cavalry.

TROUS DE LOUP.—Conical holes dug in the earth, about six feet deep, and four and a half wide at top. A sharp stake is fastened at the bottom, and the whole slightly covered, so as to conceal them from the enemy. Rows of trous de loup are very destructive to cavalry. (The name is French, and means *wolf-holes*.)

UNIFORM.—The clothing and accoutrements, the same for all the troops of a corps, by which uniformity of appearance, and easy recognition in battle, are assured.

VANGUARD.—The body of troops constituting a guard, detailed, from day to day, to march in advance of the army.

VIDETTE.—Originally, sentinels on the farthest outposts. Now confined to *mounted sentinels* on outpost duty.

VOLLEY.—The simultaneous discharge of a number of cannon, or muskets, or any firearms.

WINDAGE.—The small space by which a ball fails to fit exactly into a piece; *i.e.* the difference between the diameter of the ball and the calibre of the piece.

WINGS.—The portions of the army on the right and left. An army consists of the centre and two wings. A regiment on drill is said to consist of two wings, right and left.

WORKS.—A word used to express all kinds of fortifications and entrenchments.

ZOUAVES.—Light infantry troops in the French service,— (the name has also been adopted in the United States,)—originally composed of Arabs and Moors in Algeria, but afterwards recruited with French soldiers.

TABLE OF CONTENTS.

TITLE FIRST.

Article First.

Article Second.

TITLE SECOND.

SCHOOL OF THE SOLDIER.

Part First.

TITLE THIRD

SCHOOL OF THE COMPANY.

INSTRUCTION FOR SKIRMISHERS.

CALLS FOR SKIRMISHERS.

TITLE FOURTH.

SCHOOL OF THE BATTALION.

Part First.

Part Second.

Part Third.

THE END.

Formation of a regiment (ten companies) in

S.M.

M.

X.

F.

10th Company	9th Company	8th Company	7th Company	6th C
5th Division		4th Division		
Left Wing				

C.   Colonel
L.C. Lieut. Colonel
M.   Major
Q.   Qr. Master
A.   Adjutant
S.M. Serjt. Major
Q.S. Q. Master Serjt.
X.   Field Music
F.   Band
⊠   Color and guard
▯   Right guide
□   Left guide

Formation of a co

2nd Platoon